THE SUCCESS PAⱤ

Why we need a
social ɪ

Graeme Atᵢ

P

First published in Great Britain in 2017 by

Policy Press
University of Bristol
1-9 Old Park Hill
Bristol
BS2 8BB
UK
t: +44 (0)117 954 5940
pp-info@bristol.ac.uk
www.policypress.co.uk

North America office:
Policy Press
c/o The University of Chicago Press
1427 East 60th Street
Chicago, IL 60637, USA
t: +1 773 702 7700
f: +1 773-702-9756
sales@press.uchicago.edu
www.press.uchicago.edu

British Library Cataloguing in Publication Data
A catalogue record for this book is available from the British Library

Library of Congress Cataloging-in-Publication Data
A catalog record for this book has been requested

ISBN 978-1-4473-1634-3 paperback
ISBN 978-1-4473-2213-9 ePub
ISBN 978-1-4473-2214-6 Mobi
ISBN 978-1-4473-1636-7 ePdf

Cover design by Policy Press
Front cover image: istock
Printed and bound in Great Britain by CMP, Poole
Policy Press uses environmentally responsible print partners

Contents

List of figures and tables

Figures

Tables

About the author

Graeme Atherton has been working in the field of access to higher education for over 20 years. He has founded regional, national and local networks aiming to change people's lives through extending access to higher education, and holds visiting professorships at universities in the United Kingdom and abroad. Graeme writes extensively on issues associated with social mobility and education. He lives with his wife and two children in London and this is his first book.

Acknowledgements

This book would not have been possible without the support of my wife Sarah Adibi and my family. I thank them for their patience. I would also like to thank London Higher for their support of my work and of access to higher education and social mobility work in London and in the United Kingdom. My publishers at Policy Press have shown great patience in allowing me to complete this book and I thank the whole team who have supported me there, in particular Laura Greaves, Isobel Bainton and Rebecca Tomlinson. Finally, I would like to dedicate the book to all of those who have to fight against the odds every day to improve their lives and that of their families and loved ones. I hope this book can make some contribution to making that fight a more winnable one.

Introduction

Once upon a time, not so long ago, social mobility was an academic thing, and the concern of sociologists in particular. Although the debate around social mobility was played out in academic journals and conferences, it had little impact on the mainstream political conversation. Then something happened. Social mobility became popular.

While the rise of social mobility may have started in the early years of the New Labour government in the late 1990s, it really took off after the global recession of the late 2000s. The relatively poor performance of the UK in terms of social mobility compared to other nations, and the difficulties in penetrating a self-perpetuating professional elite, have now become a preoccupation across the political spectrum. The debate around social mobility in the UK is now starting to resemble a slow-burning moral panic (Goode and Ben-Yahuda 2009). The elite are following in the footsteps of muggers, mods and football hooligans as a metaphor through which a wider set of societal anxieties are channelled.

A convenient truth

There are a number of reasons why social mobility has gained such political prominence in recent years.

First, it captures well some of the anxieties that those in the middle class feel about the future of their children (and themselves). Since the 1980s, the middle classes have invested more and more money and effort in cementing their position through education (Ball 2002), and expect a pay-off in access to professional occupations. But when this group becomes concerned about something, then the policy makers listen. And while it might be those further down the socioeconomic ladder for whom social mobility is the biggest challenge, it would never have gained the traction it has in recent years if it had been perceived as a problem purely affecting those from lower socio-economic groups.

Second, it captures some of anger felt at the financial and political elites responsible for the economic recession that began in the late 2000s (Bennet and Kottasz 2012). These elites are perceived as separate and aloof from even the majority of those in professional occupations. And it is the lack of social mobility into this elite that has allowed it to put its own interests first, at the expense of the rest of the population.

Third, the phrase 'social mobility' itself is also appealing as a way of talking about class, inequality and poverty at a time when these terms are less palatable. The economic recession of the late 2000s has coincided with a concerted attack on the poor from the Right, while the Left, as it has been since the 1990s, is still searching for a language to articulate its core values where these issues are concerned. The latest attempt to find this language is the election of Jeremy Corbyn as leader of the Labour Party in 2015 in the UK. Neither side is comfortable, for different reasons, with speaking about class or inequality. Social mobility has represented a way of articulating the concerns of each of the three major political parties regarding class and inequality that fits with their existing ideology and policy positions.

Finally, social mobility as currently defined in the early 2010s has a personal resonance for many of the politicians in the major UK parties and the journalists who write about them. They are graduates from either Oxford or Cambridge universities or, at worst, from one of the other highly selective universities (Sutton Trust 2010). Research by Sutton Trust in 2015 showed that 26% of all MPs went to Oxford or Cambridge universities (Sutton Trust 2015). In this context, the social mobility problem is defined in a particular way, which begs a particular solution i.e. identifying able but poor young people who can make it to Oxbridge and then on to the commanding heights of society.

But while everyone might appear to be talking about it, there is little new being said about social mobility in the UK. The sociologists are adamant that their experience enables them to pronounce with certainty regarding the extent of movement up and down the class scale. The economists who have entered the fray more recently are equally convinced that their new analysis has shed a different light on social divisions that cannot be ignored. And politicians of different persuasions are in agreement that there is a problem and something needs to be done. Unsurprisingly, they do disagree, however, on whose fault this problem is and what to do about it.

The formation of the Social Mobility and Child Poverty Commission by the UK government in 2012 introduced an 'official voice' to the debate. Its role thus far has been to refract many of the perspectives above through its own lens, as it aims to become the authoritative voice on the issue. Some of the new contributions to the debate, however amount to not much more than the hijacking of social mobility to strengthen any argument related to the present economic problems or the more long-standing one of educational underperformance by lower socioeconomic groups. In 2013, Labour MP Simon Danczuk, for example, associated the increasing of business rates by the coalition government with a lowering of social mobility (Danczuk 2013). He was followed by Prime Minister David Cameron claiming that his government's flagship 'Help to Buy' housing policy was an attempt, in part, to increase social mobility (The Independent 2013).

The politicians have not strayed far from a focus on how to increase intergenerational mobility into the 'top jobs', while the sociologists remain wedded to increasing their understanding of how occupational mobility has or has not changed, usually through enhancing the sophistication of the quantitative analytical techniques used. The economists are concentrating even more on the importance of quantitative analysis. They prefer to use income or earnings as their measure of economic status as opposed to social class, and their central concern is reporting on the extent of intergenerational elasticity in earnings and where this varies more, implying greater social mobility as opposed to the more immobile places where it varies less.

The importance of this academic work cannot be underestimated, nor does any narrowness of focus denigrate its quality. And neither should the importance of politicians' attention to social mobility be downplayed. But the consequences of concentrating so much on whether something is changing or not is that what that thing actually is – and its importance – never get round to being discussed. The connections between social mobility and the wider challenges facing individuals, communities and countries in the 21st century are not being made. The lack of social mobility may be a convenient truth for some, but there are some rather more inconvenient truths, which are not yet being confronted.

The meaning of social mobility

This book aims to confront these more inconvenient truths and to present an alternative way of examining what social mobility means. It attempts to make these wider links between social mobility, the major challenges facing a country like the UK in the 21st century, and what we mean by progress at the individual and societal level. Most importantly, what is argued here is that there may be more to social mobility than we allow there to be at present. Although the focus is on the UK, examining the social mobility crisis in the context of the political and economic context of one country, the essential message can be applied across the majority of industrialised countries, in particular, those with higher levels of economic development. It is time for a new definition of social mobility.

In sociological textbooks social mobility is defined as having a number of forms: downward, upward and horizontal. Those who dominate the debate, politicians, sociologists and economists, each also have their own particular view on how to define social mobility. So achieving a consensus here is likely to prove impossible in the sense of any agreement over the extent of social mobility, or the role of education and the labour market in accounting for it.

There is some consensus though. As Goldthorpe states: 'the basic concern that economists and sociologists share is to establish the extent to which more or less advantaged economic status is transmitted across generations' (Goldthorpe 2012: 7).

While Goldthorpe does not include politicians or policy makers here, they also appear to support this definition: 'We are primarily concerned with intergenerational social mobility – breaking the transmission of disadvantage from one generation to the next. Children must be free to succeed whatever circumstances they are born into' (HM Government 2011: 11).

There are two major limitations presented by this definition of social mobility. First, focusing on intergenerational mobility is important, but equally important is looking at *intra*generational progression. By not paying sufficient attention to what happens to individuals over their lifecourse, the factors that explain the intergenerational picture are lost. The nature of the journey over the lifecourse is as important to understanding social mobility as anything that happens between generations. While the government's strategy for social mobility takes a lifecycle approach, and recognises the importance of intragenerational progression, but it remains hemmed in conceptually and practically by its concentration on the intergenerational.

This second limitation placed by the consensus position is making social mobility entirely understandable by looking at economic status. This book aims to balance the primacy of economic status with a desire to interpret social mobility in such a way as to include non-economic factors. The rationale for doing this is to recognise what everyone accepts, but for reasons of either academic belief, political judgement or methodological limitations is too shy of recognising: that there is more to understanding contemporary society at the individual or societal level than relative economic position. To repeat: economic status is crucial. It is the single most important factor under capitalism in defining the relative position and welfare of an individual in society. There is no attempt or desire to downplay the importance of economic position here. But as is being increasingly recognised by policy makers, it is not the only factor explaining societal welfare. Is it possible, then, to develop an understanding of social mobility that also recognises this fact? Would it not be more accurate, for instance, to describe the

present discourse in this area by academics and politicians as looking at economic as opposed to social mobility?

This is more than just a semantic issue. It is not good enough to continue looking at what is only a part of the picture simply because not doing so does not fit within the parameters of a particular academic discipline, or because it represents too great a political risk (see Chapter Nine), or because it is too difficult to measure. Social mobility should essentially be concerned with looking at progress at the level of the individual and at the level of society. Sociologists and economists do this, but their focus is solely on the economic progress that different groups make across generations. If we wish to use social mobility as a means of understanding how individuals and communities are changing in the early 21st century, examining this kind of progress alone is not enough.

The role of education

While there may be a degree of consensus around the wider definition of social mobility among academics, commentators and politicians, this does not extend to the role of education in social mobility. There is considerable disagreement regarding the extent to which increasing the numbers in education, especially higher education, would lead to greater social mobility. While the majority of politicians agree that it would, many sociologists take a quite different view. They believe that it is the labour market that defines the level of upward social mobility. Unless there is significant expansion in the numbers of professional and managerial occupations, which many sociologists see as unlikely given competition from emerging economies in the East, there are therefore limits on the extent to which there can be upward mobility (Brown et al 2008, Goldthorpe 2012).

As Chapter Four shows later, this is a strong argument, but it has to confront some other realities. The one constant where education is concerned across the world over the 20th century was that more and more people stayed in education longer (Cisco 2010). There seems reason to assume that this trend will halt or plateau in the 21st century. The 20th century showed us that every time it looked as if a majority of the population were going to achieve a given qualification, a new higher form of education was created. In England, the anxiety over too many young people obtaining a higher education qualification in the early 21st century will look like a quaint debate in the late 21st century – a little like the early

debate as to whether or not all children should go to secondary school appears now (Richardson and Wiborg 2010).

It looks highly unlikely that the increasing levels of education that people receive, either while young or increasingly over the lifecourse, will go into reverse. This means that the content of secondary and higher level education becomes the real area for discussion. Looking at the historical and international trends highlights some of the dilemmas where education itself, as well as education and social mobility, are concerned. It makes us consider the limitations of education when it is seen as mainly a positional good. Increasing the educational attainment of those from lower socioeconomic groups is undoubtedly an essential thing to do, but there is little debate regarding what opportunities would be offered to these young people if they achieved the equivalent results to their peers. There would be a colossal mismatch between their expectations and what society would be able to offer them. There has to be a more multifaceted understanding of social mobility in order to cope with this dilemma, which requires a debate not just about who moves up and down existing hierarchical scales, but what these scales should constitute.

The importance of social mobility

The argument for enhancing upward economic social mobility is usually couched in terms of a belief in fairness. Politicians are unwilling to countenance an argument for more downward mobility, although some outside politics see that as an inevitable outcome of more fluidity overall. But the relative importance of social mobility in contributing to any greater fairness overall in society is seldom discussed. Is social mobility more desirable and hence deserving of greater policy attention than greater equality, for example? Is the former a subset of the latter (as it is frequently described)? In the case of education, for example, there is a distinct difference between prioritising the reduction of educational disadvantage in the name of greater fairness and pursuing social mobility for young people from lower socioeconomic groups. With all good intentions, they have been conflated together, but they actually imply quite a different set of policies. The most obvious example in the UK is the creation of the Social Mobility and Child Poverty Commission. Upward social mobility and reductions in child poverty might intersect at crucial points, for example in improving the life chances of low-income children, but they are very separate, for instance, where the fortunes of those working in lower to middle

income occupations, but who are experiencing stagnant wage growth, are concerned.

For some, though, social mobility is more than a matter of values; it is essential for capitalism to function. Social mobility sits at the centre of the social contract between individual and state. In the US, in early 2013, President Obama argued that:

> 'The combined trends of increased inequality and decreasing mobility pose a fundamental threat to the American Dream, our way of life, and what we stand for around the globe.... But starting in the late '70s, this social compact began to unravel. Technology made it easier for companies to do more with less, eliminating certain job occupations. A more competitive world lets companies ship jobs anywhere. And as good manufacturing jobs automated or headed offshore, workers lost their leverage, jobs paid less and offered fewer benefits.' (The White House 2013)

Obama appeared to be referring both to the availability of opportunities for progression to elite, professional occupations, and also to shorter-range progression out of unemployment. The US is a special case, where economic mobility has always had a particular resonance. But the ability of the majority of the population to experience at least modest economic progression is a key part of the 'social contract' in capitalism per se. The periods of civil unrest in Europe in the early 2010s as unemployment and poverty have risen, and the rise of right-wing populism can be construed as examples of what happens when this social contract comes under strain.

The relationship between social mobility and broader socioeconomic changes, both actual and intended, is pivotal. The real importance of social mobility is in how it defines, and is defined by, these broader changes. What is seen as progress at the level of the individual is usually overlooked by those concerned with the overall nature of social and economic systems – especially by those who wish to posit an alternative to the present model of capitalism. The macro-level changes associated with a more progressive capitalist system – for example, greater redistribution, more commitment to climate change, or a move away from using just economic measures to capture societal welfare – depend on individuals shifting their attitudes regarding what they view as progress for themselves and, if they have them, for their children. It will be argued here that trying to instigate some of these changes will not be possible, unless our view of what social mobility constitutes changes.

The 'success paradox'

A new way of looking at social mobility means stepping back from concentrating on the measurement of social mobility to examining its nature and importance. The central proposition in this book is that social mobility is essentially about success: what it means, who achieves it and how it can be spread. However, 'success' in the early 21st century is a paradoxical thing. More money and more wealth does not guarantee a better life for the individual – as will be argued, being richer is not the same thing as improving your happiness and well-being. It can also have a detrimental effect on the welfare of others. The definition of success that dominates at the moment is at the root of increased inequality, as well as blinding us to how we tackle the big economic and social challenges of the early 21st century.

Such a paradox should in theory be unsustainable. The narrow definition of success in terms of getting a better job or accumulating more wealth does not adequately capture, on its own, what success means to the vast majority of people. What is especially worrying is that remaining wedded to this material definition alone may make it harder to adjust to the realities of the 21st century. Global economic changes and advances in technology will mean opportunities to move up the economic scale may have to become more rationed. More, not less, people will have to learn to be satisfied with a more modest slice of the economic pie. Unless we can change what success means, this scenario will lead to conflict, discord and instability. The only way to prevent this, and to overcome the success paradox, is to change how we think about success and progress. And this means changing how we think about social mobility.

The rest of this book

Chapters One to Three look at why we need a new approach to social mobility. Chapter One outlines the reasons why the present definition of social mobility is fostering unsustainability. It looks at the impact of how social mobility is defined on inequality, the capacity of advanced economies to produce success, and the relationship between success and well-being. Chapter Two explores the academic tradition in social mobility research, and the differing perspectives taken by sociologists and economists as well as those who offer explanations that sit a little outside these two schools of thought. It argues that while the work undertaken by academics across the disciplinary spectrum is rich and detailed, it is restricted in how it understands and examines social mobility. Chapter Three looks at the political discourse on social mobility, and rejects the view that there is a straightforward political consensus where social mobility is concerned. The discourse has evolved over the last 15 years and become differentiated by each political party.

Chapters Four to Six look at the challenges that need to be overcome if a new way of thinking about social mobility is to be developed. The education system is the root of social mobility, but as much for its role in communicating and instilling values as for the skills with which it imbues children and students. Chapter Four looks at how the compulsory education system is actively shaping this unsustainable idea of social mobility. Redefining social mobility in a more sustainable way will depend, however, not just on changing the curriculum and how it is delivered, but also on how education itself is understood. Chapter Five looks at higher education. It argues that higher education remains central to new thinking on social mobility. However, higher education itself has to realise its potential as an agent of change. While education is important, it cannot produce a new idea of social mobility on its own – without changes in the labour market, social mobility cannot change. Chapter Six looks at the present debate around the 'hourglass' shape of labour markets such as that in the UK, arguing that more complex concepts metaphors are needed in order to understand contemporary labour markets.

In the final chapters we start to sketch out how this new approach to social mobility could be developed. Chapter Seven looks at the shifts in the social and economic model required to address the challenges outlined to societal prosperity and well-being in the 21st century, and how a new definition of social mobility is essential to meeting them. These shifts will require political support. Chapter Eight outlines a new politics of social mobility that can go beyond the narrow parameters of the present debate. It argues that new thinking on social mobility is not only politically essential but, most importantly, politically feasible. Chapter Nine suggests where we need to go next, if the success paradox is going to be resolved and a new understanding of social mobility developed.

ONE

The need for a holistic theory of social mobility

Introduction

It is a continual refrain that we are living through a time of unprecedented change. The challenges that societies such as the UK are facing in the 21st century are not new. They echo, in fact, those of the 20th century. Coping with new technology, the movement of people, the presence of religious tensions – these are perennial problems. Nor are present-day changes necessarily any greater than past changes. Moreover for all the changes introduced by new technologies in the latter years of the last century and the early years of this one, they do not match the introduction of technologies such as telephones, cars or televisions (Ridley 2011). It is not my intention here to argue that the problems with how success and social mobility are defined are a product of an inherent or inevitable teleological process such as industrialisation. Rather, defining social mobility entirely in terms of economic progression (and narrowly at that) is a long-standing problem that has become a pressing issue because of a particular set of circumstances that have come together at this point in time. These circumstances are partly the nature of the technological developments from the latter part of the 20th century, but more the social and economic context through which they have become manifest. And the internet provides the best example. Rather than bringing the foundation for new sets of more (utopian) human relationships, as some hoped, it has become a mechanism to enable capitalism to reinvent itself, to develop new markets and to do this while reducing the demand for labour and producing a new set of all-powerful multinational global companies (Morozov 2011).

Technology itself has not led to this outcome, but rather the inability or unwillingness of governments to create structures that can effectively marshal technology for different ends, and create effective bulwarks against the power of capital, or more accurately, transnational capital. The marketisation of not just economic relationships but also (as the US philosopher Michael Sandel argues) of social relationships, which have gathered pace especially in the US and the UK since the 1970s, has created a specific context within which technological change has occurred. As Sandel put it when interviewed in 2013:

> 'If you look at it, we have drifted over the last three decades from having a market economy, to becoming a market society. A market economy is a valuable and effective tool for organising productive activity. But a market society is a place where everything is up for sale. It's a way of life, where market values reach into every sphere of life. That can be everything from family life in personal relations, to health, education, civic life, and civic duties.' (quoted in O'Malley 2013)

The way in which social mobility is understood reinforces the marketisation described by Sandel. The analysis of social mobility and some of the politics around it may, in a perverse way, be contributing to, rather than helping to solve, the problems that it identifies. It also relies on a set of circumstances and assumptions that no longer hold true (if they have ever have done). There is a reflexive relationship between social mobility and socioeconomic change – one is embedded in – and defines – the other. The academic and political discourses on social mobility have, maybe deliberately or inadvertently, contributed to a hermetic approach to social mobility, where it is separated from these broader changes rather than being an actor within them.

There are three particular reasons why social mobility at present looks unsustainable.

Social mobility is contributing to dramatic rises in inequality

A new consensus has begun to emerge that unearned wealth for a few at the top, stagnating incomes for those in the middle and deepening disadvantage for many at the bottom is not a sustainable social proposition. (Social Mobility and Child Poverty Commission 2013: 6)

On a whole range of measures, the UK is at a point in time where inequality is relatively high. Research produced by the Organisation for Economic Co-operation and Development (OECD) in 2011 shows that the top 10% of earners have incomes 12 times greater than the bottom 10%, up from eight times greater in 1985 (Ramesh 2011a). Work by Danny Dorling shows that inequality is higher than it has been since the 1940s (University of Sheffield 2012).

Research by the Poverty and Social Exclusion group in 2013 showed that nearly half the population are suffering some degree of financial insecurity, with over 10 million people too poor to engage in common social activities considered necessary by the majority of the population, and approximately 4 million children not properly being fed by today's standards. It further argues that a third of the population suffers from multiple deprivation compared to only 14% in 1983 (Gordon et al 2013). The gradual shift to a more unequal society began with the move to a more marketised society in the 1970s. It then stalled in the early 2000s before gathering pace again. The particular characteristics of early 21st-century inequality are a separation between top and bottom, with a concentration of very extreme wealth in a very small minority, along with a group at the bottom who are becoming steadily poorer (Dorling 2013).

Inequality has some well-documented negative impacts on society as a whole – success for some is leading to a range of unsuccessful outcomes for the majority. Richard Wilkinson and Kate Pickett documented this comprehensively in their 2010 book The Spirit Level. In it they outline how inequality leads to greater violence, mental illness and unhappiness among other social 'bads'. Although The Spirit Level has come in for significant criticism on the grounds of the methodology used (Saunders 2010a, Snowdon 2010), it is far from the only work pointing to the negative outcomes that inequality has on society (Rowlingson 2011). In her 2011 review of the impact of income inequality, Rowlingson argues that while there is certainly more detailed work needed here: '… the literature shows general agreement about a correlation between income inequality and health/social problems' (Rowlingson 2011:1)

Inequality is also waging a significant financial cost on society. The Equality Trust argues that inequality cost the UK £39 billion per year (The Equality Trust 2014). The Equality Trust research has estimated that if inequality was reduced to the average level seen in the OECD, the UK could expect to:

- Increase average healthy life expectancy by 8 and a half months, at a value of £12.5 billion
- Reduce mental health illness rates by 5 per cent, at a value of £25 billion
- Imprison 37 per cent fewer people, at a value of £1 billion

- Experience 33 per cent fewer murders, at a value of £678 million (The Equality Trust 2014:2)

Inequality can also lead to political conflict and unrest. Müller (1985, 1988), looking at inequalities across a number of countries in the 1950s and 1960s, argued that there was a positive relationship between inequality and death rates from political violence and regime repressiveness. It is important, however, not to see inequality in isolation here – civil wars have more to do with wider cultural and economic factors (Collier 2000). Nevertheless, the impact of new forms of entrenched inequality in the context of economic and cultural globalisation may, according to Mason (in his albeit brief analysis of discontent and unrest in Egypt, Greece, Britain, the US and the Philippines in the early 2010s), be an increasing risk if opportunities do not keep pace with expectations (Mason 2012).

Social mobility is fundamentally connected to inequality. The present concern with social mobility is motivated in large part by a genuine concern to address the increasing – and increasingly visible – level of inequality, not just in the UK, but also across the world. There is an increasing body of evidence to suggest that inequality is one of, if not the, greatest challenge facing the UK and also the world economy. In late 2014, the World Economic Forum surveyed over 1,500 leaders across all continents from business, academia, government and international organisations. Economic inequality was cited as the biggest worry and concern in the world at present (World Economic Forum 2015). As Ostry et al argue in their paper for the International Monetary Fund in early 2014, looking at the growing amount of work in the field in the early 2010s:

> Our work built on the tentative consensus in the literature that inequality can undermine progress in health and education, cause investment-reducing political and economic instability, and undercut the social consensus required to adjust in the face of shocks, and thus that it tends to reduce the pace and durability of growth. (Ostry et al 2014: 3)

Also in 2014, the OECD released its own report showing how higher inequality reduces economic growth. Figure 1.1 shows how growth has been affected by inequality over 1990 to 2010, and how much it would have changed had inequality not changed between 1985 and 2005.

Figure 1.1: Estimated consequences of changes in inequality (1985-2005) and subsequent cumulative growth

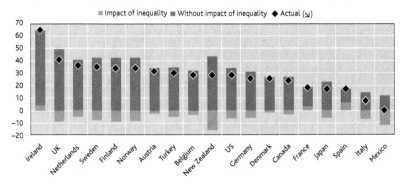

OECD, 2014a, www.oecd.org/social/FocusInequalityandGrowth2014.pdf

However, unless we confront how social mobility is understood and defined, efforts to reduce this inequality will hit a glass ceiling. The problem with concentrating on economic status as the sole measure of individual progress is that it makes it harder to persuade people to support the kind of redistribution that is necessary to ameliorate this inequality. While it appears that there is an increasing willingness to confront the reality of inequality, there is less of an appetite to confront the contradiction that if you construct an economic measure of success, how can you persuade people to give up the very thing that will make them successful? Nurturing the kind of commitment to redistribution necessary to make a big dent in the growing inequality at the national and global level depends on changing how success is defined. In turn, this means extending the definition of social mobility.

Social mobility depends on jobs that are not there

The UK, alongside most other developed (and many developing) countries, signed up enthusiastically in the 1990s to the global 'race for talent' idea – that is, the belief that the only way for economically developed nations to compete on the global economic stage is to invest in improving the quality of their labour force. In the late 1990s and early 2000s, the vision of a 'knowledge-driven economy' took root across the developed world. Its antecedents go back to human capital theory and Daniel Bell's industrialisation theories (Drucker 1959). In an era defined by economic globalisation and the power of transnational capital, developing the quality of their human capital is the only way that countries can gain a competitive advantage (Reich 1991, Michaels et al 2001, Florida 2005). This logic would then require and lead to an upskilling of the workforce and a change in its composition, so that it would be made up in the main by knowledge workers with relatively high levels of qualifications. These competitive pressures would be strong in an environment where countries were unable (or unwilling) to constrain global capital. Hence, as well as understanding that their workforces had to be upskilled, countries also had to engage in concerted efforts to ensure that this happened. They were involved in a race in which countries that failed to increase the quality of their workforce and develop the knowledge-driven economy would fall behind, the consequences of which would be stagnant living standards and higher unemployment.

It was from the belief in the knowledge-driven economy that the idea of a 'war for talent' emerged (Michaels et al 2001). The origins of this idea can be found in a landmark report from the management consultants McKinsey in 1998: 'In the 1900s, only 17 percent of all jobs required knowledge workers; now over 60 percent do. More knowledge workers means it's important to get great talent, since the differential value created by the most talented knowledge workers is enormous' (Michaels et al 2001: 2).

It is easy to see how these ideas were attractive to the political Centre Left in the 1990s in the UK and the US. In both countries the Left was actively seeking to demonstrate how traditional concerns regarding greater equality and social justice could be combined with a greater understanding of the needs of the private sector. There was also a need for a story on economic growth and social mobility that did not explicitly involve Keynesian demand management solutions. The 15 years of Labour government saw a series of White Papers that outlined investment in educational expansion framed as a response to the changing global economic landscape. Most prominent among these was the Leitch Review on Skills, produced in 2006. It argued that Britain urgently needed to increase its population's skill level:

> In the 19th Century, the UK had the natural resources, the labour force and the inspiration to lead the world into the Industrial Revolution. Today, we are witnessing a different type of revolution. For developed countries that cannot compete on natural resources and low labour costs, success demands a more service-led economy and high value-added industry. In the 21st Century, our natural resource is our people – and their potential is both untapped and vast. Skills will unlock that potential. The prize for our country will

be enormous – higher productivity, the creation of wealth and social justice. (HM Treasury 2006: 1)

Leitch encapsulated the attachment of the Labour Party in the 2000s to the global 'race for talent' idea – both the Prime Minister and the Chancellor of the Exchequer strongly supported this idea. As former Prime Minister Tony Blair stated in 2007: 'In the new knowledge economy, human capital, the skills people possess is critical' (Blair 2007).

For former Prime Minister Gordon Brown who had, it has been suggested, a much greater interest in education and skills, his words echoed those of Leitch:

> A generation ago a British prime minister had to worry about the global arms race. Today a British prime minister has to worry about the global skills race – because the nation that shows it can bring out the best in all its people will be the great success story of the coming decade. (quoted in Sparrow 2008)

Another war that Labour should never have fought?

However, it appears that this was another misguided conflict entered into by the Labour government of 1997 to 2010. The investment in education by Labour may not only have garnered a poor return, but it also led to education being put on a pedestal as the panacea for all the challenges facing the UK economy. The belief that you could educate yourself to success as a country was too simplistic (Brown and Hesketh 2004, Brown et al 2008, 2012, Keep 2013). It served to draw attention and energy away from the more fundamental challenge of creating demand and constructing a labour market that could create well-paid and meaningful work for those at all levels of skill commensurate with their levels of qualification.

Brown et al (2008) argue that the idea that increased education will drive economic progress can be traced back to a 'technocratic model of evolutionary change that has a long history in the social sciences' (Brown et al 2008: 12). For Keep (2013), education is now being expected to deliver on a range of priorities that are just too much for it to handle. In his 2013 article he quotes from the 2007 Department for Innovation, Universities and Skills (DIUS) White Paper:

> Improved skills will help individuals to improve their employability, progress in their careers and secure better

wages. It will help employers increase productivity and profitability for their businesses. It will help us reduce unemployment, tackle child poverty and improve social mobility. And it will help reduce crime, improve health outcomes, and improve civic and community participation. (DIUS 2007: 10)

Brown et al have serious doubts as to whether education can deliver on the economic aspect of these promises. In their 2008 work, they draw on research with nearly 200 senior managers from leading transnational companies to point to what they see as the major changes in how economic globalisation is developing, which seriously undermine the idea that a country like the UK can achieve economic success through winning the 'knowledge wars'. Their research indicates that there is a 'second wave of globalisation' occurring. In this second wave, multinational companies are able and willing to locate the knowledge-based parts of their production processes in the parts of the world where costs are lowest, not just (as in the first wave) those aspects of the process that were more routinised. The developing world is trying to expand education as quickly as it can (University of Oxford 2015). In this context it is impossible for a country like the UK to compete effectively on the basis of the number of skilled, knowledge-based workers alone. This does not mean that knowledge is without value, but it is the very skilled and talented who prosper. Without broader changes in the labour market and the economy that stimulate the demand for more skilled labour, the rest of the population is likely to experience diminishing returns for their educational qualifications.

There is certainly evidence to support this view. Data from the Office for National Statistics (ONS) show how the percentage of those in lower-skilled jobs increased from around 26.7% in 2001, or just over one in every four recent graduates, to around 35.9% in the final quarter of 2011 (ONS 2012a). Similar data have also emerged in particular from the US, and also from mainland western Europe and Australia (OECD 2010). Nor are the concerns about the ability of education to deliver social mobility restricted to undergraduate students. Research has also pointed to a similar oversupply problem among research doctorate students (Group of Eight 2013). While the research focused primarily on Australia, it is supported by research from the US regarding the number of graduates with doctorates in low-status employment. This message is one that must be heeded by other countries.

Brown et al (2008) argue that what countries like the UK are heading toward is a 'highly skilled: low wage' economy, where the ability of large firms to move their more knowledge-intensive work to developing countries depresses the returns available to education. The nature of knowledge work may also be changing, to resemble not a kind of intellectually fulfilling, creative activity, but a more routine, regimented scenario, which they describe as a form of 'digital Taylorism', taking their lead from the restrictive management techniques developed by Frederick Taylor in the late 19th century (Brown et al 2008). There will always be opportunities for those with high levels of ability and/ or the right forms of education to access high-paid and high-skilled work, but these opportunities may be far more sought-after, could be fewer and are more likely to be filled by those with the social and economic capital to secure entry to the more prestigious global universities where they can build on the networks that they will often already have through friends and family.

There will be an increased demand for high-skilled workers, but this may still be exceeded by demand for those with medium- or lower-skill requirements, and who do not, at this point in time, require degree-level qualifications, for instance. Table 1.1 is taken from the work of Clifton et al (2014), who use data from the 2014 work by the UK Commission for Employment and Skills (UKCES). It shows that there remain a significant number of employees in mid-range as well as low-skilled occupations. While the increase in high-skilled occupations may be predicted to be more rapid, overall, they still represent the minority of occupations. Low- and medium-skilled work is not disappearing.

As worrying as these conclusions sound, they are being taken a step further by a number of writers who argue that we are undergoing a quite fundamental shift in the way in which advanced capitalist economies are being organised, which is analogous to that experienced with the invention of the steam engine. Routinised and knowledge-based work is not just being shifted from West to East, and nor are we seeing changes in the nature of employment confined to the routinisation of knowledge work. Rather, in the longer term, large swathes of skilled jobs (not low-skilled ones) will disappear, and those that are left will be quite different in character, with new ones yet to emerge.

The US economist Taylor Cowen argues that the consequences of these changes will be to exacerbate the kind of inequality described earlier (Cowen 2013). He argues in his 2013 book Average Is Over that the US is becoming a form of 'hyper-meritocracy', where the very able who can exercise control over the new technologies that are defining the trajectory of the economy are becoming exceptionally successful while everybody else is becoming worse off. There will be

Table 1.1: Changes in employment demand 2012–22

	Expansion demand (000s)	% change	No in 2012 (000s)	No in 2022 (000s)
22 Health professionals	332	25.0	1,328	1,660
11 Corporate managers and directors	493	22.5	2,191	2,684
21 Science, research, engineering and technology professionals	354	20.4	1,735	2,089
24 Business, media and public service professionals	337	19.8	1,702	2,039
23 Teaching and educational professionals	152	10.1	1,505	1,657
High skilled	1,668	19.6	8,461	10,129
32 Health and social care associate professionals	102	30.7	332	434
35 Business and public service associate professionals	384	17.0	2,259	2,643
34 Culture, media and sports occupations	88	14.5	607	695
31 Science, engineering and technology associate professionals	47	8.9	528	575
12 Other managers and proprietors	93	8.3	1,120	1,213
53 Skilled construction and building trades	73	6.6	1,106	1,179
52 Skilled metal, electrical and electronic trades	-103	-7.7	1,338	1,235
33 Protective service occupations	-39	-8.7	448	409
51 Skilled agricultural and related trades	-41	-10.2	402	361
54 Textiles, printing and other skilled trades	-236	-35.5	665	429
Medium-skilled	368	2.4	8,805	9,173
61 Caring personal service occupations	594	26.9	2,208	2,802

	Expansion demand (000s)	% change	No in 2012 (000s)	No in 2022 (000s)
72 Customer service occupations	138	20.8	663	801
62 Leisure, travel and related personal service occupations	55	8.5	647	702
82 Transport and mobile machine drivers and operatives	-3	-0.2	1,500	1,497
41 Administrative occupations	-159	-5.7	2,789	2,630
71 Sales occupations	-202	-10.0	2,020	1,818
81 Process, plant and machine operatives	-211	-26.1	808	597
42 Secretarial and related occupations	-327	-34.6	945	618
92 Elementary administration and service occupations	-44	-1.6	2,750	2,706
91 Elementary trades and related occupations	-23	-4.0	575	552
Low-skilled	-182	-2.6	14,907	14,725

Source: Clifton et al (2014)

10–15% of workers who will be very wealthy, and the rest will have to become used to at best a stagnant – and at worst a declining – standard of living. Cowen alludes to the power of technology to enable scrutiny over work performance to increase significantly. The result will be, borrowing from Brown et al's work, a form of 'hyper-Taylorism'. Cowen does not believe that there will be an impact on economic stability as a result of these changes, pointing to how in the 1960s, for instance, at a time of relative equality and affluence, the US saw extreme social unrest. However, as others argue with reference to the US: 'Even if only a fraction of Mr Cowen's vision comes to pass … [i]n a country founded on hope that would require something like a new social contract' (The Economist 2013a).

Erik Brynjolfsson and Andrew McAfee capture much of this thinking in their 2014 book The Second Machine Age. They have a very optimistic view of the economic future, however, arguing that we are on the brink of realising the potential gains for society that computer processing can bring. But they also point to a period of disruption this could cause and implications for the labour market:

Rapid and accelerating digitization is likely to bring economic rather than environmental disruption, stemming from the fact that as computers get more powerful, companies have less need for some kinds of workers. Technological progress is going to leave behind some people, perhaps even a lot of people, as it races ahead. As we'll demonstrate, there's never been a better time to be a worker with special skills or the right education, because these people can use technology to create and capture value. However, there's never been a worse time to be a worker with only 'ordinary' skills and abilities to offer, because computers, robots, and other digital technologies are acquiring these skills and abilities at an extraordinary rate. (Brynjolfsson and McAfee 2014: 11)

Frey and Osborne (2013) argue that 47% of jobs in the US will be susceptible to automation in the next 20 years and, as Cowen says, it is not just the kind of low- to medium-skilled routinised jobs that are under threat, but also skilled, knowledge-intensive ones. Changes in the nature of the demand for human capital present important questions for social mobility. The present social contract between citizen and state – based on education, occupational progression and social mobility via redistribution or labour market reform – cannot be repaired. It is inherently unsustainable in its present form, and must be replaced with something new.

Critics of these apocalyptic visions of the labour market point to the fact that previous periods of technological change have always produced more and better jobs (Walker 2007). In the past, capitalism has always found a way to monetise technological change to create more complex and skilled jobs. Technological change affects the composition of the labour force rather than actually reducing the number of jobs (Autor and Katz 2010). However, the concerns regarding the future of the labour market cannot be easily dismissed with reference to either the present or the past. While there is a hysteria and hyperbole in some of the literature on the impact of technological change, it is also quite focused on the US, where divides between different groups in the labour market are much starker than, for instance, in Europe, with its stronger role for intermediate institutions. However, the pace at which technological capacity is increasing is far in excess of previous time periods. As Brynjolfsson and McAfee argue, the power of computer processors is doubling every year. This is happening at a time when (as Dorling 2013, Brown et al 2008 and others argue) private capital has significant latitude to turn these innovations into profit, especially in the UK (which resembles the US far more than Europe in this regard).

It would be naive to think that this will not have profound implications for what social mobility means. The changing nature of the labour market is only one part of a wider picture, according to writers such as King (2014), Gordon (2012) and Piketty (2014). In his 2014 work, Capital in the Twenty-First Century, Piketty argues that the rates of growth that the US and other Western countries experienced in the 20th century were an anomaly. The shift toward greater inequality and lower growth overall is a return to the trend inherent to capitalism, where capital earns a greater return than labour. Piketty predicts that growth will slow to between 1% and 2% – 19th-century levels – by the end of the 21st century.

Does social mobility lead to a better life?

Even if the inequality could be tamed by redistribution and the concern over employment reduced to 'lump of labour' hysteria (i.e. the idea that the amount of work available in the economy is fixed, when history suggests that when one area of work contracts another expands to take its place) there would still be a case for revising how social mobility is understood. Academics and politicians, with few exceptions, take as read the idea that economic progression alone defines welfare and progress at the individual and societal level. The evidence refutes this assumption. The 'Easterlin paradox' argues that as societies become more economically developed, their level of happiness does not necessarily increase. As the economist Richard Easterlin, on whose work this claim is based, outlines: 'Simply stated, the happiness-income paradox is this: at a point in time both among and within countries, happiness and income are positively correlated ... But, over time, happiness does not increase when a country's income increases' (Easterlin and Angelescu 2009: 1).

Easterlin argues that there is a correlation between income and happiness, but that there is a limit to this correlation. There are points beyond which increases in income do not lead to happiness. Easterlin first formulated his position in the 1970s, when looking at income progression in different countries from the 1960s onwards (Easterlin 1974). He has since built on this work, with more recent research looking, for example, at data running up to the mid-2000s from across 37 countries collected over various time periods, from 12 to 34 years. His sample included nations that are developed and developing, rich and poor, ex-Communist and capitalist (Easterlin et al 2010).

There have been numerous attempts since the 1970s to disprove the Easterlin paradox, which point to either the methodological (and philosophical) problems with proving happiness or the frailties in the data or analysis used. Stevenson and Wolfers (2008) strongly refute the claims made by Easterlin that there is a cut-off point beyond which happiness does not increase with income. Drawing on a range of large-scale surveys looking at happiness, they argue that: 'Our key result is that the estimated subjective well-being-income gradient is not only significant but also remarkably robust across countries, within countries, and over time' (Stevenson and Wolfers 2008: 10).

However, there has also been a range of other studies that support Easterlin's argument, that higher income does not necessarily imply progress. Protoa and Rustichini (2012) argue that above an income level of approximately £22,100 in countries such as the UK in 2011 happiness does not increase. Beyond this 'bliss point', the desire for a better 'standard of living' in terms of housing, education and consumer goods leads to anxiety and stress. It appears, then, that the idea of success embodied in the present social mobility discourse actively leads to a loss of welfare. It is not a neutral force but a damaging one. Easterlin himself rebuffs the doubters, by accusing them of not differentiating between short-term and long-term happiness:

> … the dissenting view appears to be largely the result of failing to distinguish between the short- and long-term temporal relationship between happiness and income. Over the short term, when fluctuations in macroeconomic conditions dominate the relationship, happiness and income are positively related. Over the long term, happiness and income are unrelated. (Easterlin and Angelescu 2009: 13)

The ONS, in its work on well-being in the UK specifically, found that those in higher-income groups do report higher levels of life satisfaction and happiness – and lower levels of anxiety. However, for those in the lowest-income groups, increases in income matter more, and there are diminishing returns to income increases as we people move up the scale (ONS 2014a).

Yet more evidence looking at life satisfaction over time in the UK at the societal level also offers further support for the Easterlin paradox. Figure 1.2 illustrates that while over the last 40 years gross domestic product (GDP) has risen considerably, life satisfaction has remained relatively constant.

The implications of the Easterlin paradox are off the radar of the present academic and political social mobility discourse. The idea that economic progression may not necessarily bring increased welfare, or in

Figure 1.2: Life satisfaction versus GDP in the UK, 1973–2011

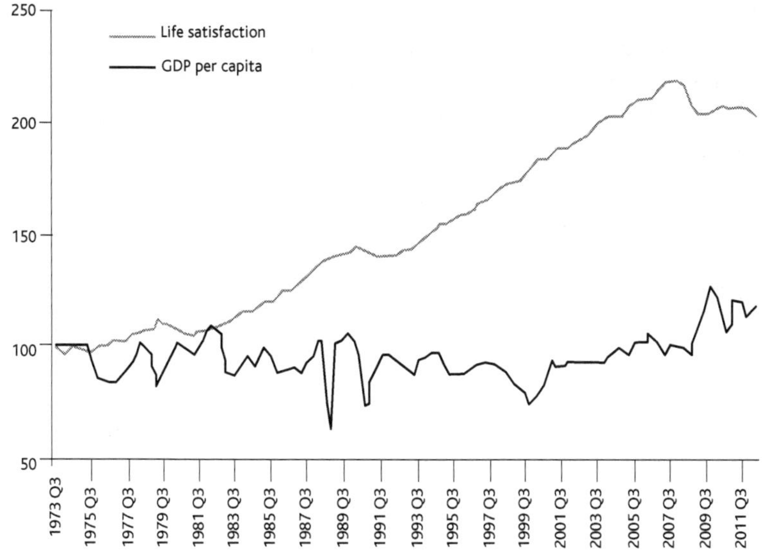

Source: www.behaviouralinsights.co.uk/blogpost/measuring-national-wellbeing

particular may not fully capture what increased welfare may constitute, is not being considered. It cannot be assumed either that the paradox is the function of an inability of individuals to earn as much as they would like or to get that better job, so they adjust to where they are. There is a conscious aspect here that actually belies the term 'paradoxical' altogether, which must be taken into account.

As Friedman (2013) argues, there is no room in the present social mobility discourse for those who do not wish to progress beyond their present economic position or for those who do, the losses may outweigh the benefits. This is not to say that anything but the minority of individuals would say no to more income. The extent to which they actively pursue such gains – and what they are willing to sacrifice – varies greatly. Upward social mobility is not all gain. Friedman points to the social dislocation that can come from moving up the occupational or educational ladder, as the 'beneficiaries' of these moves lose the attachments to the community they come from and never really belong in the one they become part of. For some people, even the potential losses of this nature are not worth it. While it may sound strange in the present discourse, many people like their existing jobs and lives. They want to improve them for sure, but are not necessarily looking for new ones.

As Easterlin himself argues, if happiness is not increased by economic growth, the rationale for building a social and economic system around economic growth has to be questioned. However, questioning the importance of economic growth when inequality is at such high levels has to be done carefully. Economic growth is a necessity if inequality is to be combated. (Chapter Eight looks at the research into well-being, alternative ways of examining stratification in society, and different approaches to organising the social and economic system – and whether this balance between focusing on equality and moving away from purely economistic ways of conceiving of success can be struck).

Holistic social mobility

The present approach to social mobility focuses primarily on the question of 'how much?', with little attention being paid to 'why?'. This would be permissible if the definition of social mobility had a neutral impact, but it does not. As this chapter has shown, how social mobility is defined is intertwined with the great challenges facing early 21st-century societies. The present understanding is contributing to a potentially dystopian future of an increasingly unequal society, chasing a dwindling number of 'high quality' jobs and with a distorted view of its own welfare.

A different approach is suggested in the rest of the book. 'Holistic social mobility' is both a method of looking at issues of progress and success, and an alternative way of conceiving of these things. As a method it implies broadening the parameters of social mobility analysis. If social mobility cannot be interpreted in isolation from wider social forces, neither can a new way of understanding it be constructed without reference to the institutions and structures that make up society. A holistic approach to social mobility does not imply rejecting the analysis of changes in income or occupation. It does mean bringing firmly within the remit of social mobility studies an examination of the very nature of the education system, labour market and social economic model. It also means exploring philosophical approaches that underpin this model in any given society. The holistic method is a multidisciplinary one that makes a virtue of crossing theoretical and thematic boundaries.

As a way of conceiving social mobility, the holistic approach attempts to proceed on the basis of the fault-lines within the existing understanding of social mobility identified here. It attempts to fuse the reality of income and occupation (as the forces that define the progress individuals can make) with another set of realities – both existing and required. The latter realities are that progress in life is not just an economic phenomenon, and it depends on factors that can be separated from the economic. This has always been the case. Measuring progress in purely economic terms is a function of social and economic context. It is not an external given that exists outside such forces. As argued in later chapters, it is possible to construct progress in different terms, if we choose to do so.

The evidence suggests a sense of urgency in the holistic approach. While it is easy to become apocalyptic here, it is crucial to point out at this stage that the UK is richer than it has ever been. Poverty, while extreme for the few, still does not compare to that of even 100 years ago (never mind the centuries before), and we are safer than we have ever been (Pinker 2011, Ridley 2011). Ridley, in fact, makes a strident case for greater optimism in how we see the global futures, arguing in 2012:

> 'Compared with 50 years ago, when I was just four years old, the average human now earns nearly three times as much money (corrected for inflation), eats one third more calories, buries two thirds fewer children, and can expect to live one third longer. In fact, it's hard to find any region of the world that's worse off now than it was then, even though the global population has more than doubled over that period' (Ridley 2012:5).

Pointedly, Ridley also argues that history suggests that we will find solutions to the challenges of our time, such as climate change and global deflation, as we have found solutions to past challenges. Research on happiness and well-being also shows that we are generally happy with our lot (ONS 2014a).

However, even if we do find a way of creating better jobs, living with inequality while chipping away at the edges and continuing to remain optimistic in the face of challenges, this does not mean that the definition of social mobility is necessarily fine as it is. It remains more important than ever to understand the wider issues of inequality, welfare and economy, regardless of the trajectory they take, than is currently recognised. While we may be safer, richer and happier than in the past, this does not apply to all groups in society. As outlined in this chapter, it is not present practices where social mobility are concerned that are failing too many people both in the UK and globally, but the ideas that underlie social mobility itself.

Finally, there is no reason why the relatively benign state of affairs that the majority of people in the UK still enjoy should last. The conditions that produce them – economic, environmental and social – while not under immediate threat, neither are they guaranteed ad infinitum.

The rest of this book examines what a holistic approach means, and why it is needed. It shows how the education system, the labour market and the political system in the UK all depend on a certain idea of success, and suggests ways in which that idea can be moderated and changed. The objective is not to turn away from the present conception of success completely, which would be unrealistic. Rather, it is to show that it is possible and desirable to shift what success and social mobility mean, so as to incorporate what is actually a more realistic view, and to curb the excesses that are causing the problems identified in this chapter. To do this, though, we need to start at the beginning. And so Chapter Two examines the academic discourse surrounding social mobility – what is the history of social mobility, and why are academics unable to agree on what is happening to it?

TWO

Social mobility: rising, falling or staying the same

Introduction

For most of those who study social mobility, it is interesting because it is a vital part of a bigger picture. For sociologists, it enables them to be able to better understand how society is structured. One of the most important contributions to such sociological research was Erikson and Goldthorpe's Constant Flux in 1992. This book was a major comparative study of social mobility across nine different countries. However, one of the most revealing parts of the book with regard to why social mobility should be studied at all is on the very first page: 'Discussion of social action requires reference to actors who have, in the last analysis, to be recognized as individual men and women: we must as Stinchcombe has put it, see the social structure as being "peopled"' (Goldthorpe and Erikson 1992: 1).

The question is whether sociological research manages this 'peopling' successfully or not, or whether it falls back on a preference for the creation and analysis of structures within which people are slotted. This same question also applies to the work of economists. Throughout the different theories outlined in this chapter, how social mobility is examined is always a product of a broader set of beliefs or principles within which it is positioned. This applies to sociologists with their adherence to providing macro-level structural explanations of how society works, or economists and their commitment to mathematical modelling as the route to understanding better how scarce resources are allocated.

The problem with this approach to social mobility is that, as a concept, it is always defined – and thus trapped – within this broader set of principles. Hence, the understanding of what social mobility is and its importance is always partial.

Pitirim Sorokin and the meaning of 'stratification'

The major pre-war sociological contribution to understanding social mobility came from the work of Pitirim Sorokin. The way in which Sorokin considered social mobility was broader. Less trammelled by the development of an academic discourse in the area (which, as in any area of established academic discourse, can close off debate by setting parameters to discussion), Sorokin was able to consider the meaning of social mobility.

For Sorokin: 'by social mobility is understood any transition of an individual or social object or value – anything that has been created or modified by human activity from one social position to another' (Sorokin 1959: 10).

The schema he developed gave equal weight to the importance of downward, upward and horizontal social mobility. Sorokin was equally concerned with social mobility in a range of forms, not just the upward social mobility that concerns our present-day politicians. But he was also concerned with structures of stratification per se, rather than structures defined by social class, occupation or income, unlike our present-day sociologists and economists.

Sorokin did not deny the importance of economic position in defining social mobility, particularly in Western capitalist economies, but he also saw society as politically stratified when its social ranks were hierarchically structured with respect to authority and power as well. Stratification was economic, political or occupational. It was not necessarily a unitary concept but had different facets. As his scope was social mobility and stratification as a concept, Sorokin also looked at different countries and cultures, pointing to the way in which the caste system in India, for instance, as a form of stratification differed from those systems based on occupation in Western economies. This scope allowed him to see social mobility as context-specific.

Sorokin also recognised the critical importance of the movement of groups. While he fully acknowledged that the study of social mobility needed to concern itself with the movements of individuals, it also needed to pay close attention to the impact of these movements – for the social groups who are mobile, those who are not, and for the structures within which these groups exist. This concern for the interaction between social mobility and the society in which it occurs also extended to ambivalence regarding the merits of mobility. Sorokin described a price to be paid for social mobility in dysfunctional outcomes for society, in terms of negative psychological impacts, social isolation and loneliness for individuals who move away from their familiar cultural context into one where they feel less of a sense of belonging.

The great value in starting with Sorokin is to illustrate that there is a precedent where different ways of considering social mobility are concerned. By focusing on the importance of context in understanding social mobility, Sorokin highlights that stratification is not static. In the UK, for example, the significant changes in ethnic composition that have occurred at the same time as the rise in the study of social mobility do not appear to have been able to penetrate the academic orthodoxy where social mobility is concerned. A more reflexive 'Sorokinesque' approach may have enabled greater discussion, in the UK context at least.

Finally, this kind of approach also allows what is understood by 'stratification' to change over time as societies change. This insight is extremely important. The objective of the holistic approach is to take a forward-looking perspective on social mobility in the 21st century. The likelihood of social, economic, technological or political change shifting how stratification is understood must be recognised.

David Glass and the dominance of class

As Payne (1990) argues, Sorokin's pluralistic approach did not find favour in the study of social mobility of the UK mainly due to the influence of Glass's landmark work, which was the first real attempt at defining the field of enquiry in the UK. Social Mobility in Britain, published in 1954 (Glass 1954), drew mainly from national research conducted in 1949 with a random sample or 10,000 adults, which was the largest study of its kind undertaken at the time. In selecting occupation as the indicator of social status and concentrating on intergenerational differences between father and sons as the measure of social mobility, Glass frames the rest of the sociological study that has been undertaken since then and up to the present day, accepting the relatively recent increase in attention given to the position of women. However, Glass's study may actually take a wider view than Payne gives it credit for. Two of the chapters look at the stratification in voluntary organisations. The rationale for this is the argument that leadership in such organisations offers an alternative form of social prestige. While this line of enquiry was not taken forward by stratification sociologists post-Glass, it does reveal that this study was still searching for the dominant definition of status in the UK, and was at least open to the possibility that there were complementary forms of stratification to class.

Glass's book also contains chapters looking at the influence of educational background on intergenerational mobility. It was produced in the wake of the Education Act 1944, which ushered in the biggest transformation in the English school system in its history. In his opening commentary, Glass felt that the increasing importance given to education by the Act would lead to education itself driving greater social mobility. Hence, his book also laid some foundations for the present political discourse and its belief in the power of education.

However, Glass was also sensitive to some of the potentially negative implications of social mobility. He argued that the three-track system of grammar, secondary modern and technical schools could lead to some being left behind. He was concerned about the resentment that those who did not make it to grammar school, and hence who did not progress to higher prestige occupations, may feel, compounded by the fact that their failure to do so was not due to some hidden mechanism of exclusion, based in nepotism or economic disadvantage, but due to their public inadequacies as they were unsuccessful in the 'fair' selection system of the 11-plus exam. Glass suggested that to reduce this risk, ways of increasing the social prestige of the occupations that such young people did enter should be considered.

The willingness to consider the implications for social mobility on society itself, as well as an acute awareness of the case for action to change what prestige means for the good of society, illustrates that Glass is not only part of the evolution of academic and political discourses, but also of the holistic one being developed in this book.

Michael Young, meritocracy, industrialism and historicism

Payne (1990) also goes on to describe a dearth in research into social mobility in the UK for the 20 years after Glass until another landmark piece of research, the Oxford Mobility Study, conducted in 1972. However, this did not mean that nothing was produced over that period germane to the social mobility debate in the UK.

The Rise of Meritocracy, written by Michael Young in 1958, was a satire warning against the dangers of building a society where status is based entirely on merit, when that society is already stratified by wealth and power. While it is not a piece of sociological research, it has had a significant impact on how social mobility is conceived. Young picks up on the worries that Glass expressed of the danger of frustration and injustice becoming even more pronounced as society moves to becoming 'fairer', with rewards not distributed by ascription but by education. His narrator describes how, over the mid-part of the

21st century, society became ossified into a number of self-selecting classes based on measures of intelligence. As what Young describes as the 'bureaucratic system' becomes more efficient, intelligence can be measured with greater and greater accuracy in ever younger children. By 2030, the potential of children would be accurately identified in children as young as three. The continual advances in the ability of society to identify and reward merit only serves to produce a self-recruiting elite, who use their moral authority to further cement their power and rewards. The narrator describes the breakdown of society as those whose inferior abilities exclude them from the higher classes' revolt.

This dystopian vision of meritocracy, while widely read and quoted, has had something of the opposite impact on the discourse around stratification, social mobility and education that Young intended. Rather than acting to warn against the dangers of continual educational expansion in a stratified and unequal society, the need to create a more meritocratic society in Britain has been at the centre of the political social mobility discourse since the 1990s. Writing in The Guardian in 2001, Young says: 'It would help if Mr Blair would drop the word [meritocracy] from his public vocabulary, or at least admit to the downside' (Young 2001).

The inability or unwillingness of politicians to confront the extent of change necessary to make meritocracy viable is Young's major concern. Several of the developments that Young foretold in fiction have come to resemble reality. As well as the earlier identification of potential in children, which is quite prescient of the extensive work that has been undertaken into measuring ability among infants from different groups in the last 20 years (see Chapter Four), Young's book also describes how higher education would come to be essential for admission to higher class groups, which it now is. The rise of a powerful, self-recruiting, self-aggrandising elite is exactly the problem that tasks the majority of politicians as well as many academics looking at social mobility today. Other elements of the book remain fictional, however, and have yet to resemble fact. Young describes how competition would wither away, and the discontent that comes from a system that is unequal but now justly so has yet to come to pass, and probably will not do so by 2030. There may well still be the kind of negative outcomes from a justly unequal system, in terms of alienation, frustration and resentment among those who see themselves as failures in this kind of society but who are not minded to revolt – at least not in an organised, political way. In highlighting so clearly the particular nature of meritocracy, and its difference from equality of outcome, Young's book is extremely important. As with Sorokin's work and, to an extent, Glass's work, it reinforces the idea that the study of social mobility should place at its centre the impact (or lack of impact) that it has on the society in which it occurs.

In a similar vein to Young, a number of US writers from the 1960s onwards sought to make an explicit link between upward social mobility and industrialisation (see, for example, Blau and Duncan 1967, Kerr et al 1973). In the US, a theory was also being developed which had a significant impact on the understanding of social mobility, and which attempted to place it in the context of the 'development' of society. There is an inherent 'logic' in the shift from pre-industrial to industrial societies that brings with it a common pattern of mobility across such societies. This common pattern is an increase in both absolute and relative mobility, and these changes are necessary parts of the development of industrial society. It is an approach driven by a historicist account of human development. There is an inevitable move to pluralist democracy, as it is the form of political arrangement most functional for the equally inevitable progression of all societies from the industrial to the pre-industrial. Social mobility takes the particular form it does within this context due to the role of technology in increasing the skill requirements of employment, creating more of the kind of managerial, administrative positions that Young also describes. This shift is coupled with a move to achievement and indeed meritocracy as qualifications become far more important in the recruitment of staff, and as we move away from an ascription economy where upward social mobility is based on social backgrounds towards one based more on the qualities of the individual.

Finally, while mobility is only part of a more comprehensive story, it is an important one. Social mobility contributes significantly to the stability of liberal democracies, by providing a justification for their existence. By being based on achievement, inequality is legitimised, and with the bias towards upward mobility, presumably the majority of the population will feel satisfied with what the state offers them.

Such 'liberal theories of industrialism' (Bell:1973) have been heavily criticised by other sociologists, in particular Goldthorpe and Erikson (1992), on the grounds of their historicism and inaccuracy. The relationship between economic growth and progression and social mobility is more complex than the liberal industrial theory assumes. For example, the role of technology in social mobility, assumed to be benign, may in reality be anything but (as argued in Chapter One).

John Goldthorpe and the importance of measurement

The 1972 Oxford Mobility Study was reported in the 1980 book *Social Mobility and Class Structure in Modern Britain*, by John Goldthorpe and colleagues, which marked the beginning of the period of dominance in the study of social mobility in sociology which continues to the present day. Goldthorpe et al's analytical techniques, conception of what the study of social mobility entails and their arguments surrounding the extent of it have set their own parameters around how the vast majority of sociologists look at social mobility (Goldthorpe et al 1980; Goldthorpe 1996, 2007, 2012; Goldthorpe and Jackson 2007; Goldthorpe and Mills 2008), as later acknowledged by Payne and Roberts (2002).

The Oxford Study was not dissimilar to Glass's study in the early 1950s, as it was a major national representative survey of over 10,000 men aged 20 to 64 in England and Wales. Respondents were asked to report their current occupation and employment status and those of their father when the respondents were about 14 years old. An assumption was made regarding the degree of career mobility across the lifespan. Goldthorpe et al take father's occupation at the age of 35 as what they describe as 'occupational maturity'. Beyond that, it is assumed there would be relatively little career mobility.

Occupation and employment status data were then coded into a seven social class schema designed by Goldthorpe himself, based on market situation (source and level of income, security of employment, promotional aspects) and work situation (degree of control and authority in job). There was, however, a simplification of these social classes into three groups: service class, intermediate class and working class. While the service class included experts and specialists filling important positions in the dominant institutions of society, it is far broader than what could be understood as a conventional elite; Goldthorpe, however, felt that there was a significant level of social distance between the two groups with an intermediate group in between.

Goldthorpe's major conclusion is that at the time of this study there was significant upward social mobility in the absolute sense as the occupational structure was changing. Service and intermediate group jobs were expanding creating more 'lower middle' and 'middle' class' jobs which needed to be filled. But the relative levels of mobility were not increasing. The chances of these new jobs being filled by those from the existing working and middle class locations were not changing. It was still the case that the chances of middle class jobs being taken by working class people was far lower.

This distinction between absolute and relative mobility is a crucial one for Goldthorpe, and the failure (in his eyes) of politicians to grasp it is his major bugbear. He defines these two concepts as: 'Absolute rates refer to the actual proportion of individuals of given class origins who are mobile to different class destinations, while relative rates compare the chances of individuals of differing class origins arriving at different class destinations and thus indicate the extent of social fluidity' (Goldthorpe 2012: 3).

It is the relative, intergenerational mobility of those from different social classes that has been Goldthorpe's major concern, and for him, it is what social mobility means. The 1972 Oxford Mobility Study showed that while in the early 1970s there may have been 'room at the top', some social groups were more likely than others to take advantage of the new opportunities that were emerging. Whatever the chance of a working-class boy reaching the service class, a boy from the intermediate class had twice the chance and a boy from the service class four times the chance. Relative mobility rates had remained remarkably constant – there had not been reductions in class inequality or increases in social mobility. Those in higher social positions were still far better off than those in the working classes. Overall, though, Goldthorpe did find a significant degree of this absolute mobility. Over 70% of the children in the study were in different social classes to their fathers. On this reading there was significant social mobility in the UK, but it did not, in Goldthorpe's view, imply greater equality of opportunity.

This 'room at the top', however, was not a permanent phenomenon. As the century progressed, later cohort research shows a levelling out of absolute mobility. This led Goldthorpe to conclude that the 'change observed in absolute rates was in very large part structurally determined' (2012: 6). In the same 2012 article, Goldthorpe summarises his position on social mobility across the 20th century, and it is clear that it has also remained relatively consistent over a 30-year period. On the basis of his later work, for example, Goldthorpe and Mills (2008), which brought together data from 13 representative surveys of the adult British population carried out between 1972 and 2005, and that of others such as Paterson and Iannelli (2007) who looked at both men and women born between 1937 and 1946 comparing them to those born between 1967 and 1976, Goldthorpe states:

> Absolute rates of inter-generational class mobility ... appear
> quite high ... rates of upward mobility increased in the

course of the twentieth century primarily as a consequence of class structural change ie of the expansion of professional and managerial positions creating more 'room at the top'. However, immobility at the 'top' also increased, and there were indications that towards the end of the century rates of upward mobility among men were stabilising, as the growth of professional and managerial positions began to slacken and as men faced greater competition for these positions from women. Relative rates of intergenerational class mobility ... showed a basic constancy over most of the twentieth century, or at all events no sustained directional change, with the possible exception of some recent slight increase in fluidity among women. (Goldthorpe and Mills 2008: 88)

Those sociologists who do not agree with Goldthorpe come at his work from a number of angles.

Geoff Payne, for example, has been writing about social mobility in the UK for about as long as Goldthorpe, but he parts company with him mainly by stressing the importance of class – as opposed to occupational change – in understanding inequality and social mobility, refuting the lesser importance that Goldthorpe places on absolute mobility. Payne argues that the fact that large numbers of people have moved out of lower socioeconomic groups is of greater consequence than Goldthorpe allows for. Its major implication has been that the actual size of these different groups has changed, so that there are actually far fewer people at the lower end of this stratification system. These changes in the composition of the overall class structure are important for both the individuals involved and society itself. As Payne states (1990: 297): 'mobile people and indeed the immobile too, do not encounter mobility as a relative chance, but rather as mobility or non-mobility.' This attention to the lived experience of mobility and the role of occupational change in both driving and defining lifecourse mobility makes Payne's contribution very valuable in the context of the ideas being developed here. Understanding the nature of changes in the structure of the economy and labour market are legitimate and vital parts of the study of social mobility. Payne (1990: 295) describes the problem with Goldthorpe's work here as being not that it is 'interested in class, but to narrowly interested in class'. This narrowness means that while Goldthorpe's work is, in many ways, the starting point for understanding social mobility in the UK in the last 50 years, it should not also be the end point.

The commitment to a class-based understanding of social mobility is based in Goldthorpe positioning his approach within a broad Marxist context. This commitment, though, leads him, in Payne's opinion, not to tackle some of the implications of his findings. The extent of social mobility that the 1972 study found, for example, calls into question the cohesiveness of the different class groupings. If they are subject to what Goldthorpe himself described as 'constant flux', then how could they develop the kind of class consciousness that is a prerequisite for collective action, which is the driver of social change in any Marxist-inspired framework?

Payne's critique is again very useful, in turning the spotlight on how class is understood by those who experience it. Goldthorpe remains firmly committed to the primacy of class as the best way of understanding stratification and the major determinant of life chances into the early 21st century. This is a contentious commitment in a number of ways, but none more so than in the area of consciousness. The evidence suggests that 'the subjective significance of class has declined considerably over the past 30 years' (Park et al 2013:180), that the class that people think they are in is far less useful in understanding their attitudes. Nor is socioeconomic group as measured by occupation a very strong predictor of their views on welfare or politics, for example. Rather than the invisible hand of the market in the 21st century (which, given the rampant competitive ethos now extending to all aspects of life, is now in quite open view), it may make more sense to talk of the invisible hand of the class system, which is structuring our everyday lives but in a way that we are far less conscious of. To the success paradox we must add what Savage (2000) describes as the 'paradox of class'.

Payne does not confine himself to offering a critique of Goldthorpe. In 2002, Payne looked at a different set of data to that of Goldthorpe's in 1972, and argued in Payne and Roberts (2002) that social mobility, in both absolute and relative terms, was increasing at a greater level than work in what the paper describes as 'the Nuffield tradition' (inspired by Goldthorpe and colleagues from Nuffield College) allows. Expanding on the critique offered in 1990, Payne and Roberts argued that the longitudinal survey data they used in their paper, drawn from the British Election Study (BES) carried out at each general election, was superior to the 'one-off' cohort analysis used in the 1972 study. The problem with such cohort comparison work (and it is a criticism that Goldthorpe himself applies with some force to the economistic approach to social mobility pioneered by Machin, Blanden and others, as we shall see later in the chapter, is that it is difficult to hold age constant, so that those of different ages are compared when they are actually at very different points in their careers. Payne and Roberts also point to the extreme limitations of a survey that focuses only on the experiences of men. While later work by Goldthorpe and others does look at women separately (Goldthorpe and Mills 2008), Payne and Roberts bring home the importance of maintaining this distinction in the very nature of social mobility analysis.

Absolute versus relative social mobility

The final critique of Goldthorpe offered by Geoff Payne and Judy Roberts returns to the issue of absolute and relative mobility. They argue that the separation of these two forms of mobility is taking the study of the field down the wrong direction, and that it is the interaction of these different phenomena that should be the focus: 'Equally, although the odds-ratios used to express "relative mobility" may be statistically calculated independent of the marginal totals, the numbers of people following particular origin-to-destination trajectories are not sociologically independent of changes in the distribution of origins and destinations' (Payne and Roberts 2002: 13).

Looking at the BES, Payne and Roberts find that Britain was more open than the work from 1972 suggests. At the same time, however, their conclusions do not look hugely different in some ways to the overall summary of the UK mobility history offered by Goldthorpe in 2012:

> 'The patterns of mobility that we have reported suggest that Britain became a more open society between 1972 and 1992 for men but then the picture changed. On the basis of the BES evidence, opportunities for upward mobility for men decreased in the mid-1990s. The changes in openness are demonstrated both by absolute and relative mobility measures. The gate to the service class was pushed wider open for a while, but then swung-to again.' (Goldthorpe 2012: 8)

What Payne and Roberts do, though, is place the changing nature of the occupational structure as the key explanatory variable, and it is the detailed understanding of specific occupational changes that is important. Payne builds on this theory in his 2012 paper Labouring Under a Misapprehension. In it he presents a different way of measuring social mobility, which combines the measurement of absolute and relative mobility that he calls a 'conditional disparity ratio'. He argues that the probability of being in a particular class considerably affects one's chance of leaving it. Again, the explanation that this begs is not completely dissimilar to what Goldthorpe has suggested before. Goldthorpe has explained the resilience of relative mobility in terms of differential decision making at particular points in the educational and employment trajectory by different class groups. Such an explanation could fit with a number of sociological explanations of differences in mobility, but it also remains in the realm of the broadly descriptive. Payne argues that the working class is decreasing in size, but there is a danger of those in it being left behind and experiencing frustration, alienation and presumably (although Payne's 2012 paper does not mention this explicitly) financial hardship.

Searching for consensus

What is becoming clear is that while Goldthorpe and his colleagues may have exerted a great influence, there is certainly no complete or comfortable consensus among sociologists regarding social mobility. It makes sense to talk of a sociological viewpoint grounded in class analysis, biased towards the intergenerational and descriptive, but this does not imply that there is agreement among those examining social mobility. It is possible to identify research that describes relative mobility and absolute mobility as increasing, decreasing or constant, and it appears that all scenarios are a possibility, depending on the data analysed, the techniques used and the position on what mobility means taken by the researchers. However, none of those researching the field point to big changes, excepting the upward mobility into the service classes in the mid/late 20th century. Any change is gradual and takes time.

As Lambert et al argue (2007), the studies that look at longitudinal data as opposed to examining cohorts tend to point to increasing social mobility. They go on to perform a meta-analysis of 31 different contemporary social surveys going back to 1800, arguing that this shows that social mobility has increased, albeit slowly, over this period. The rate of increase appears relatively constant when comparing data from those born in the late 18th and early 19th centuries to data concerning those born in the 20th century. While the focus of much of the article is on the rates of social mobility per se, they recognise that it is important to try to differentiate between downward and upward mobility: 'increasing magnitude of upward moves has fallen off over the period, whilst the downward mobility magnitudes have increased [this] suggests that younger cohorts tend to experience relatively more long range downward mobility than long range upward mobility, in contrast to the experience of older cohorts' (Lambert et al 2007: 14).

The legitimacy of downward mobility as a cause for concern may seem a non-issue from the political standpoint (or, you could argue, even from the non-sociological standpoint): it is clearly a bad thing if some people lose social status. However, from the pure meritocratic position, this is not a problem if it means the most able are rising to the top, which will actually strengthen society. There may also be other factors at play here, meaning that downward mobility is not portrayed as the problem in sociology that it is in politics. First, there is an almost inherent tendency in sociology to see advancement of the interests of those in lower socioeconomic groups as more important than any detrimental outcomes for those in higher positions. This tendency, rooted in the history of the discipline, will affect in some way what researchers say and how they look at an issue like this. And second, the desire of sociologists to position themselves as scientists reporting on phenomena in the social world as opposed to quasi policy makers can make them shy away from any detailed attempts to explore the merits of either downward or upward mobility. This does not stop socioligists criticising politicians for their lack of understanding of social mobility. Sociologists see the obsession with upward mobility as being to the detriment of a better understanding of the issue.

There are those who offer a rapprochement with the views of politicians, in contrast to the cynicism with which most of the other sociologists treat political interventions in the field. Li and Devine take what has to be a more productive approach, as they state in the conclusions to their 2011 paper 'Is social mobility really declining?'.

[T]his preoccupation with upward social mobility facilitated by major structural change may be somewhat galling for academic sociologists who place a high premium on the distinction between absolute and relative mobility and are exasperated that most politicians and media commentators do not acknowledge that a genuine meritocracy involves downward mobility as well as upward mobility on the basis of merit ... it is more constructive to recognise that politicians, policy makers, media pundits and, most importantly, voting parents have different preoccupations to academic researchers on social mobility. Upward mobility, rather than downward mobility, is the name of the game. The ongoing challenge for social scientists of whatever discipline is to understand how and why the debate on social mobility is conducted in the way that it is and to contribute to discussions of policy that improve the life chances of working-class men and women in the lower echelons of the class structure in contemporary Britain. (Li and Devine 2011: 17)

Li and Devine do, however, revert to sociological type in the final sentence, and place a concern with how those from the lower classes can be helped to move up as the priority, as opposed to helping the middle classes who may move down. It could be argued that if social scientists are serious about recognising the different preoccupations of politicians and others, they need to confront the fact that the need to avoid downward mobility is at least of equal political importance to improving the life chances of the working classes.

Li and Devine's paper makes another valuable contribution beyond their thoughtful conclusions. They look at cohort surveys from 1991 and 2005, comparing these to try to ascertain whether social mobility was improving or getting worse at these two points in time. They found that upward mobility for men had declined when comparing the two surveys, and downward mobility had increased, but the upward mobility still outweighed the downward mobility for men (40.6% in 1991 compared with 31.3% in 2005). However, while women's upward mobility was increasing over the period, downward mobility remains slightly higher than upward mobility among women (36.8% in 1991 compared with 35.9% in 2005). Women, then, are more likely to be downwardly mobile than men.

Li and Devine also point to increasing relative mobility in line with what Lambert et al argue, but in contrast to Goldthorpe's position. In particular, they find an increase in long-range upward mobility for men. So, while in one way this research may lend weight to the concerns of politicians, in another way it does not, as it shows that the rags to riches journey that politicians so readily associate with social mobility is not in decline but actually increasing.

Finally, Devine and Li also share Payne's concern with the changing sizes of different groups, and show that men and women occupy different parts of the occupational structure. Men still dominate the positions in the top two socioeconomic groups, for example, and the proportion of all women in working-class positions is 40%. The percentage of men in such positions is 27%. This analysis shows clearly that social mobility is located in a different context for men and women.

The entry of the economists

The sociological analysis of social mobility in the UK has a history stretching back to the 1950s, while the economistic tradition is more recent. It is the contention of several sociologists, in particular

Goldthorpe (2012) and Saunders (2012b) that this is not a tradition as such. They argue that the claims regarding social mobility that economists have made are based on a limited amount of data, that these data are analysed incorrectly and that the use of income is inferior to occupation-based class categorisations as a basis for understanding stratification.

The research that has sparked the ire of the sociologists so much has been produced in the main by a group of economists from the Centre for Economic Performance at the London School of Economics and Political Science. Building on a growing international interest in intergenerational mobility research based on income and not on social class (some of which is discussed later), research began to emerge in the early 2000s which looked at mobility in the UK in this way (Blanden et al 2001, Blanden and Machin 2004). The main finding, based on comparisons of children born in 1958 and in 1970 using the National Child Development Study and the British Cohort Study respectively, was that 'social mobility' had declined. For those born later, in 1970, there is a stronger relationship with family incomes when they reach their early 30s than for those born in 1958. More specifically, Blanden and Machin (2004) found that 42% of sons born into the richest quartile of families in 1970 achieved incomes at this level themselves when they grew up, while just 11% ended up with incomes in the bottom quartile. However, for those born in 1958 the corresponding figures were 35% and 17%. Rather than the odds ratios, which define the relative mobility analysis of the sociologists, the economists use elasticity as their measure. On this basis the 'coefficient of elasticity' rose from 0.21 for the 1958 cohort to 0.29 for those born in 1970. There was, therefore, a slight increase in the association between family income and child income across the two cohorts.

In terms of explaining this change, Blanden et al (2007, 2011) point to widening income inequality in Britain in the 1970s, caused by children from higher income groups benefiting disproportionately from the increase in numbers going on to higher education. Further research undertaken by this group of economists shows that the earnings premium related to graduate study has remained significant despite the expansion in numbers, hence the argument that higher education expansion is actually driving a slowing down in social mobility (Blanden et al 2005).

Goldthorpe is rigorous in his critique of the position of this group of economists in Understanding – and Misunderstanding – Social Mobility in Britain (2012). In this critique (or more accurately, caveat, as it does not in itself render the work of Blanden, Machin and colleagues invalid), he is correct to point to the limitations in the size of the body of work compared to the sociological studies. However, the strength of this research has to be based on the rigour to which these academics have subjected the data to analysis, rather than its existence within a wider set of complementary work that looks at different data sets over longer periods of time.

The more substantive methodological critique concerns missing data and the biases that might result, and the fragility of the measure of family income variable. Stephen Gorard (2008) takes the missing data criticism forward. The first thing that he reminds us, which is especially pertinent to the argument being developed here is that the economistic research does not measure 'social' mobility but 'income' mobility': 'A child who became a university lecturer, born to a father who worked as a fireman and earned as much in real terms as a lecturer, might be an example of social mobility based on education. But this would not show up as income mobility?' (Gorard 2008: 320).

Gorard goes on to examine the actual number of cases analysed from the two cohort studies, and outlines that when a number of categories of respondent are removed, including, for example, the long-term unemployed, we are left with only around 2,000 cases in each cohort, which represents only just above 10% of the whole cohort for each one (Blanden et al 2005). Gorard goes on to argue that the majority of the difference in incomes of those across the two cohorts is actually attributable to factors other than parental income, and finally, that a detailed reading of the research by Blanden et al indicates that there is actually a high level of income mobility. As Gorard states:

> … 17% of those born to the poorest 25% of families end up in the richest quadrant, and vice versa. If there were no financial inheritance, no inheritance of talent, no nepotism, and perfect social mobility then the maximum this figure could be is 25%. The difference from the ideal of perfect mobility in these tables containing 2,000 cases is represented by only about 25 cases in each of the 'wrong' extreme cells. Taken at face value, a key policy message could be that Britain has a quite staggering level of social mobility. (Gorard 2008: 322)

Finally, not satisfied with deconstructing the actual research, Gorard turns his attention to the explanations. His issue with the argument that this alleged slowing down in social mobility was due to increased university attendance is quite simply that it does not square with the evidence. An acceleration in university attendance occurred in the early 2000s, which would have been too late for the majority of those born in 1970.

These criticisms add up to a quite formidable set of caveats regarding the strength of the work by Blanden and colleagues. Gorard's main point, also echoed by Goldthorpe and Saunders, is that this research is just not robust enough to justify a claim that social mobility in the UK has stalled. This is a crucial point to make when a whole political bandwagon has been built around it, which is influencing a whole range of policy areas.

Goldthorpe's criticisms of this work go beyond caveats. He argues that the measures of income used are 'one shot' – they are taken from one point in the lives of correspondents in the survey, and may not reflect their income over their individual lifetimes. The specific problem is that the transitory component of family income in 1958 is higher than in 1970 (Erikson and Goldthorpe 2010). The picture in 1958, then, of family income is less reliable than that in 1970, which means the ability to compare cohorts is impaired significantly. Blanden et al respond to this in a 2011 paper where they build a model of permanent income to get over the 'one shot' problem. They then claim that current earnings are a good predictor of permanent income, and even if there are greater transitory errors in the 1958 research (which there may be some evidence of), it may reduce the fall in mobility but it does not imply that the data are not statistically significant. They also seek to address Goldthorpe's assertions that class is a better predictor of income, and a superior mechanism for delineating social stratification.

This debate between the different academic groups will continue. Much is down to interpretation and belief in the relative superiority of different analytical techniques, but this aspect of it has a wider resonance. The issue of whether class or income per se is a better measure of stratification is a broader one, and while it will not be solved by this exchange, the separation of the two ideas as proposed by Blanden et al (as opposed to one being the product of the other) does have some appeal. They offer a conciliatory conclusion to their 2011 paper: 'intergenerational income and social class mobility measure different things. Social class reflects wider job autonomy and wider social capital while income and earnings reflect economic opportunities. In this study we find limited common ground between the two approaches' (Blanden et al 2011: 26).

The extent to which we can be satisfied with this conclusion is important. Accepting the significant caveats placed by Gorard, it is necessary to decide whether the area of income-based social mobility analysis is in itself a separate thing from work based on social class. While it may be much less mature than its sociological cousin, should work be done to support its growth? The decision is actually already being made, as this work continues to be produced and, as outlined later, seems to have gained a significant foothold in the political psyche. Despite the imperfections in this work, looking at income as a factor in the stratification mosaic in its own right is valuable and essential.

The UK, the 'sick man' of social mobility

The political foothold that the work of Blanden et al has secured is also a consequence of how their research findings on UK income mobility sit in the international context. Comparing the UK to other countries, they have produced several pieces of work suggesting that the UK is not doing well, and is at best mediocre in this regard. Blanden (2009) examines a range of different studies across the world and produce a composite table that positions the UK as the second most immobile of 12 countries behind, notably, France, Canada and Scandinavian countries, with Brazil and the US above the UK. There are considerable caveats to allow for here, however. This is not the outcome of one distinct international cohort survey, but the product of assessing 12 different pieces of work with their own methodologies, delivered at different times.

In his 2012 pamphlet Social Mobility Delusions, Saunders is virulent in his criticisms of Blanden (2009) .Despite acknowledging the limitations in the comparisons that can be made internationally where income mobility is concerned, Saunders feels that the Blanden paper still stretches too far in its claims, going on to say that, on all measures examined, the UK 'tends to the immobile end of the spectrum' (Saunders 2012: 20). The UK only appears in one of the measures – looking at the relationship between educational achievements and income and children, the UK appears to be performing around average rather than poorly.

Gorard (2008) also has something to say here. He points to the decision to compare Britain with others, using data from the 1970 Oxford Mobility Study work as opposed to the 1958 survey undertaken by Glass when several of the other countries used surveys from 1958 or closer to it. Given that the 1970 survey shows greater immobility in the UK, it is fair to assume that it will inevitably mean the UK looking as if it is doing worse than it would be doing if the 1958 results were used.

It is worth lingering on these points. They are more than just another disagreement between academics because, as both Saunders and Gorard point out very well, this research is inherently politically appealing. In such globally competitive times, it compares the UK to its rivals and shows bad news, which always offers more political capital. Because of this, and possibly because (as Saunders argues) this research has benefited from influential sponsorship in the guise of the educational charity the Sutton Trust, the research by Blanden and colleagues over the mid to late 2000s has enjoyed much interest from policy makers.

The constant flux

There certainly appears to be a view among several of the sociologists listed here that the economists could have been more circumspect and considered in the conclusions they have drawn from their work. The sociologists (unsurprisingly) take a different view where comparative social mobility is concerned.

Goldthorpe and Erikson, in their 1992 book The Constant Flux, looked at data from nine different countries in the 1970s. They argue that absolute mobility varied between these countries but there was no trend as such to this, while relative mobility showed no such variation and was far more stable. The factors accounting for the changes in absolute mobility are related to the nature of the political regime and to differences in how countries adapt to external influences in the international political economy. In effect, Goldthorpe and Erikson (1992: 388) argue that cross-national variation in social mobility largely reflects 'effects specific to particular societies at particular times'. The 'constant flux' idea supports the conclusions that Goldthorpe has reached over his career on social mobility in the UK. The comparative position of the UK where social mobility is concerned is less of an issue in this context, as there is much less difference between nations – or at least any differences that are subject to systematic explanation. Goldthorpe and Erikson were particularly concerned in The Constant Flux to confront the industrialisation ideas of Blau and Duncan (1967), and find conclusively against the idea that as societies become more economically developed, they become more fluid.

However, as with Goldthorpe and Erikson's domestic conclusions, their views on international social mobility have not been accepted uncritically. In 2004 Breen and Luijx look at later data from the same countries as Goldthorpe and Erikson going up to the mid-1990s, but over a longer time span, utilising several different surveys and including information on women. Breen and Luijx argue that there is a tendency for increases in absolute social mobility over time as occupational structures change. While there may be big differences between countries in these rates, they are systematic, and Breen and Luijx come out broadly in favour of the industrialisation thesis. They also give some weight to the role of politics. In countries where there is greater 'direct political intervention of the kind associated with state socialist and social democratic societies' (Breen and Luijx 2004: 401), mobility is higher.

Further work looking at data collected since The Constant Flux also supports the industrialisation thesis. Yaish and Andersen (2012) utilise survey data from 20 countries collected in the 1990s as part of the International Social Survey Programme (ISSP). Their focus is on the relative importance of individual and macro-level variables in explaining any differences in rates of intergenerational occupational mobility between countries. They also support the idea that greater economic development exerts a positive impact, but that levels of economic migration – and also having a communist past – have a role to play. In their conclusions they compare the relative contributions of individual-level influences, in particular educational attainment and political/historical differences. They argue that their model can account for almost 80% of the differences in absolute mobility between countries. Unfortunately, the UK does not feature in the survey that informed their work, but the interesting aspect of their study is this attempt to look at the individual and societal levels in explaining social mobility.

The debate over structure and agency – or the extent to which individuals have the ability to shape their own destinations relative to the frameworks within which they live – should be at the crux of understanding social mobility. The preponderance of sociological research, though, looks at measuring social mobility rather than explaining it.

The fact that the sociological research above is dated, that some of it does not include the UK, and that it does not enjoy the influential patronage of income-based measures of inequality all combines to mean that, while it may offer a strong rejoinder to the view that the UK is the 'sick man' of Europe (or the world), it has not taken hold like that of the economists.

Additional work from influential sources has supported this 'sick man' position. Miles Corak, a Canadian economist, has written a number of influential papers on international mobility (Corak 2006). He has produced what he describes as 'the Great Gatsby Curve', which shows the relationship between intergenerational elasticity in income and national income inequality, as measured by the Gini co-efficient for 12 of the richest countries in the world, which is reproduced in Figure 2.1.

Figure 2.1: The Great Gatsby Curve

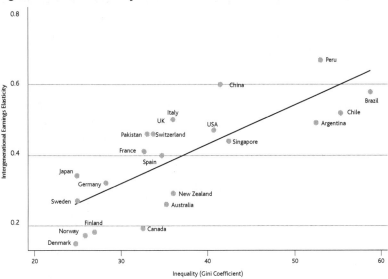

Source: Corak (2012)

This diagram features in President Obama's 2012 economic report (White House 2012).On both sides of the Atlantic it is the income-based analysis that has entered the political mainstream, shaping the view on social mobility, and in both cases portraying the UK and the US as problem cases. It shows there is a strong relationship between higher levels of inequality and lower levels of intergenerational economic mobility among fathers and sons. Predictably in social mobility analysis there are those who disagree with this link between inequality and immobility. Scott Winship (2012) from the Brookings Institute in the US, points to the fact that (as with the work of Blanden and colleagues discussed earlier) the graph is assembled from different surveys with contrasting methodologies, done at different times. Nevertheless, despite these criticisms, the power of the message that income-based social mobility in the US has stalled shows no sign of diminishing.

The momentum of this argument is less surprising when it is supported by analysis from heavyweight international research bodies such as the OECD. In 2010 the OECD examined the influence of parental background, as measured by educational achievement of parents, on wages and educational attainment of various cohorts of adults for 14 European OECD countries. They also examined the influence of parental background on the cognitive achievements of 15-year-old students in 30 OECD countries, and report a strong link between parental and children's earnings for the UK, that is low mobility. However, at the same time they recognise that:

> … intergenerational social mobility is measured by several different indicators, since no single indicator provides a complete picture of social mobility and the United Kingdom seems to be less mobile in terms of wage persistence (measured by the summary indicator of wage persistence) than in terms of education persistence. (Causa and Johannson 2010: 24)

This seems only to reaffirm the point that, as with studies of intergenerational social mobility that look at the UK alone, there is a lack of consensus where the extent of social mobility is concerned.

Is inequality a problem?

What unites these sociologists and economists is the view that social mobility reflects some form of structural inequality in society, and these inequalities are things to be combated. But there are alternative perspectives that reflect differences in natural ability and effort and, as such, are far less problematic.

Peter Saunders has been writing on social mobility since the 1990s (1997, 2010a, 2010b, 2012). In recent years, he has subjected the work of Blanden et al to heavy criticism, siding far more with the view that social mobility is relatively static over time, in keeping with Goldthorpe et al. Where he departs from the majority of the sociologists and economists whose work has been described so far, is in his explanations for the stability of social mobility. He argues that this is a function of differences in IQ, and that sociologists and politicians have ignored research showing the importance of IQ and hereditary factors because it does not fit with their beliefs. Differences in IQ are solidified by the increasing likelihood that couples will form among those of similar educational and occupational backgrounds. This leads to middle-class homes where children are both more intelligent and also work harder, as they are inculcated with a belief in the importance of education. As social mobility patterns are the result of genetics (which cannot be affected) and effort (which should not be affected), there is little that policy makers can or should do here. If there is a problem, according to Saunders, it is with an underclass whose 'feckless' behaviour is placing a burden on the rest of society and the dilution of the quality of elite universities, which are being forced to admit students who are just not good enough to be there.

There is a voluminous critique of the use of IQ as a way of measuring or determining social outcome (Heckman 1995, Korenman and Winship 1995, Kinchelloe et al 1997, Breen and Goldthorpe 1999). It is hard to measure, and the relationship between IQ and future outcomes is fragile. Saunders, however, remains robust in his views. There remains too much doubt regarding the use of IQ and natural ability for it to be a form of external justification for differential outcomes. Saunders' interpretation of the relationship between IQ and outcome also needs to take into account research showing the malleability of genetic predisposition (Lee Hotz 2011, Collins 2012). In a sense he does, when he talks about differences in effort and mating patterns between social groups, but accepting the existence of this malleability then places greater weight on nurture as opposed to nature. What Saunders' work does do, though, is demonstrate the need to think through questions regarding the extent to which parental influence should be countered (or not) to produce greater social mobility and where lines should be drawn. Hence, what level of immobility is acceptable and what is not?

Swift (2004) offers one of the few serious philosophical interventions into the social mobility discourse. He considers what the actual goals for social mobility should be, and examines some of the assumptions that underpin the social mobility academic and political discourse but that are not adequately theorised. He asks whether perfect mobility, which he defines as 'where a person ends up is random with respect to where she starts out' (Swift 2004: 4), is both possible and even desirable. In his 2004 article he examines five different issues that those researching social mobility need to consider when thinking about the normative implications of their work. The most interesting of these issues is his analysis of where natural ability figures in social mobility and where the legitimate boundaries regarding family intervention in the life chances of children are concerned. What is the difference between an individual's chances, depending on social background and on natural ability? Both are due to factors out of the control of the individual but one is seen as fair and one not. For example, few begrudge David Beckham his millions, based on his natural talent; compare this with the resentment felt towards many old Etonians. It is where the blurring of talent, background and effort occur that the difficulties emerge for social mobility.

Swift adopts the position that perfect mobility would not be 'perfect' because of the sacrifices it would demand. Where the transmission of advantage is concerned, Swift argues that the moral cost of expecting parents not to speak to their children at dinner, for example, or not to read to them at bedtime would be too high (as well as impractical to police). Swift's work identifies the limits to mobility and forces academics and policy makers to engage with more difficult terrain; hence it is in keeping with the goals of this book. It does not provide any answers as to where the boundaries between acceptable and unacceptable transmission of disadvantage are concerned – in terms of either talent or parental support. But his work does make the examination of these issues the legitimate business of social mobility analysis.

Conclusions

The academic study of social mobility is a growing field, drawing in researchers from different disciplines who are taking up a more diverse range of positions.

On one level there is little consensus about the discourse. Depending on who you believe and the definition of social mobility you adopt, the discourse has been increasing, decreasing or static.

However, on another level the discourse remains both consensual and also conservative. It is constructed within a conception of stratification that is based around narrowly economistic measures of welfare. In one way, this is entirely appropriate. Occupation and/or income exert a fundamental hold on the relative welfare of individuals and groups. However, there is little appetite for assessing the extent of this relative hold. The emphasis is predominantly on the measurement of rates of change in social mobility within schemas that are taken as read by their protagonists or criticised by their opponents on the grounds of their methodological weaknesses. For sociologists in particular, the importance of social class as the anchor around which the whole discipline is secured implies that more fundamental questions regarding what social mobility may actually mean – or how important it is – are largely untouched.

It takes the intervention of those operating mainly outside the field, such as Swift, for the issue of how much mobility is desirable to be debated. The inability or unwillingness to invite such questions, and the narrowness of focus around class or income alone, mean that while the existing approach to social mobility study does a comprehensive job in explaining part of the picture, it does not portray the whole of it.

THREE

Unpicking the political consensus on social mobility

Introduction

Sociologists have been keen to portray a cross-party political consensus on social mobility (Goldthorpe 2012, Payne 2012) – the idea that it has stalled at best, or is going backwards at worst, appears to be shared by all the major political parties in Britain. However, politicians always arrive at their interpretation of an issue from the context of their own party and its ideology. Bracketing together different politicians' views hampers an understanding of how and why social mobility has become such a high-profile issue. Crucially, it also masks the possible trajectories that social mobility could take into the future.

This chapter shows that while all the main political parties in the UK subscribe to some 'truths' on social mobility, they arrive at these by different routes, which then gives hope that they could leave in different directions too.

Social mobility and New Labour

The origins of the present concern about social mobility can be found in the 1990s and Labour's desire to find a way to articulate the party's core concern around inequality and poverty in a way that seemed to resonate with late 20th-century Britain. Labour had to find a way back to government as it was staring at what some thought was perennial opposition.

Where its views on inequality and poverty were concerned, this process began with the Commission on Social Justice report produced for the Labour Party in 1994 when in opposition (Commission on Social Justice 1994). It continued through the 1990s with the two dominant figures in Labour politics in the UK of that and the following decade, Tony Blair and Gordon Brown, seeing social exclusion as a way of redefining what was once poverty and equality of opportunity (Levitas 1998). They were both keen to place education at the centre of how social exclusion would be addressed and equality of opportunity increased. Blair gave a famous speech in 2001, proclaiming that: 'If we are given a second term to serve this country, our mission will be the renewal of our public services. There is nothing more important to making Britain a fairer and stronger country. Our top priority was, is and always will be education, education, education' (Blair 2001).

Brown was also not slow to emphasise the role of education. Throughout the 2000s, he argued that education was the driver of not just equality of opportunity, but also of economic growth (Johnson and Floud 2014).

In taking this road, Labour was not in the business of questioning broader structural inequalities (McKibbin 2007). They saw that the way to retain power was to work within the framework set by globalised capitalism. In this context, it is not surprising that they were less likely to entertain any notions of downward mobility or to look at how more fundamental, deep-rooted issues may need to be tackled (Goldthorpe 2013).

Social mobility itself, though, did not rise in prominence until the early 2000s. The Labour government's Performance Innovation Unit produced an overview of social mobility that was a much more even-handed treatment of the issue than what became the rhetoric of the 2000s (Aldrich 2001; see also Goldthorpe 2012).

In Goldthorpe's eyes, things began to go wrong when the work of Blanden and colleagues emerged. By presenting a problem that was at the core of what Labour's values should be about, and giving the Conservatives at the time a much-needed stick to beat the government with, it is clear to see how Blanden et al's work could have such an impact. As a problem that germinated over time, it was also one that each party could accuse the other of not dealing with, with first Labour and then the Conservatives being able to take advantage of this opportunity. It also resonated well for Labour with the rhetoric of modernisation that they continually pushed in the early to mid-2000s. It could be argued that this was a positive message: the aim was to increase social mobility as opposed to reducing social exclusion. It is noticeable how in two of Tony Blair's most high-profile contributions to the debate in the early 2000s, he associates social mobility with a vision of a better society. In 2004, for example, he states that he wanted to create an: 'an opportunity society [where] the aim was to put middle class aspirations in the hands of working class families and their children to open up opportunity to the many and not the few' (quoted in Wintour 2004).

The early 2000s also saw the start of the diffusion of the social mobility goal across government. As Nunn et al argue in their 2007 review of social mobility for the Department for Work and Pensions (DWP), increasing upward social mobility was a goal that could be used to justify work across different departments including that of the Department for Education in upskilling the population; the Treasury and its work on addressing low pay; the Sure Start initiative, also originating in the Treasury; area-based regeneration work via the DWP itself; and the Cabinet Office, with its focus on social exclusion (Nunn et al 2007). It became a very effective 'meta-narrative', which could weave together what the government was doing to create a more 'dynamic' society.

Further evidence of the shift in language on the Left towards social mobility, and the emergence of social mobility as meta-narrative, was seen in 2005 when the IPPR (Institute for Public Policy Research) produced Maintaining the Momentum (Reed et al 2005). This reinforced the fact that responsibility for the issue was dispersed across different government departments.

The IPPR report was preceded by the government's White Paper on higher education, The Future of Higher Education (DfES 2003). It framed the government's commitment to increasing participation in higher education (HE) by those from lower socioeconomic groups in terms of social mobility. While this was an issue that cut across departments, it was skewed towards those dealing with education. This interplay of government policies framed around social mobility in the policy community seeking to use the language of social mobility continued throughout the 2000s.

It was not until the mid-2000s, however, and the election of David Cameron as leader of the Conservative Party, that the political Right entered the social mobility fray. In an article for The Guardian newspaper in 2006, Cameron stated that 'we will carry the banner of sensible, centre-right reform into territory which Labour should never have conceded: social mobility and the role of schools in enabling every child to reach their potential' (Cameron 2006).

The Conservatives have readily bought into the idea that social mobility has slowed down. The Education Secretary in the early 2010s, Michael Gove, referred to this frequently to support his own personal beliefs on education (which had a significant impact on government policy) (Paton 2012). But it was the Liberal Democrats, as the junior member of the coalition government that ruled Britain in the early 2010s, which took ownership of social mobility, building on Labour's work. Their former leader, Nick Clegg, described it as 'the long term social policy goal of the government' (Clegg 2010).

The White Paper *Opening Doors, Breaking Barriers* (Cabinet Office 2011) was very much the Liberal Democrats' contribution to the coalition's work. It is surprising that they were able to do this given that the focus on social mobility only increased in the final years of the Labour government up to 2010 (HM Government 2011). When Gordon Brown became leader of the Labour Party in 2008, it became clear that he was a strong supporter of the social mobility idea. In an interview with the Telegraph in 2008, Brown stated that:

> My whole argument is that Britain is ready for a new wave of social mobility – upward mobility – people being able to do better than their parents, the next generation doing better than the last, because there are more opportunities in this new world economy. We've got to help people climb the ladder of success, we've got to give them the opportunity to make their aspirations and dreams come true (quoted in Hennessy 2008)

Brown was not just using social mobility for sloganeering effect; it sat at the centre of his view of the world. Education was the driver of a nation's future prosperity. It would unlock people's ability to take advantage of an increasing number of knowledge-intensive jobs. In 2009, Brown's government commissioned the then ex-Labour Minister, Alan Milburn, to conduct a review entitled Fair access to the professions (Cabinet Office 2009). This contained 88 different recommendations, which extended far beyond its initial remit, including the abolition of the whole Connexions service (the national service introduced in England in 2001 to support young people in progressing to adulthood). Its effect and the subsequent follow-up reports from Alan Milburn was both to cement his place as the leading political authority on social mobility and to locate progression to elite occupations via more selective universities as the primary definition of social mobility.

Social Mobility and Child Poverty Commission

After the 2010 general election, Alan Milburn took on the role of head of the quasi-autonomous Social Mobility and Child Poverty Commission. Its main role is to produce an annual report to Parliament highlighting the government's progress, or lack of it, against the targets in its 2011 social mobility strategy. Milburn saw the role of the Commission as what he described as a 'bully pulpit', from where it could advocate for social mobility (Grice 2013). The focus of the

Commission is certainly wider than just access to the professions. As its major remit was to monitor government policy, it retained the lifecourse approach to social mobility, first developed in the early 2000s via the IPPR, and embedded in the Opening Doors strategy (Cabinet Office 2011).

The Commission evolved from the earlier Milburn reports in how it defined social mobility, to incorporate the problems of the low paid as well access to elite universities and professional occupations. In its first annual report in 2013, the Commission made a number of wide-ranging policy recommendations, including reallocating resources from the old to the young; eliminating youth unemployment; and improving childcare (Social Mobility and Child Poverty Commission 2013a). These recommendations serve as the start of an approach to social mobility that is broader and could develop over time into something more coherent.

But exploring the nature of social mobility is less a priority for the Commission. What constitutes social mobility is both explicit, in that its role is to report on what government does, therefore they de facto accept the UK government's intergenerational definition, and also to a degree implicit, interpreted through the policy recommendations above. Any broader debate on what is meant by social mobility, or its relationship to broader political and economic issues, has thus far been avoided. Neither has some of the potential internal contradictions in bringing together child poverty and social mobility been confronted. In addition, the relative priority or importance of the two issues needs to be breached. The reduction of child poverty and upward economic social mobility are not the same thing. Nor is it clear why child poverty, as opposed to poverty per se, is the priority and how this relates to social mobility – other than to lock the Commission's work into a primarily intragenerational framework.

The Commission has so far steered clear in its policy recommendations from any consideration of the kind of labour market challenges described in the following chapter. By doing this, though, it leaves its work far too open to the criticisms of the sociologists, who argue that expansion in higher earning/higher socioeconomic positions is axiomatic to the kind of social mobility that the Commission advocates, but who are sceptical about whether this is a realistic expectation.

Social mobility, politics and the 2010s

The political 'consensus' on social mobility of the 2010s has evolved since the early 2000s. What began as an attempt to position Labour's core concerns in the context of global economic changes became a way of the Liberal Democrats expressing their commitment to fairness and social justice, and a means of the Conservatives assuaging their guilt regarding the composition of elite professions. Labour is less active now in defining this discourse. The leader of the Labour Party from 2010 to 2015, Ed Miliband, flirted in the early 2010s with the idea of a British promise – a British equivalent of the American dream. In a 2011 speech he stated that:

> 'We have always assumed that our kids, the next generation, would do better than us. Not just the well off, the vast majority can expect that their kids will do better than them. It is a promise that each generation will pass to the next: a life of greater opportunity, prosperity and wellbeing. In many ways that is the promise of Britain. We may not have given it a name in the way that Americans talk about the "American Dream", but it is there nevertheless. (Labour Party 2011)

This idea has yet to be pursued with any real vigour. Unlike his predecessors, in particular Tony Blair, Miliband has shown less appetite so far for building the kind of 'big picture' narrative about the future that has within it an idea of success and what it means. Nor, as will be explored later in Chapter Nine, have the Left-leaning political think tanks shown much appetite to develop the idea of social mobility.

It is telling that an All-Party Parliamentary Group (APPG) on Social Mobility was set up in 2011 chaired by a backbench Conservative MP. Such groups serve to raise the profile of an issue and to help shape the discourse on it. The APPG has produced a series of reports on social mobility and has had an important part to play in keeping the issue on the political agenda. Its perspective has thus far followed the social mobility orthodoxy in emphasising the importance of progression to elite occupations and the critical role of education in social mobility. As will be seen in Chapter Four, though, it has also added its own twist to these themes.

The APPG's 2012 seven key truths about social mobility lays out the group's core position, however:

- The point of greatest leverage for social mobility is what happens between ages 0 and 3, primarily in the home.
- You can also break the cycle through education ...

- ... the most important controllable factor being the quality of your teaching.
- But it's also about what happens after the school bell rings.
- University is the top determinant of later opportunities – so pre-18 attainment is key.
- But later pathways to mobility are possible, given the will and support.
- Personal resilience and emotional wellbeing are the missing link in the chain. (APPG 2012: 10)

While these key truths only echo much of what has been heard before, the APPG is also making its own distinctive contribution to the political discourse on social mobility. It has produced further reports focusing on the role of character and resilience in promoting educational attainment and trying to identify what makes social mobility more likely in one area than another (APPG 2013, Paterson et al 2014).

These truths broadly echo, however, the priorities identified in the 2011 HM Government White Paper *Opening Doors* (referred to earlier). These are shown in Figure 3.1. This illustrates that while politicians may wish to interpret social mobility differently, and in politically partisan ways, many of the concerns regarding how to affect it – and indeed, what it is – remain within a set of given parameters. This also shows quite clearly how social mobility has come to embrace a broad set of policies and departments with the lifecycle approach. In this sense, then, it has evolved since the 2000s as a policy area.

In contrast to the 2000s, social mobility is not an issue that the Prime Minister of the Conservative-led coalition from 2010 to 2015 invested great store in (Helliker 2010). David Cameron was conscious of his own background, coming from a wealthy family and having attended Eton and Oxford. He was careful of doing anything that drew undue attention to this background, as it is something that has repeatedly been used as a weapon against him by the media and political rivals. He has been drawn into the social mobility debate, rather than entering into it willingly, like both his predecessors. In late 2013, for example, former Conservative Prime Minister John Major publicly criticised the lack of diversity in positions of power (Wintour 2013a). Cameron duly expressed his concern about the fact that his own Cabinet contained a relatively high number of those from public schools. He also took a very wide view of what social mobility meant and how to increase the upward part of it. As alluded to earlier, he argued that the government's 'Help to Buy' scheme, which gives preferential financial support for

Figure 3.1: Social mobility across the lifecycle

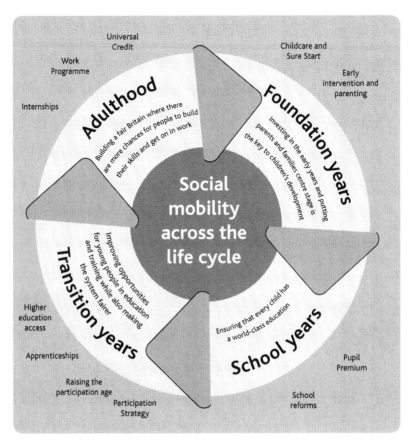

Source: HM Government (2011: 9)

first-time house buyers, was 'about social mobility' (The Independent 2013). It was about helping Britons to 'move on and up in life'.

In associating home ownership with social mobility, Cameron has broadened how it could be defined. This may have been done inadvertently. It was certainly the product of political opportunism as much as any philosophical reasoning, but it is an interesting observation as it supports the view that social mobility may be an issue that goes beyond who is (and who is not) a member of the Cabinet. As with the idea of the 'British promise', which was not developed by Labour, it illustrates that politicians are able to connect social mobility with wider issues in British society in a way that academics have been less inclined to do.

Other senior Conservative figures have been more willing to speak about social mobility, though. In early 2014, Michael Gove, the former Minister for Education, described the dominance of Eton in public life as 'ridiculous' (Cohen and Bloom 2014). However, exactly what difference a more diverse Cabinet would make was never explored. There has been no more staunch an advocate of the Conservative's policies than Gove, who has no regrets about what the government has done since 2010 (DfE 2014).

If Gove didn't want to see policy changed, what difference could a more diverse Cabinet make, other than to make the Conservatives electorally appealing to a broader constituency? The principle of more diversity in public office does seem consensual, but the lack of any developed thinking regarding what difference this diversity would make in practical terms is also consensual. (This issue of the rationale for elite diversity is tackled in more detail in Chapter Eight.) This episode shows that while politicians might be willing to link social mobility with a broader set of societal challenges when it suits them, they are also happy to support the orthodox view when that fits their priorities better.

Miliband and Cameron's contribution to social mobility, though, pale in comparison to those of the Liberal Democrat leader Nick Clegg (Skelton 2013). He made social mobility a personal vocation and his office repeatedly attempted to keep the coalition government focused on this agenda (Clegg 2013). A considerable part of Clegg's desire to be associated with the social mobility agenda may stem from it presenting a safe way of differentiating his party from the Conservatives in the ruling coalition government. The Liberal Democrats' decision to form a government with the Conservatives was not welcomed by many of its supporters, who saw themselves as closer to the political Left than the Right. To try and bolster its appeal to these disgruntled supporters it then tried to act as the 'conscience of the coalition', defending the interests of those from lower socioeconomic groups. And taking the lead as the champion of social mobility became one aspect of this strategy, giving the Liberal Democrat take on social mobility a particular character.

The focus was less on positioning social mobility as part of a broader vision of society and the economy (as did Labour in the 2000s). There was also far less of the anxiety surrounding membership of elites (although Clegg's personal background has been raised in the media several times), as this is far less of an issue for the Liberal Democrats. Neither was social mobility seen as part of a drive to reduce inequality. Somewhat controversially, Clegg argued in 2012 that inequality and social mobility were not linked (an example of politicians falling foul not just of sociologists but also economists) (Ramesh 2012).

Rather, it appears that social mobility took on a particularly personal association for Nick Clegg. As he stated in his speech to the Liberal Democrats annual conference in 2013:

> 'And now, as a father with three children at school, I have come to understand even more clearly than before that if we want to live in a society where everyone has a fair chance to live the life they want – and to bounce back from misfortune too – then education is the key. The gifts we give our children – self-confidence, an enthusiasm to learn, an ability to empathise with others, a joy in forging new friendships – these are instilled at an extraordinarily young age. That's why I made social mobility the social policy objective of this Government – and I will want it to be the same for any Government I'm in.' (Clegg 2013)

For Clegg, social mobility became a motif of a policy. It represented something he stood for as a politician, conceived in a distinctive way: not part of a commitment to historic Labour goals of greater equality, but emblematic of a commitment to fairness and opportunity that the Conservatives could never possess.

Conclusions

At the broad level of problem and definition, there has been a consensus on social mobility between political parties in the UK from the early 2000s to the mid 2010s, but there are also evident differences.

Each party has its own distinctive position on social mobility, a product of its history (both recent and more distant), the personal views of its senior politicians and how each party wishes to position itself at any particular point in time. This scenario of difference within consensus provides grounds for both pessimism and optimism. Pessimism comes from the extent to which a particular understanding of what social mobility is and how to fix it has become embedded in a political discourse that is, in reality, focused on securing a fairly narrow political centre ground (at least this is what a party does if it wants to be successful – witness what happened to the Labour Party in 2015 when it was perceived as straying from this centre ground). The more attention is placed on social mobility from within this narrow frame, the more this definition is reinforced. Optimism can be found in the spaces that exist within, between and around parties to shape different ideas around social mobility.

As we enter a new 5 year parliament, it is likely that these spaces will change again. The Conservative government has renewed its rhetorical commitment to social mobility. Prime Minister David Cameron spoke about it in his first speech to the Conservative Party conference of the new parliament (Kirkup 2015) and a new prime ministerial target for access to higher education for those from disadvantaged background has been created (HEFCE 2015). It is still not clear though yet what a distinctive Conservative position on social mobility will look like. Labour has the most left leaning leader for over 30 years and he has used his power to position advocates for his policies in powerful positions in the party. Given his commitment to a new politics this may mean that Labour will develop a more robust approach to this issue up to 2020. Whether this extends to questioning the nature of the concept and confronting some of the issues outlined in this book remains to be seen.

The most important thing that this chapter has shown is that this is not a static discourse. It is constituted of different actors, making distinct forms of contribution, causing subtle changes over time in how social mobility is interpreted. How it will evolve in the next five or ten years is still contested ground. This dynamism illustrates that, in theory at least, potential opportunities for shifting the discourse exist, if the right arguments can be developed and the right strategies adopted.

FOUR

Going beyond attainment

The children that are at the schools in Shanghai are doing three years better than children at schools in England.... That's the reality of the situation. I've seen it for myself.... We have stagnated in terms of our maths performance for the last 15 years, while other countries like Germany and Poland have been learning from the East. (Gander 2014)

Zhang Yang, a bright 18-year-old from a rural town in Anhui province in China was accepted to study at a prestigious traditional medicine college in Hefei. But the news was too much for his father Zhang Jiasheng. Zhang's father was partly paralysed after he suffered a stroke two years ago and could no longer work. He feared the family, already in debt to pay for medicines, would not be able to afford his son's tuition fees. As his son headed home to celebrate his success, Zhang Jiasheng killed himself by swallowing pesticide. (Sharma 2013)

Introduction

These two quotations highlight the problem faced in developing an educational system that supports these broader (as opposed to narrower) forms of social mobility. China is lauded in the West for its achievements in the international PISA (Programme of International Student Assessment) tests. However, this obsession with attainment comes at a cost for countries such as Korea and China. Nor are those in these countries entirely happy with what their own education systems are doing. Yet they are greatly admired by education policy makers in the UK. Increasingly we now share their obsession, but the idea that England should emulate these countries should be considered carefully.

Academics and politicians both see educational achievement as central to social mobility. Even accepting the doubts outlined in previous chapters regarding the limitations of education in terms of the problems it can solve and the returns it provides, it would be perverse to suggest that improving the attainment of learners from lower socioeconomic groups is not crucial. It would be equally perverse to criticise or ignore the efforts that are going into closing the gaps in attainment between social groups. While the coalition government slowed down investment in education, from 2010 to 2015 it built on Labour's commitment to reducing attainment gaps through initiatives such as the Pupil Premium, which has allocated funding to every child from a disadvantaged background, and the creation of the Education Endowment Foundation, which works to fund, identify and disseminate innovative, leading practice in work to raise educational attainment. But it is not the intention of this book to document the work on closing these attainment gaps; there is an ever-growing body of research that looks at this and links these efforts with reducing social mobility. The focus here instead is to examine what that success should look like, not to look at how to make individual pupils and the system itself more successful.

Education will become increasingly important to social mobility, however it is defined. While doubts regarding the returns to education are well founded, the alternatives are both unrealistic and undesirable. Do we wish to return to a nepotistic regime, where labour market reward is based entirely on family or community ties? Our present brand of meritocracy may have a huge strand of nepotism of the cultural variety running through it, but the ability of education to break down much of what would otherwise be more rampant inequality means that it is impossible to see a way round it as the route to more sustainable societies. The realisation by the majority of the public that education is the better of two evils means that it is highly unlikely that we will see a reversal in the extent of educational participation in Western countries, or indeed globally.

Such a reversal would anyway imply a dramatic reversal of what happened in the 20th century (Schofer and Meyer 2005). Over 70% of 17-year-olds were in full-time education in England in 2102, compared with less than 10% in 1953, while over 80% have five A–C GCSEs or equivalent, compared with less than 10% in 1953 (Bolton 2012). We are a far more educated society now than we have ever been.

Like most advanced capitalist countries, the UK has moved inexorably, as Young predicted in 1958 in The Rise of the Meritocracy, from an ascription economy, where economic opportunities are mainly awarded on the basis of the financial and cultural influence associated with socioeconomic position, to an accreditation economy. Influence still matters, but it is now translated into economic opportunity through qualifications.

Finally, increases in healthy life expectancy (ONS 2012b) and a need to work to an older age to pay for an ageing society will pull up the age at which young people enter the labour market. It will also imply the need for more lifelong learning as workers seek to retrain and (hopefully) participate in education to enhance their quality of life.

There should not be a reverse in participation in education, though. A broader, sustainable conception of social mobility requires an education system that supports that goal, but this means aiming to prepare young people for progression across a number of domains. At present, it is not doing this – a narrow definition of what success means in the educational system is acting as the foundation for the unsustainable definition of social mobility.

This chapter looks at how the idea of success in the education system in England is arrived at, and what may need to be done in order to adapt this idea so that social mobility can be defined differently. It examines the interaction between the three essential parts of the system: what is taught explicitly in the curriculum; what is taught implicitly through schooling; and what happens in the home. In particular, this chapter concentrates on how these three elements are being made manifest in the 2010s in the context of social mobility debates. Where the curriculum is concerned, this is via the debate around the classical curriculum versus 21st-century skills. In the nature of schooling, the rise of character as a defining feature of educational success is examined. We begin, however, by exploring the increasing importance placed on the early years and the role of parenting in shaping what happens over the lifecourse.

Home, school and the 'early years' evangelists

In the 2000s, detailed research started to emerge that focused on the importance of what happens in the early years of a child's life in defining how well they will do in the education system. Research in the UK purported to show that differences in aptitudes for academic success can be identified as early as three to four years old between children from different social backgrounds (Feinstein and Duckworth 2006). These differences in achievement never close over the lifecourse (Goodman and Gregg 2010); in fact, they widen. This evidence has had a significant impact on the educational policy discourse (Saunders 2012). It has brought a real focus on what happens in the early years of a child's life in terms of both policy and investment. This work in the UK has been combined, as we have seen before in the social mobility debate, with work from the US, to make a policy case.

James Heckman is a US economist who has become one of the leading academic advocates for early investment in the development of non-cognitive skills. He argues that such investment prevents poverty, crime and school/college drop-out. He starts from the position that US society is becoming even more polarised and divided, and is fearful of the consequences. Rather than solutions based on distribution, however, he favours pre-distribution-based approaches centred on prevention. Drawing on a range of studies, he argues repeatedly that attitudes and personality traits are at the basis of differences in life trajectories by social group. Heckman offers a broad definition of these non-cognitive skills: 'character skills such as increasing self-confidence, teamwork ability, autonomy, and discipline which are often lacking in disadvantaged youth' (Heckman and Mosso 2013: 9).

Heckman paints a pessimistic picture of the chances that young people who come from disadvantaged backgrounds have of social progression at present in the US. Family backgrounds have 'deteriorated' over recent decades as incomes have stagnated for the poor and there has been a fragmentation in family and community structures making parents from some social groups less equipped to instil in their children the attributes necessary for success (Heckman 2008). However, Heckman also believes that if interventions can be made early enough, in particular to improve parenting, then things can change. His analysis of the pay-offs in terms of income and career benefits of the national Perry programme in the US has been used to justify significant investments in pre-school education in the US (Heckman et al 2009). This programme combined both additional schooling with low pupil:teacher ratios for three- and four-year-old African American children from disadvantaged backgrounds with home visit support, to encourage parents to work with their children.

Heckman is keen to point to the financial pay-off in terms of higher wages and economic growth in raising the skills level of all young people. However, he ignores the labour market side of education, and does not engage with the evidence outlined earlier in Chapter Two, that future labour markets will not generate unlimited higher-earning graduate jobs without a battery of non-education-related interventions, if indeed at all.

The kind of non-cognitive skills that Heckman focuses on also remain hard to define. In his 2006 paper, he states that: 'Common sense suggests that personality traits, persistence, motivation and charm matter for success in life' (Heckman et al 2006: 15). The subsequent analysis draws on standardised studies of self-worth used in the US to examine how this range of traits relates to wages and adolescent risky behaviour (Heckman et al 2006). In the conclusion Heckman adds to the list of non-cognitive skills to include motivation, persistence and self-esteem.

The lack of real clarity regarding what these non-cognitive skills are – and how they are accumulated – also means that it is not clear what the balance between investment in formal pre-school education and parenting should be. While there is a weight of international evidence to support the impact of pre-school education, there are also exceptions – especially in Finland, where children do not start school until the age of six. It appears that there are broader cultural factors associated with the way in which children are raised from birth, and the role of educational activity and education within this culture, that are most important here.

To a significant extent, the common-sense proposition that Heckman makes above is one that he can support through evidence. The concept of investing in the 'whole child' through pre-school home and family activities offers a glimpse of an alternative understanding of what success could mean. He does not address, however, the broader questions of where the increased intensity in parenting at early years could lead and the nature of the parenting model. To a degree, his work is a little like that of the sociologists and economists cited earlier in Chapter Two: there is a greater focus on measuring the extent of difference between groups than explaining what could cause this difference. This means that the potential of the Heckman approach is not being fully realised. If the focus on the importance of parenting and what that means could be developed in such a way as to see the outcomes as broader than just economic success, then the drive to enhance non-cognitive skills could be a springboard for a different view of what constitutes success.

The rise of 'hyper-parenting'

Unfortunately, rather than opening up a debate around what parenting means and its different forms, the focus on the importance of early years has actually narrowed the understanding of 'good parenting'. It has contributed to the intensification of the efforts of those in middle-class positions to parent in ways that can be described as not just economically defensive, but also economically offensive.

The central importance of parenting in the early years model has been embraced enthusiastically by many parents in the UK and extended across and into post-secondary education. Aware of the importance of educational attainment to future success, those in higher socioeconomic groups are investing more time and resources in explicitly educationally focused activities for their children at a younger age. This is a kind of 'hyper-parenting', where success in parenting is not measured by the quality of the relationship between parent and child, but by the quantity of effort put in to ensure that children are able to participate in as many stimulating activities as possible and to succeed in school in comparison to their peers. The goal is not just to ensure that the child does well enough to maintain the social position of the parents, but that the child beats the other children and actually does better than the parents. To paraphrase Cowen from Chapter One, average is over in a quite different way here (2013). This manifests itself most clearly in the much greater attention being paid to school choice from primary level entry onwards. And the importance that parents place on school choice is well documented by research (Vincent 2012).

This kind of 'hyper-parenting' is focused mainly in higher socioeconomic groups, but it has become the dominant model of 'good parenting' that all groups are being compelled to adapt to. The consequences of this model are an 'educational arms race' that all cannot possibly win. Furthermore, as this model extends to all socioeconomic groups, it only intensifies the efforts of the more affluent to gain advantage. The concept of all schools being good ones, for example, and therefore it not being an issue which one a child attends, does not work in the 2010s. Even in areas where all the schools score above the national average in all metrics, the competition to enter the best is still fierce. House prices in areas where the 'best schools' reside in London are up to 245% the average (Tobin 2014). This model is not one where 'excellence for all' works; it is excellence for some that is at the heart of it.

Pierre Bourdieu, Raymond Boudon, parenting and cultural capital

Differences in parenting by socioeconomic group are not new. Pierre Bourdieu (1992) built a comprehensive theoretical framework to explain not just parenting, but the whole nature of how inequality is perpetuated via the behaviour of individuals based around the ideas of capital, field and habitus.

Archer et al (2007) describe habitus as: 'an amalgamation of the past and the present that mediates current and future engagement with the world, shaping what is perceived as ab/normal, un/desirable and im/possible' (Archer et al 2007: 220). Habitus is deeply rooted in the culture of particular groups in society (Bourdieu 1992). For middle-class groups, their habitus fits easily with the education system, while for those from working-class groups there is a friction, which leads to the view that education is always somehow unnatural for 'the likes of us'. Cultural capital is the manifestation of habitus. The attitudes and dispositions that form it are translated into knowledge and skills, which middle-class groups can use to succeed in the education system.

Addressing disparities in cultural capital is not straightforward, if indeed it can be done within the context of a capitalist economic system (which many writers in this area seem to doubt). Cultural capital is also hard to measure and define (Goldthorpe 2007). Goldthorpe prefers to explain the differences in educational progression by reference to Raymond Boudon's work (Goldthorpe 2007) who sees two different kinds of impact on educational success arising from social class background (Boudon 1974). The primary effects relate to children's academic ability, which stems from economic differences that are both cultural and material, such as access to computers or the internet. The secondary effects pertain to class-related factors that affect educational decisions for children with the same level of academic ability. It is the latter on which Boudon focuses. He was interested in why young people with the same level of ability would choose educational progression in the case of those from higher socioeconomic groups, and leaving the system in the case of their peers from lower socioeconomic groups. He explained it in terms of rationality – the fear of downward mobility is what motivates decision-making and underpins what is perceived as rational. Those in the middle-class groups saw the loss in terms of economic and social status as higher than the costs in terms of tuition costs, extra work and so on; the reverse was the case for those from lower socioeconomic groups. Boudon proposed that the only way to address these problems was to make society less unequal and to reduce the number of 'branching points' where students could exit the system.

Boudon's theory provides a more than plausible description of the behaviour of the hyper-parents described above. However, much of the investment (both in money and in time) that more affluent groups place in education is not defensive: it is also offensive. There is a strong element of wanting to progress as much as not wanting to slip down any social scale. Boudon's work may need augmenting in the 2010s by the idea of 'hyper-parenting'.

The theoretical debate among sociologists regarding the merits of Bourdieu versus Boudon is a long and complex one (and there is no space to tackle it here). Both Bourdieu and Boudon provide a rationale for differences in approach to parenting that is grounded in economic inequality at the societal level. In both cases it is a 'rational' response to the environment within which parents parent and their children live. Hence, it is less amenable to change by exhortation – and indeed, why should it be? By contextualising parenting, Bourdieu and Boudon open up the debate regarding the merits of different models of parenting and their worth. Is it possible, for instance, to develop models of the 'good parent' in the present context that do not necessarily prioritise academic attainment in schooling above all else?

Schooling and confusion over character

A consequence of the increased focus on early years education has been the rise in the importance of 'character' in understanding educational attainment. Shaping the 'character' of pupils was one of the central concerns of the education system in England at its inception in the 19th century (Owen 1813, Newsome 1961). It continued to be an important theme in what education should seek to achieve to the mid part of the 20th century. In the latter half of the 20th century it became associated with particular kinds of challenge-based outdoor activities, and featured less prominently in mainstream education. It is no coincidence that, as the state started to exert greater control over the education system, it returned to prominence.

However, the more recent interest in character differs somewhat from that in the 20th century and when it first reappeared under New Labour. The interest in character is now less to do with the formation of a set of citizens with certain moral attributes, and more to do with character and now also 'resilience' in terms of how they can support attainment in schools and then progression afterwards. Supporters of the role of character draw on the work of Heckman and Feinstein as well as that of US writers such as Paul Tough and his best-selling 'popular sociology' book, How Children Succeed (2013) to justify its importance in defining success.

However, what character actually means is contested. The APPG is a group of politicians who have come together from across political parties to contribute to the social mobility debate. They have no formal role, but have been able to influence the debate. They have been vocal proponents of the importance of character, linking it explicitly to what happens in public schools as well as to Heckman's work. Their 2014 Character and Resilience Manifesto is vague on exactly what they mean by character, however: 'character and resilience is used here as an umbrella term for a range of concepts variously categorised as aspects of social and emotional development and as non-cognitive or – somewhat incongruously – soft skills' (Paterson et al 2014: 11).

They quote a 2011 report by Demos (Birdwell et al 2011) to try to give a more accurate definition:

- Application – the ability to stick with tasks and see things through.
- Self-direction – the ability to see one's life as under one's control and to effectively shape its future course; the ability to understand one's strengths and weaknesses accurately; the ability to recognise one's responsibilities towards others.
- Self-control – the ability to monitor and regulate one's emotions appropriately.
- Empathy – the ability to put oneself in other people's shoes and be sensitive to their needs and views. (Paterson et al 2014: 11)

It is noticeable that empathy is at the bottom of this list. There is an echoing of the Heckman problem here, where the actual skills or capabilities described are done so in overlapping and interchangeable ways. There is also a real shortage of detailed considerations of how they might differ and what the order of importance may be. It is quite possible that character could be an educational trend and could fade in the medium term (a little like personalisation in the 2000s, for example). In the mid-2010s it is certainly in vogue, being picked up by both major political parties offering different, and in some cases new, examples of what character means and its importance to fuel the debate (BBC News 2014a).

The basic idea at the heart of the quest for character – that there is a broader range of capabilities that young people need to develop via schooling than learning about particular subjects – supports holistic social mobility well in principle. However, the risk is that while the potential is there for character to do this, it is not being realised. It is becoming a way of encouraging the development of a very narrow set of skills purely in order to drive better attainment. Calling for improvements in character does not acknowledge that there could be differences in character by social background and that they could be quite valid. The existence of character is being measured by a set of standards constructed on the basis of what very affluent and powerful people do. Resilience, self-control or any other components wedged into the character 'box' are being associated with what happens in private schools. When politicians and others make this link, they only contribute to the 'character problem' that they are allegedly setting out to solve, as they ignore where the real 'character' is being displayed on a day-to-day basis. Those in lower socioeconomic groups show determination, character and resilience every day to survive on low incomes and in unrewarding, low-paid jobs.

To borrow from the ideas of Bourdieu outlined earlier in this chapter, this resilience is not translated into success in the same way in the educational system; and to borrow from Boudon, such success is not seen as important as for higher socioeconomic groups. This does not mean, though, that they lack character. For sure, young people in private schools experience problems. Adolescence is no respecter of class, and these problems should not be ignored. But it would be bizarre if those in schools which cost thousands of pounds to attend had bigger problems to overcome than those in schools beset by challenges of poverty and inequality.

However, it may not just be politicians and those on the political Right who do not recognise the above. In the desire to apportion responsibility for educational inequality with the system, it could be argued that sociologists especially have not paid enough attention to the strengths of working-class culture as opposed to what it lacked. There is a long history of working-class achievement in working-class-led education going back to the 19th century (Simon 1998). Research commissioned by the government and produced by Siraj-Blatchford et al in 2011 argued that parents from children in lower socioeconomic groups were able to provide just as much educational support for their children as those from higher socioeconomic groups. This research looked at how children who succeeded 'against the odds' from lower socioeconomic backgrounds had to show determination, belief and resilience.

The deficit model of education, where those from lower socioeconomic groups are concerned, is damaging and counterproductive. The idea that those from such groups do not have educational aspirations for their children, for example, continues to inform policy. As Cummings et al (2012) found in their review of the literature on educational aspirations, the reality may be somewhat different to the perception:

> [C]hildren and parents from low income families have high aspirations and value school, and … parents by and large try their best to support their children's education. There is evidence that teachers and other professionals may underestimate the aspirations of socio-economically disadvantaged children and parents and not appreciate the

importance with which school is viewed. (Cummings et al 2012: 8)

There are some fundamental issues with using the term 'character' to encapsulate the non-cognitive skills that young people are supposed to accumulate through schooling. It refers to something that is unique to every individual. Everyone has a character; it is not, as such, something that has a set, unitary definition that you can develop. (When the development of uniformity of character has been attempted before, it has been called 'indoctrination'.) This is not to say that the capabilities that the supporters of character advocate developing are undesirable, but to describe the process as the accumulation of character is wrong. It would be far better to explicitly define the capabilities that young people should develop in far more detail and to stop associating them with qualities that are, to an extent, inherent and should be individual.

There is a role for character-related education, but it should focus on supporting the development of the individual's distinctive character rather than on the accumulation of a set of skills called 'character'. This means enabling young people to better understand the kind of person they are and want to be. This kind of work would support holistic social mobility, and would give young people the tools to work out what success means for them in life, and to understand that it comes in more forms than the one they are being sold at present.

The return of the classical curriculum

The changes introduced into the school curriculum in England in the 2010s, driven forward by the very interventionist and very powerful former Education Secretary Michael Gove, is a radical departure from the existing template left by the previous Labour government. Gove adopted a philosophy that you need to go back to go forward, and was happy to use the 'global race for talent' metaphor to support his position (Gove 2013). In order to prosper in this context, it is necessary to return to a curriculum that has a narrower range of subjects, more rigorous testing and a focus on learning facts. The changes that Gove introduced have been radical to an extent: reducing the numbers of qualifications offered and changing the way in which examinations are to be graded. These changes have drawn from a history of conservatism in the school curriculum in England that began to reassert itself robustly in the late 1980s with the introduction of the national curriculum (Ball 2011).

During the 1990s and 2000s Labour did not move far away from the template they had inherited. While there may have been a broadening of the curriculum offer, they lacked the political courage to move to a national baccalaureate when the opportunity presented itself in the mid-2000s. In 2003, the government commissioned the former chief inspector of schools for the Office for Standards in Education, Children's Services and Skills (Ofsted), Mike Tomlinson, to look at how the overall system of assessment from primary to post-16 could be revised. His recommendations, while not accepted universally, garnered a relatively large degree of cross-sector support (Working Group on 14-19 Reform 2004). Central to these recommendations was that the existing examinations be replaced by a national baccalaureate, giving much more equal weight to academic and vocational qualifications. It was rejected, in the main because it would involve the scrapping of the academic A-levels, perceived to be very popular among middle-class voters (Porter 2007).

Nor did Labour do anything to reduce the role of competition as the driver for system improvement introduced by the Conservatives and manifested in the form of league tables. The introduction of league tables, together with the accumulation and dissemination of ever-increasing amounts of data on schools in combination with the ever-increasing power of the school inspecting body Ofsted, did more than anything else to reinforce a narrow idea of success in education. Schools responded as predicted to the incentive structure within which they operated. Unless a particular element of the curriculum was measured, be that by league tables or Ofsted, it was hard for it to be prioritised.

The best example here relates explicitly to social mobility. The government invested heavily in the 2000s in activities to support progression to higher education for those from lower socioeconomic groups via the Aimhigher programme (Atherton 2012). However, much of the funding and control was with higher education institutions (HEIs). It was a constant difficulty to try to get schools to find the time in the curriculum for visits to HEIs. One of the primary reasons was that such work did not usually relate to attainment, and was therefore not measured. The coalition government from 2010 to 2015 recognised this issue and introduced a new measure of progression at post-16 (SecEd 2014).

The product of a zealous minister building on a culture of educational conservatism in England was a narrow curriculum prioritising a small range of academic subjects, with little room for subjects that fall outside this narrow range, and/or for activities to support the explicit development of the non-cognitive skills deemed so important by some for academic achievement (Garner 2013). Non-cognitive skills, parenting and the classical curriculum form an imperfect storm where holistic social mobility is concerned – they combine to close off alternative ways of thinking about success in the educational system. For those who lack the ability or desire to conform to a certain set of culturally constructed behaviours and attitudes, they offer little hope. A blog post by a member of staff from the Social Mobility and Child Poverty Commission courted controversy when he suggested that the way to succeed now was for everyone to become 'middle class' (Brant 2014). However, he was only saying what many others were thinking but we're afraid to say.

Are 21st-century skills solving or adding to the problem?

The chances of navigating a course to a form of education that embodies a different idea of success depend on coming up with a different way of understanding parenting, non-cognitive skills and the curriculum. This will inevitably mean reforming the curriculum.

There is no shortage of ideas here. For the last 20 years or so, there has been a constant flow of research, reports and policies aiming to imbue learners with '21st-century skills'. On the surface it offers a good starting point for holistic social mobility. It is at least looking forward (as opposed to the present curriculum, which is looking back). It could also be interpreted as meaning a range of competencies that enable young people to progress in the 21st century. This means skills for life as well as work. However, in the main it does not do this. Despite claims of being new and forward-looking, the traits within it echo much of what has gone before. It appears that the 21st century continues to be seen as a way of better preparing learners for a changing labour market, and not a changing society.

As with the other areas of non-cognitive skills examined before, the discourse on 21st-century skills is a confusing form of consensus, where a range of similar terms are repeatedly deployed in slightly different combinations, and what these terms mean is usually not explored. Again, as with the non-cognitive skills described by Heckman, and with character, the difficulties with measuring this range of skills means that they are not defined to the same degree of precision as more 'cognitive' ones. The Assessment & Teaching of 21st Century Skills (ATCS) project at the University of Melbourne (sponsored, interestingly, by Cisco, Intel and Microsoft) pulled together the work of 250 researchers from across the world in an attempt to define better what 21st century skills are. It came up with 11 skills divided into four categories:

Ways of thinking. Creativity, critical thinking, problem-solving, decision-making and learning

Ways of working. Communication and collaboration

Tools for working. Information and communications technology (ICT) and information literacy

Skills for living in the world. Citizenship, life and career, and personal and social responsibility (Brinkley et al 2010: 18)

Suto, writing for Cambridge Assessment in 2013, takes a more detailed look at the work analysed by the ATCS project, examining specifically reports from the US, the UK and Europe. A similar scenario emerges as was observed regarding character described earlier. The same terms appear repeatedly but with slightly different interpretations and emphasis. The evidence base to support the proposition that such skills are more important in the 21st century is usually constructed from an analysis of present employer skill demand, and then extrapolation of such trends into the future. As with the classical curriculum model, however, there is less of a willingness to consider the implications of the changing labour market demand for skills (mapped out in Chapter Two). There is no provision for the possibility that, in the medium term at least, there could be a change in the nature of the overall demand for knowledge-based workers and/or the kind of 'digital Taylorism' that Brown et al (2008) describe.

Neither are the skills described above 'new' as such. As Silva (2009) argues, critical thinking and creativity are skills that were identified as important to success as long ago as the time of Socrates and Plato. They have appeared repeatedly in government policy since the 1980s, especially in relation to the needs of employers. The 21st-century skills discourse is being constructed as a mechanism by which young people can become more employable. It reinforces the exclusivity of the association between education and employment, and not necessarily in a positive way. Skills such as flexibility, which while not in the ATCS list is ubiquitous in most of the 21st-century discourse, as well as communication and collaboration (which are on the list) are also frequently hijacked in this way.

The development of these skills in young people could be construed as a methodology to prepare young people for more insecure employment and to adjust to the kind of labour market described by Brown, Cowen and others earlier in Chapter Two. It is obviously important that young people are adequately prepared for a changing labour market – social mobility of any form would be difficult without such preparation. The danger is that 21st-century skills become a way of repeating 20th-century problems. Employers are continually pointing out the inadequacies of those leaving education in the UK (Federation of Small Businesses 2013, Paton 2014). This is not new, contrary to how it is presented in policy discourse; they have been doing this throughout the 20th century (Payne 1999). Unlike their counterparts in some other countries, employers have been less willing to become involved in a more constructive dialogue with education providers, and bear joint responsibility for the skills that workers obtain. The view predominates in the UK that it is the employers' needs that should be served by the education system. As long as this remains the case, it will be difficult to extend what social mobility means. To reiterate, this is not to say that young people should not be prepared for the vagaries of the 21st-century labour market – but that is a different objective from meeting the needs of employers. It implies developing skills that enable young people to cope and deal with risk and uncertainty in the 21st-century labour market, starting from the employee up, rather than the employer down.

But such a change in itself is not enough. The purpose of education in the context of the challenges outlined in Chapter Two should be to enable young people to meet the challenges of 21st-century life – not just the labour market. The 21st-century skills discourse has the potential to make a positive contribution to how social mobility is understood, if it can empower young people to navigate a more uncertain labour market and a more risky society. However, it could also take things in the opposite direction, and act as a mechanism to narrow even further the objectives of education.

Is there more to school than attainment?

The theory of 'maximum maintained inequality' was developed with reference to higher education participation, but it applies well to the secondary education system. Maximum maintained inequality, or MMI, was defined by Boliver (2010) as 'expansion in and of itself is unlikely to reduce educational inequalities simply because those from more advantaged socioeconomic backgrounds are better placed than others to take up the new educational opportunities that expansion affords' (2010: 1). Shavit and Blossfeld (1993) tested the MMI theory and undertook research in 13 different countries covering a range of political regimes, looking at educational participation over long periods of time. They found that only when the higher socioeconomic groups had colonised a point in the system would participation increase by those from lower socioeconomic groups increase, by which time, advances in technology and increases in supply had reduced the relative value of these qualifications. Even at the rate of increase in GCSE attainment of the late 2000s (which has now stalled), it would be well into the mid-part of the century when all young people achieve five A-C grades at GCSE (or any newly demarcated equivalent 'matriculation' point in the education system in England). As Lupton and Obolenskaya (2013) show through the 2000s the gap between learners from different socio-economic backgrounds in terms of 5★ A-C GSCE increased when English and Maths were included. While the percentage of learners in receipt of free school meals achieving this level increased from 20% to 30% from 2006 to 2010, the percentage of learners not in receipt of free school meals who achieved at this level increased from just under 50 to 60%.

By the time those most disadvantaged learners reach this 'matriculation stage', the point of labour market differential between groups will be at least degree level. Having five A★-C GCSE grades or any new equivalent will be akin to being able to read and write – an essential skill, but not one that enables significant economic progression on its own. It is possible that there could be a significant acceleration; for instance, London has significantly outperformed the rest of the country since the early 2000s (GLA 2013). If the London phenomenon spread, universal matriculation at 16 could possibly be reached much sooner. But by then the more affluent groups would more than likely have pushed their way even further ahead.

The present focus in schools on social mobility, which is to drive up attainment of those from lower socioeconomic groups, is at best not fully thought through and at worst a deceit. It will help the minority, who will be able to access the knowledge-rich, well-paid jobs available, but it cannot assist the majority to access such jobs, as there are simply not enough of them. This is a difficult problem to address – too difficult for politicians (this is an area where there is a consensus), who will not admit that educational inequality will always exist, and that the number of knowledge-intensive jobs is finite.

The only realistic approach is to try to change what educational success means, so that inequalities in achievement can become differences in achievement. This means looking beyond attainment as the sole defining feature in how compulsory education is designed.

The vocational problem

Vocational education has always been subjugated to narrow, academic-based curriculum models, and suffers in the eyes of many parents because of its association with 'lower status' job outcomes. One of the accusations levelled at the English system since its inception has been the weakness of its vocational routes (Wolf 2011, Green 2013), especially in comparison with countries such as Germany, which England has been repeatedly encouraged to mimic in this regard. Setting aside some of the inherent problems in 'policy borrowing' stemming from the cultural and structural embeddedness of education (Phillips and Ochs 2004), there is no doubt that vocational education could be better.

However, the assumption that it is somehow ideally positioned both to ensure that a country will be able to compete in the global economy and meet the needs of those who do not achieve a certain set of academic qualifications is seriously flawed (Keep 2013). Improving clarity regarding what vocational qualifications can do and what they lead to would be beneficial, as would improving their quality by regulating who delivers them. But they will always be a victim to the bigger problem of what constitutes success and achievement in compulsory education. Until this can be changed, vocational education will not provide a panacea any more than attainment will, but enhancing its status does present part of the way forward.

The biggest step that could be taken in the medium term to enhance the vocational route would be to reform the assessment system and introduce a baccalaureate that covered a broad range of capabilities and gave them more equal weight. This was proposed both in the 2000s and in the 2010s (Anderson 2014). But it has to be one baccalaureate for all students, and it must contain more than just a narrow range of academic subjects and include non-cognitive skills as well as the kind of character-building described earlier.

Education for holistic social mobility

Curriculum reform alone, though, will not dampen down the desire of the more affluent groups to help their children progress – it will just change what they focus their energies on. It is noticeable that one (political) metric of success for the investment in the government's new apprenticeship programmes in the early 2010s has been the willingness of middle-class parents and their children to engage in apprenticeships rather than higher education (Paton 2014).

Alongside any curriculum reform there needs to be a national debate on parenting that is unprecedented in its scope and longevity. It cannot just be about early years and school readiness. What comes from this debate must be backed up by long-term policy commitment. The focus of the debate should be on getting parents from higher socioeconomic groups to think about adapting how they parent just as much (if not more so) than those from lower socioeconomic groups. The aim should be to get them to focus as relentlessly on the emotional well-being of their children as they currently do on their academic attainment. This might mean doing less, as opposed to doing more, and creating the space for engagement and consultation with children regarding their future wishes and desires, rather than assuming that parents can always define this.

Education for holistic social mobility requires underpinning everything that is done with a step-change in the engagement of young people. This needs to begin from a very early age, making children partners and co-producers in their own learning experience. This means practical strategies to integrate the 'student voice' into curriculum development and delivery, pedagogy and institutional strategy. It means drawing on examples of work from across the world in the informal educational sector, such as the 'children as change agents' model (see Atherton and Jenkins 2015).

The benefits of co-production with student voice work are well documented, as are its shortcomings (see, for example, Raymond 2001, Rudduck and Flutter 2004, Noyes 2005, Street and Temperley 2005); it is not another panacea. But if young people have a much stronger voice in education, it is highly likely that what constitutes as success will be seen differently, as we know that the reality is that what success means differs from individual to individual.

This will be particularly effective if student voice is supported by the establishment of a comprehensive and universal system of information, advice and guidance (IAG) on post-school opportunities. The decline in IAG support in England in recent years has been startling (Langley et al 2014), even though it began from a low point – it is not an area where England has excelled historically. However, this dialogue with learners from primary age upwards on their futures after school is fundamental. The space for it does not exist at the moment, nor do the resources to support it. Each young person should have the individual one-to-one support to talk regularly about what they want from life, why they want this and how to develop the capabilities to think about these issues. This is more important than the achievement of a slightly better grade in the end-of-school examination. (However, for this statement to be true in practice, the entrance system to higher education may need to be addressed; ideally, it does not have to be one or the other, of course.) The views of young people are much more considered, serious and varied than the popular misconception often presented by policy makers and the media (Hannon and Tims 2010). The evidence shows that young people are already having these conversations about success, progress and life from primary level, but unfortunately it appears that they are not being supported in doing so (Atherton et al 2009).

Conclusions

The study of social mobility has largely ignored any critical analysis of the nature of the educational system. A holistic approach to social mobility requires a break from such an approach. Any attempts to broaden the discussion on social mobility, and also any aspirations to make it genuinely attainable, depend on broadening the goals of education. The unquestioning pursuit of higher attainment in a narrow range of subjects provides the basis for the narrowness of the social mobility discourse. The scope of the challenge cannot be underestimated.

Education is located within a historical set of institutional and cultural relationships (which is why it is so difficult for one country to transplant the approaches of other countries into their own). In some respects, the education system in the UK has changed very little since the 18th century. Green (2013) examines the historical roots of education in England, France, Germany, the US and the Pacific Rim countries. He argues that the relatively late realisation in England of the importance of education to the development of nationhood has undermined its position as a public good. The marketisation of the system in the last 30 years has only built on the idea that it is appropriate for the state to have an arm's-length approach to how education is delivered. While this passivity with regard to the role of the state may now have reversed, the regressive reforms introduced by the coalition government since 2010 have been possible because they mine a rich vein of sepia-tinted nostalgia mixed with ignorance where education is concerned.

Bringing education into the 21st century from the mid part of the 20th (where it is seems to be stuck) requires a more systematic and more honest engagement with social mobility. Equally, if social mobility is to remain relevant to the 21st century, it requires a quite different approach to education.

FIVE

Unbundling, diversification and the ecological university: new models for higher education

> Our belief is that deep, radical and urgent transformation is required in higher education as much as it is in school systems. Our fear is that, perhaps as a result of complacency, caution or anxiety, or a combination of all three, the pace of change is too slow and the nature of change too incremental. (Barber et al 2013: 3)

Introduction

In the long run, an increase in the overall level of education in the population may well be almost inevitable, despite the variable returns it may have for many. It is not as clear, however, how this education will be delivered. Higher education (HE) is cast in the present discourse as the main route for upward social mobility by the majority but, as has been shown in previous chapters, there are an increasing number of naysayers doubting its ability to confer benefits on all who participate. At the same time, HE is changing. As the number of (different types of) students entering HE increases, new forms of provision and new providers are entering the sector. This is leading to a battle within HE itself to define what it is and what it does, as external educational, economic and social forces pose both threats and opportunities.

This chapter looks at the relationship between HE and social mobility. It explores whether HE as it is presently constructed can provide all students with the skills they need to progress in work and life. Can and should HE move from becoming something for 40 to 50% of the population to something for 90%? Should it remain where it is, or is something new needed, to provide the greater post-secondary education that this century will inevitably see? Under a holistic view of social mobility there is a need for a post-secondary education route that can enable individual progression throughout life. Can HE do this for some, any, or all? Participation in HE increased from 19% in 1990 to close to 50% by the early 2010s (Bolton 2012, BIS 2013a), but, as argued later, the economic benefits remain robust, and most students are still very satisfied with their decision to enter HE despite fees increasing (Grove 2014). However, tensions are showing. If there is to be another step-change in HE participation in England, changes bigger than those that enabled the last increase in participation to work may be required.

Access to higher education

There has been considerable progress in England in the last 20 years in terms of narrowing the gap in participation in HE between those from higher and lower socioeconomic groups. Those from 'high participation' neighbourhoods are 2.7 times more likely to progress to HE than those from low participation neighbourhoods in 2013 compared to 4.3 times more likely in 2004 (BIS 2014). This change represents steady but impressive progress, but it has come at a cost. As an estimate, over £900 million was invested in activities to widen access to HE in the 2000s (Atherton 2010). Investment in activities to support wider access to HE and also to support students entering HE from underrepresented backgrounds was close to £1 billion per year in the early 2010s (BIS 2014).

However, there are still huge differences in the numbers attending HE from lower and higher socioeconomic groups. There is also a range of 'fault lines' of inequality in HE by social background. Socioeconomic group measured especially by geography is the dominant way in which access to HE is conceived in England, but as Watson points out in his 2006 paper for the Higher Education Funding Council of England (HEFCE), 'widening participation' in HE encompasses quite a range of groups:

> Widening participation is taken to mean extending and enhancing access to HE experiences of people from so-called under-represented and diverse subject backgrounds, families, groups and communities and positively enabling such people to participate in and benefit from HE. People from socially disadvantaged families and/or deprived geographical areas, including deprived remote, rural and coastal areas or from families that have no prior experience of HE may be of key concern. Widening participation is also concerned with diversity in terms of ethnicity, gender, disability and social background in particular HE disciplines, modes and institutions. It can also include access

and participation across the ages, extending conceptions of learning across the life-course, and in relation to family responsibilities, particularly by gender and maturity. (Watson 2006: 1)

To illustrate Watson's point, progress in terms of narrowing access gaps at the most selective universities in the last 20 years has not been anywhere near as impressive as across the sector as a whole (Harris 2010). Significant differences also exist in terms of participation by ethnic group, especially regarding type of institution (HEFCE 2013). There is also growing concern regarding the participation of older learners and those who study part-time, who themselves, to an extent, represent an underrepresented group but also include a disproportionate number of students from lower socioeconomic groups. When HE tuition fees were increased in England in 2012, part-time participation immediately fell by a quarter (HESA 2014).

Furthermore, the focus has also turned recently to include not just getting students from different backgrounds into HE, but what happens to them when they enter HE. Research from the HEFCE shows that distinct differences remain in the trajectories of students from underrepresented groups through HE (BIS 2014). The research examined the performance of those from lower HE participation neighbourhoods in terms of classification of degree, course completion and employment six months after graduation. After controlling for prior attainment and institution attended, it shows that those from lower participation neighbourhoods perform below average on all these measures. It appears, then, that even if progress is being made in getting students from lower socioeconomic groups into HE, their background is hampering them when it comes to progress through HE and 'success' afterwards.

There are also some deeper cultural and structural barriers to overcome, if outcomes for students from underrepresented groups are to be improved. While there has been considerable investment by the state in England in widening access to HE in the last 15 years, it has not met with universal support. HE serving as the mechanism to equalise the life chances between individuals between different groups makes some people uneasy. It is part of an agenda for HE that is taking it away from its core purpose. As David Willetts, former Minister for Higher Education and Skills under the coalition government from 2010, stated:

> … the primary role of universities is to enrich our knowledge and understanding. That is the fundamental value of teaching and research. We will not compromise on that. *You don't usually become an academic to raise the national growth rate or to improve social mobility.* (Willetts 2011; emphasis added)

There are structural and cultural ceilings in HE where access is concerned. At the institution level (and those who represent institutions), the limits of the university's responsibility where access is concerned are forever being drawn in the sand. The following quotation is taken from the Russell Group, the body that represents the most selective HEIs in England:

> Of course, our universities have a role to play in helping students from under-privileged backgrounds to overcome the barriers they face, and we have never claimed otherwise. But we cannot solve this problem alone and there is also a vital role here for schools, and other agencies. (Russell Group 2011)

This doesn't just apply to the more selective institutions – the regulatory regime in England is based around written 'access agreements' between individual institutions and the Office for Fair Access. These agreements outline the measures that institutions need to take each year to promote wider access to their institutions. Other countries, where access might not even be remotely on the radar of universities, look at these with envy. But this has also helped to consolidate the pre-existing idea that access work is something that universities have to do, rather than want to do. This can clearly be seen in the case of those institutions that admit higher numbers of learners from underrepresented groups, arguing with complete justification that they are doing the 'heavy lifting' where access is concerned. But few ever express a desire to admit more. They have 'done their bit' and are often more concerned to improve their academic standing, so they are not perceived as being an 'access university'.

This is where the old (or existing) ideas on social mobility and the new ones being described in this book come together. If HE is to be a route to upward social mobility for the majority of the population, at some stage it is going to have to admit the majority into its fold. And this means those from lower socioeconomic groups. The idea that working with schools and the wider community to support access to HE through outreach based work such as summer schools, peer mentoring and HE information activities should be a core part of what academics do appears far away,, as does the university leader who is happy to proclaim that at his or her university would like there to be 60, 70 or 80% of its students coming from lower socioeconomic groups still appears far away. As presently constructed, HE is not in a place where it can be the route to 'mass' social mobility. The question is, should it ever aspire to be, or be encouraged to be, such a route? Is there a case for HE being the engine for social mobility in the 21st century?

The first case for higher education

In spite of the changes in the labour market described earlier in Chapter Three, the economic case for HE remains robust overall. While there is evidence to support the pessimistic view regarding the role of HE in the 21st-century economy expressed by Brown and colleagues in Chapter One, there is also counter-evidence showing that for the majority of people, going on to HE is the rational thing to do. To borrow from the economists' view, if going to HE provides any benefit, no matter how small in comparison to the opportunity cost of not going, then it is rational. And overall it does so.

In the mid-2000s, the UK government estimated that graduates would earn over £100,000 more over their lifetime than non-graduates (DfES 2003). However, more recent research commissioned by the government argues that this average return may be even higher (Walker and Zhu 2013).

Furthermore, the economic benefit is not restricted to the individual. The state also, through higher taxation contributions, profits greatly from students entering HE. Walker and Zhu, in research published in 2013 for the Department for Business, Innovation and Skills (BIS), estimate that: .the private benefit of a degree, in terms of lifetime earnings net of tax and loan repayments, is large – in the order of £168k (£252k) for men (women) on average. The social benefit to the government is also large (of the order of £264k (£318k) from men (women) graduates – far in excess of likely exchequer costs (Walker and Zhu 2013: 5).

Walker and Zhu's work is supported by international evidence. Data from the OECD show that there is an earnings premium attached to tertiary education across countries (OECD 2013). While this premium differs markedly across countries, it is on average 1.5 times that of those with upper secondary education. Nor may the problem be as bad as some make out regarding unemployment. Research released by the ONS in 2013 shows that graduate unemployment was actually lower in 2013 than it was in 1992. It was also higher than in the 2000s, but the UK has been experiencing the worst recession since the 1930s (ONS 2013).

Moreover, these data look at 19- to 24-year-olds. What really matters is the labour market position of those in their early 40s, not those in their late 20s (especially for graduates who also start families later, according to ONS research). This is a fundamental point that is missed by the majority of the public discourse on graduate employment. While earnings may be similar for all groups when they enter the labour market, as people get older, it is graduates who earn significantly more (ONS 2013). Looking specifically at occupational mobility, Savage (2011) examined the relationship between being qualified to the graduate equivalent of NVQ Level 4 in the 2000s and progression in the earning scale – those who graduate from HE are more likely to move up the occupational scale.

While benefits are important, though, necessity is usually a more powerful force in driving behaviour. The evidence shows that young people know that the returns from education are fragile, and it may be a long road to a rewarding graduate job. But as more and more employers ask for a degree for jobs that previously did not require one, young people see little choice. For the first time in 2012, the number of jobs requiring a degree in the UK outweighed the numbers that did not (Felstead et al 2012). The majority of these jobs are also ones that demand high skills. The 2013 ONS report also shows that graduates are nearly four times as likely as non-graduates to be in high-skilled jobs. And there is evidence to show that the future demand for graduates is likely to be strong. The UKCES predicted in 2012 that up to 80% of new jobs created would be in professional and managerial occupations, with another 2 million such jobs by 2020. Looking internationally, a report by the McKinsey Global Institute (2012) predicts a potential shortfall by 2020 of up to 40 million workers qualified to degree level.

Education is not yet seemingly losing all its power as a mechanism for transmitting economic advantage, but how it does this may be more complex than the data above imply. The research on average returns to education may be interesting, but it hides as much as it reveals. It is a fairly safe assumption to make that returns vary greatly by subject and also by institution, and the evidence bears this out. Work from the ONS shows that the average annual gross wage differs from £21,000 to £46,000, dependent on the subject studied (ONS 2013).

The ONS research also shows that earnings differ by institution. Those from the more selective Russell Group universities, favoured so much in the social mobility discourse of the early 2010s, earn approximately £4 per hour more on average than those educated in the rest of the sector. And inequalities in the graduate labour market certainly appear to be growing. Walker and Zhu, in their work on average returns to HE described above, acknowledge that one of the reasons why the returns are so high is because they factor in the disproportionate impact that very high earners with degrees have. They also find differences in earnings by institution attended, but that these are largely accounted for by differences in the background of students who attend particular institutions in terms of gender, subject studied and prior qualifications. Further work from Macmillan et al at the Institute of Education (2013) also points to the importance of institution in defining progression to the top jobs. It is more important, for instance, than any advantage that those from more affluent backgrounds obtain because of their background alone. Hence, even for the powerful, education is crucial in translating this power into economic return.

The evidence outlined here clearly shows that the ability of education to confer advantage remains strong. HE still offers the best available route to stable employment that provides above-average earnings. Where the employment question is concerned, while for those educated in the 1980s and 1990s the data show that by their key employment years their education is paying off, we do not yet have data for those being educated in the era of near mass HE from the early to mid-1990s onwards. What does appear to be the case is that for the latter it might be a longer and harder road after HE until stable graduate employment is reached. The importance of this should not be underestimated. It starts to make post-graduate education appear more important, and it also puts more pressure on those who enter HE from less affluent backgrounds.

It could be argued that HE is more important than ever. It acts as the mechanism now by which entry to the vast majority of better jobs is controlled and, furthermore, even powerful, affluent groups retain their labour market advantages. The expansion in HE since the 1960s in the UK has primarily benefited middle-class groups (Elias and Purcell 2012). They understand that the jobs they want their children to enter now almost universally require a degree (whether the job needs one or not). So while going on to HE may be a gamble, many young people think they cannot afford not to make it.

The second case for higher education

While the demise of HE as a provider of economic benefit may be a little premature, there are still warning signs that cannot be ignored. Taking forward a new vision for HE is dependent on there being an empirical evidence base to draw from, and the signs are concerning here. The percentage of graduates in lower-skilled jobs rose over 2001 to 2011 (ONS 2012a). Similar data have also emerged in particular from the US, and from mainland Europe and Australia (OECD 2012a). Graduate unemployment in the UK is also higher than most would deem desirable, at over 20% for young graduates (ONS 2014a). There is also research to show that average graduate starting salaries fell by 11% from 2007 to 2012 (BBC News 2014b).

The concerns about the ability of HE to deliver social mobility are not restricted to undergraduate students. A 2008 study pointed to a similar oversupply problem among research doctorate students (Group of Eight 2013).

While the research focused primarily on Australia, and quoted research from the US regarding the number of graduates with doctorates in low-status employment, the message is one that must be heeded by other countries. The economic risks associated with obtaining a degree are also far higher when the costs of HE are taken into account. The prospect of ex-HE students labouring under a significant debt for 20 to 30 years as they struggle ever to earn enough to make real inroads into that debt will be a fact of life for many (Crawford and Wenchao 2014).

At the same time as there being a need to address the education/ employment relationship, however, the limitations here must be acknowledged. Education offers both less and more than the 'global race for talent' discourse allows. It does not guarantee economic security or progression, but at the same time it may offer more. It provides a range of other benefits that are essential to both the individual and society.

A surprising source of real support for this view has been the government in England in the early 2010s – or at least one minister and his department. BIS produced a paper in late 2013 examining the benefits of HE participation, aiming to give a systematic overview of the benefits of HE study to both individuals and groups, and to the economy and society. It argues strongly for a more holistic view of the benefits of HE study. Figure 5.1 is taken from this paper.

The BIS report is a very thorough exposition of the extent of the benefits of HE. It provides an extensive bibliography of research from across the world that supports every one of the benefits in shown in

Figure 5.1: The market and wider benefits of HE to individuals and society

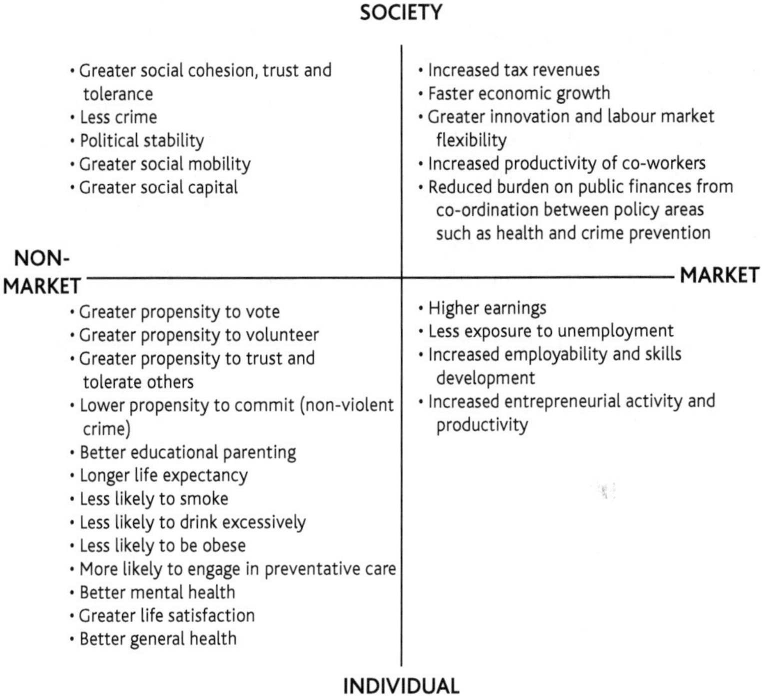

SOCIETY

• Greater social cohesion, trust and tolerance • Less crime • Political stability • Greater social mobility • Greater social capital	• Increased tax revenues • Faster economic growth • Greater innovation and labour market flexibility • Increased productivity of co-workers • Reduced burden on public finances from co-ordination between policy areas such as health and crime prevention

NON-MARKET ————————————————————————————— MARKET

• Greater propensity to vote • Greater propensity to volunteer • Greater propensity to trust and tolerate others • Lower propensity to commit (non-violent crime) • Better educational parenting • Longer life expectancy • Less likely to smoke • Less likely to drink excessively • Less likely to be obese • More likely to engage in preventative care • Better mental health • Greater life satisfaction • Better general health	• Higher earnings • Less exposure to unemployment • Increased employability and skills development • Increased entrepreneurial activity and productivity

INDIVIDUAL

Source: **BIS (2013b)**

Figure 5.1, and hence the more 'holistic' view of the benefits of HE. It is also careful not to exaggerate what is known here, especially where HE itself is concerned. Some of the evidence refers not to HE as such, but to the length of time actually spent in education. Despite the number of benefits listed in the bottom and top-left quadrants of Figure 5.1, it is still those on the right-hand side (especially the lower right) that gain most attention. One way of addressing this has been an attempt to put a monetary value on non-market benefits.

McMahon attempted to do this in the US, and estimated that the value of private non-market benefits was 22% higher than private market benefits, and the value of social non-market benefits was up to 88% higher (McMahon 2008). The New Economics Foundation (nef) (2011) estimates that universities contribute £1.31 billion to society. Using .social return on investments techniques, nef assesses the value of the greater political interest, higher interpersonal trust and better health that result from HE attendance.

The work by BIS, McMahon and nef is crucially important. These ideas frame a different understanding of what HE does, but they have to be handled carefully. There has to be an economic return of some description to HE study. When the economic present and future is uncertain, it is politically unpalatable to have any understanding of the role of education that does not recognise this. Emphasising the multifaceted nature of the benefits of education could easily alienate policy makers and the public, whose primary concerns are financial. What good is the ability of education to enable improved trust or even better health if it cannot alleviate poverty, or worse, if it might exacerbate it by burdening students with debt that they cannot repay? There has to be a level of economic return that is satisfactory enough to answer this question, but it is this level that is not being discussed in the present discourse.

There is a prevailing short termism in how the benefits of HE are understood (Hackett et al 2012). If it does not guarantee a job in the first six months – or even six years – that is clearly fulfilling and substantially better paid than non-graduate work, then it is claimed it must not be worth it. However, it is what happens in your 30s and 40s that matters most where the impact of going on to HE is concerned and, as argued earlier, the evidence holds up well here.

However, the economic benefit agenda remains strong – and will become even more important as the cost of HE in England is so high. While championing the broader benefits of HE, since 2010 the government has been exploring ways of funding HE based on the economic returns to graduates, building on work done in the US in this area (The Economist 2014). The problem with such approaches – or the one that occurs in this case – is that they embed in policy the view that the returns to HE should be defined in purely economic terms.

However, nef and McMahon are individual voices. There has not been the kind of developed, empirically based thinking regarding what the benefits of 21st-century HE are, when they occur and how they can be developed to enable the economistic ideas to be countered.

Beyond access and the battle for the soul of higher education

There is still a strong case for HE participation as a societal/individual social and economic good. It may be an even stronger one in the early 21st century, but this does not on its own mean that HE is positioned to be the vehicle of holistic social mobility.

The increase in number and diversity of learners has combined with a sort of marketisation similar to that described by Sandel in Chapter One, to bring a wider malaise to HE itself. The increasing numbers of students going on to HE as it becomes massified have challenged of the relationship of HE to the state (Trow and Burrage 2010). Funding HE entirely from public funds becomes an ever more difficult proposition. Virtually all countries that are experiencing mass HE are relying on some form of non-state contributions from the individual or private sector (Usher 2009). In England, the answer has been to implement one of the highest levels of tuition fees in the world (OECD 2011).

Combined with this massification has been marketisation. The default response to these twin forces, many argue, has been the rise of new managerialism in HE. New managerialism is defined by Deem et al (2007: 5) as: 'the detailed restructuring of public services delivery, organization, and management in a way that facilitates a flexible, and changing balance, between "strategic control" and "operational control"'.

The impact of new managerialism has been to challenge the very ideas and practices on which HE is based. The organisational reality of everyday university life seems to suggest that for many, if not most, academics there has been a fundamental loss of control – over work organisation and professional culture – as universities have been transformed from 'communities of scholars' into 'workplaces'. Activities designed to promote social mobility via widened access have been associated with this shift. As Deem et al argue:

> Unfortunately, work to further social mobility via the access to higher education work described earlier has come to be perceived as part of this agenda, where outside forces in the guise of senior management and government impose on the academic community responsibilities and tasks which curtail what it means to be part of a university. (Deem et al 2007: 12)

Closely related to this change in how universities are managed are further threats to the idea and practice of the university in the form of their marketisation. Brown and Carasso's forensic analysis of the changes in the way that HE is funded in England over the last 30 years illustrates the reach of the market and market forces into academia. They argue that the funding of HE has changed to push universities to compete and behave in ways akin to businesses (Brown and Carasso 2013).

This push to marketisation is more than just a function of how the funding and regulatory system has changed in one country; it is also a function of how HE itself is part of the global economy and how it has changed since the 1970s. As with social mobility, HE itself is not just the subject of socioeconomic change but also its architect. As Marginson and van der Wende argued in their 2007 paper for the OECD:

> Being deeply immersed in global transformations, higher education is itself being transformed on both sides of the economy/culture symbiosis. Higher education is swept up in global marketisation. It trains the executives and technicians of global businesses; the main student growth is in globally mobile degrees in business studies and computing; the sector is shaped by economic policies undergoing partial global convergence, and the first global university market has emerged. (Marginson and van der Wende 2007: 5)

The massification of HE, the questioning of its role and the way in which HEIs, their leaders and the state have responded have provoked a broader struggle for the soul of HE in the UK. Academics such as Collini have argued that the very purpose of HE is under threat from the actions of politicians and the drive to show that what universities do has to have external and measurable benefits. He argues that those in HE: 'are merely custodians for the present generation of a complex intellectual inheritance which we did not create – and which is not ours to destroy' (Collini 2012: 199).

In 2012, the Coalition for the Defence of British Universities was formed. It is an alliance of primarily individual academics who believe that the focus on employability, the encroachment of performance targets into academia and successive governments taking an instrumental view of the role of HE in society have distorted what HE is. The pursuit of knowledge as an end in itself by both researchers and students has been lost. There is an urgent need to defend this principle and the practices that go with it. It is tempting to dismiss the Coalition as some disgruntled academics concerned about threats to their own welfare. However, regardless of whether the changes in HE are a threat to any mythical soul of HE, the views of the Coalition are real. They also, to some degree, reflect the views of many academics in the UK (Parr 2014).

Imagination and the role of higher education

HE is being pulled in different directions. It is attempting to balance retaining its ability to develop critical, reflective thinking and thinkers but also to provide the kind of tangible skills that enable its students to not just survive but to prosper in the 21st century. Attempts to keep faith with a classical vision of the university without recognising the changes that HE itself is undergoing look doomed to failure, but rushing to become an 'education business' and rejecting the history of HE and the intellectual and social capital that comes with it also looks to be a risk-laden route.

Barnett has written extensively on the mission and model for contemporary HE. He is very critical of the way in which the university is now 'imagined'. He argues that: '[the] conceptual journey that the idea of the university has undergone over nearly one thousand years has gradually shrunk. [It]... has closed in...' (Barnett 2011: 1).

Barnett sees those who espouse visions for the university at present as being reactive in the response to globalisation and what comes with it. They offer either the defensive responses described earlier or some version of the 'entrepreneurial' university, which inevitably (in Barnett's view) trail behind the forces that they respond to. Each response also suffers, according to Barnett, from either too much pessimism (in the case of those concerned about the threat to the university) or too much optimism, as those who see economic and social changes as offering opportunity rush headlong to grab what might not be there. He feels that we need a 'feasible utopia' (Barnett 2013). His preferred attempt at such a utopia is the ecological university. Barnett argues that the university should embrace an idea of interconnectedness. A vision for it should not be afraid to seek to include individuals, institutions and communities in its thinking. Barnett describes such an institution as 'the ecological university':

> The ecological university would be intertwined – at very deep levels of its being – with the global knowledge economy and with forces for marketisation and competition. But it would look for spaces in which it could live out the values and ideas deeply embedded in the university – of truthfulness, inquiry, critical dialogue, rational dispute and even iconoclastic endeavour. (Barnett 2013)

Barnett firmly positions the ecological university between the polar extremes of the optimists and pessimists that he criticises. For Barnett, it could give life to the ideas embedded in the university by public engagement through intellectual endeavour, the opening up of physical space, and so on. The most important manifestation of this public role, however, would be in what the ecological university seeks to achieve. It would seek to 'promote well-being at every level' (Barnett 2013)

This idea clearly connects the ecological university with holistic social mobility. A commitment to well-being creates the space for a pedagogy that could enable students to leave university with not just the ability to earn more money, but to have 'successful lives' along a number of dimensions.

In positioning the university in this way, Barnett further sees it as being prompted not purely by economic changes, implying that it should act more like a business or that its students should become more employable. More important are the wider challenges that globalisation implies – global warming, global terrorism and crime, energy crises and global diseases and hunger (Barnett 2012). This rationale presented for the ecological university strengthens the connection of the idea with holistic social mobility; it links HE directly to the sort of societal challenges that are also shaping the need for a new approach to social mobility.

Disruptive forces and massive open online courses

However, as appealing as the ecological vision is, realising it will be a challenge. As Figure 5.2 shows, the expansion of undergraduate HE in England in recent years has focused very much on undergraduate first degrees as opposed to different forms of HE provision at this level. Some signs of change can be detected at the end of the period up to 2012 but they appear temporary, as undergraduate first degree participation has increased again post-2012. There is clearly a huge way to go to develop a far more diverse form of undergraduate HE where provision is concerned.

There are significant cultural and structural rigidities within HE that, despite the protestations of those concerned about the threats to the academy from new managerialism and marketisation, act as barriers to innovation in HE (Bourdieu 1996, Huberman 1973). Martin Hall, drawing on his experience leading a large institution in England, points in his 2012 paper for the Leadership Foundation to the challenges in building the consensus for organisational change in complex institutions such as universities.

The extent of these rigidities implies that initiating the shift in thinking required to open up access to far more students may need

Figure 5.2: Participation in undergraduate higher education, 2005–2011

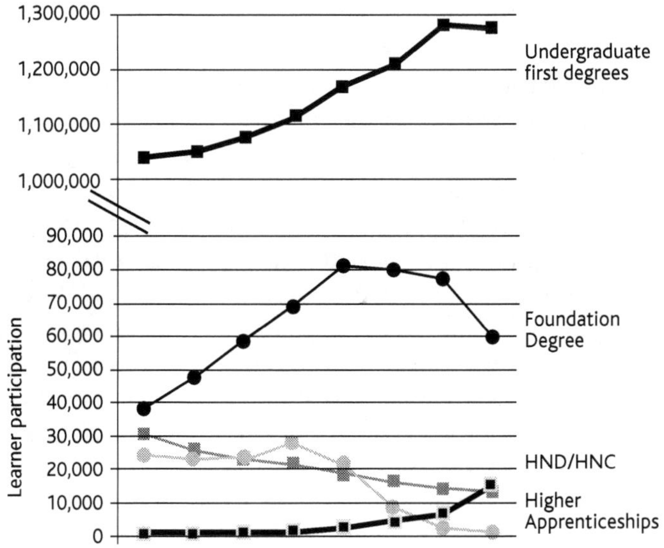

Source: UKCES (2015)

an external force (or forces) to initiate change. Online technology may have such a role. The most high-profile example of what such technology could do to HE is found in massive open online courses (MOOCs). These have brought huge number of learners in contact with what HE has to offer very quickly.

Some have described MOOCs as a 'disruptive technology'. Christensen (1997) describes a disruptive technology as one that unexpectedly displaces an existing technology (UUK 2013). For others, however, MOOCS have all the hallmarks of a 'bubble" where the interest and investment will rise quickly before bursting leaving little significant afterwards (Scott 2013). The evidence shows that, thus far, the majority of those who have signed up for MOOC-related courses already have significant amounts of education. And the majority do not complete the course they sign up for (DeBoer et al 2013). On their own, MOOCS are not necessarily mechanisms to make HE available to a more diverse group of learners. Neither is the ability of MOOCS to confer on students the benefits of conventional HE yet clear. If the courses are not accredited, will they have any labour market currency? They illustrate that the learner is at least committed to self-development, and past evidence where the trajectory of learners who have left HE early shows that they can still go on to progress in the labour market. But there are no formal entry requirements, so, unlike in the standard HE case, entry itself is no marker of achievement to potential employers.

MOOCs do, though, represent a fascinating opportunity to understand better what it is about HE, if indeed anything, that leads to the non-economic benefits of the quadrant diagram (see Figure 5.1). They 'strip out' the normal experience of HE, leaving it in its purest form as subject. Even the kind of social experience that is associated with traditional distance learning is usually absent. The 'social capital' that some argue is as important a gain from HE as any form of intellectual capital does not work the same in the MOOC context. Many of these courses are taken by those who are already qualified. The majority of those who take them do not receive qualifications comparable to, say, a 'real' university accredited degree. This implies a huge rise in HE as a form of personal enrichment activity. Taking an HE course becomes explicitly something one does to enhance non-economic well-being. It opens up the possibility that different forms of HE could be a driver of both the economic and non-economic aspects of social mobility. The early evidence looking at why learners take up MOOCs shows that the majority are taking them mainly to learn, rather than for any form of economic benefit (DeBoer et al 2013).

But for MOOCs to act as a disruptive technology, as Christensen describes, they would have to have an impact on the mainstream of the HE offer. To do this would mean that core courses, for which either the state/employer/student were willing to pay, would have to 'go MOOC'. Alternatively, MOOCs would have to grow in importance to such an extent that they become the core of what HE offers. For that to happen, there would have to be a viable business model underpinning them.

Where the disruption may be more likely is in MOOCs acting as a 'Trojan horse', forcing HE to embrace online learning in ways it had not previously thought possible. The more innovative models inspired by MOOCs are already going 'post-MOOCs' – seeking to combine what MOOCs offer with more concerted learner support. Harvard, for example, is already moving from MOOCs to SPOCS, or small private online courses (Coughlan 2013a).

The generic benefit of online learning is that it offers greater flexibility in how HE is delivered. This flexibility is what is necessary, if HE is going to be able to meet the challenge of further massification. The dominant model of full-time study over three to four years after the end of compulsory education is unlikely to suit everyone, and so there must be a greater range of provision. But the kind of shift in mission described above via the ecological university model will also be required. If part-time, one- or two-year degree MOOCs are seen as add-ons to the full-time 'gold standard', they will never be able to deliver on holistic social mobility. There has to be a vision of HE that strives to see different forms of provision as equal. This equanimity is only likely to prove possible if different modes of delivery exist within a more overarching set of goals, which means establishing a narrative for the content of curriculum that is powerful enough to transcend these different modes.

Finally, while technology has the potential to enable a redefining of HE, the risk is that dividing lines will remain. As Geoffrey Crossick, ex-Vice-Chancellor of the University of London, stated in 2012:

> The division may no longer be between those who get a higher education and those who don't, but between those who get a higher education in a comprehensive traditional university and those who access it through a myriad of providers in often small learning modules…. [U]nless we think about the issues now as we imagine the new system, we might end up with a clear social dividing line between the two forms of receiving higher education. (Crossick 2012: 12)

A pedagogy for holistic social mobility

Realising a model of HE that can drive holistic social mobility requires not only a shift in how the university is imagined at the macro level, but also a shift in how it goes about its business at the micro level.

The dominance of the subject discipline as the mode through which HE is delivered does pose questions about the benefits of HE and how they equate to social mobility. There has been much written in recent years on 'graduateness' and graduate skills, as well as the alleged mismatch between what graduates can do and what they are expected to do (CBI 2009).

The conundrum of how to inculcate students with generic skills through a model that is predicated on subject-specific skills has not been solved. While online learning has huge potential to instigate change in delivery, it is not clear how it will overcome the subject/skills disjuncture.

There are a number of possible ways to address the disjuncture, although none would guarantee success.

The first step would be to try to ascertain more clearly what skills HE students really need to develop. As in the case of schooling, the subject/skills disjuncture is construed almost entirely as a subset of a bigger HE/employment disjuncture. The idea that HE graduates lack skills is constructed as a lack of skills that employers need (Archer and Davidson 2008).

The BIS report Supporting Graduate Employability (The International Graduate Insight Group Ltd 2011) encapsulates this approach. It frames the discussion around the development of skills and attributes that will enable students in the 21st century to progress and therefore be entirely socially mobile in terms of employability. Even in terms of employability alone, it paints a worrying picture; only a minority of HEIs focus on this area separately. For the majority of those that do, it remains in reality a peripheral concern.

But the desire to fit the 21st-century skills discussion into the employability straightjacket is the real concern. This is never clearer than in its use of the example of Macquarie University's work in Australia in the employability context. Macquarie is attempting to develop a set of holistic skills in their graduates that go beyond preparing them for work. All students have to take a module in 'People, Planet and Participation' over the course of their degree. The module 'provides opportunities for students and staff to actively contribute to more just, inclusive and sustainable societies through activities with communities locally, in regional Australia and overseas' (The International Graduate Insight Group Ltd 2011: 36). This is interpreted in the report as a leading-edge example of how Macquarie is developing employability.

As with the secondary system, the danger with employability is that it 'crowds out' discussion about whether and how HE can help students to develop skills that may support progression outside the economic sphere, such as the ability to reflect on and formulate life goals, to cope with personal and emotional setbacks or to develop a sense of control over both work and non-work life. Returning to Figure 5.1 above, the question should be what skills graduates need so society can reap the benefits in the top-left quadrant as well as those in the bottom-right. However, as illustrated by the BIS employability report, the thinking required to really link what HE does, and how it does it, to these broader outcomes is not there yet.

The second issue in the skills/subject disjuncture is whether the development of such generic skills is viable through the teaching of specific subjects. Are there limits to which English, for example, can be a vehicle for the development of teamwork, workload organisation skills or the kind of resilience described earlier? Should graduate programmes therefore be remodelled to provide students with this broader range of skills and include specific modules that focus on these issues, thus allowing subjects to concentrate on being subjects?

To an extent, subject disciplines, if taught creatively with a focus on the development of dynamic interaction between student and staff rather than using didactic, top-down teaching models, can enable some of these other skills to be developed. Part of the issue is their translation – there is evidence to suggest that one of the major contributory factors to the HE/employment disjuncture is that students are not always aware of the skills that they do have (Mourshed et al 2012). They have developed the ability to communicate and work in teams, for example, through their subject work, but the students do not pick out these skills when applying for jobs. There is a case for greater support approaching the point of exit from HE, to help students better appreciate and articulate their skill set (Mourshed et al 2012).

Third, the importance of subjects themselves as vehicles for upward economic social mobility cannot be ignored. The focus on generic skills obscures both the value of the subject itself and the extent to which they act, in themselves, as a vehicle for the development of wider sets of skills. The emphasis on the importance of these generic skills has provoked a response from established subject disciplines. The STEM (Science, Technology, Engineering and Maths) disciplines argue for 'embedded employability' where it is within the discipline itself, as opposed to delivered via an additional or specialised course that employability skills will be developed (National HE STEM Programme). A further value in the subject-based approach, at least as expressed in the National HE STEM Programme report, is the emphasis on a student-centric (rather than an employer-centric) view of employability.

Established subject disciplines remain in themselves an essential part of any idea of 21st-century skills. Aside from the value of embedded employability as a concept, the HE offer itself is highly vocational in subject terms. The subjects with the most demanding entry requirements – medicine, veterinary science and law – are also the most 'vocational'.

Accepting the importance of subjects, however, and the extent to which they may naturally incline students to develop the generic, there is still a major challenge to be faced. It is difficult to see how this can be done by subjects alone. The major problem with initiatives like 'People, Planet and Participation' from Macquarie (and other attempts to introduce personal development on a compulsory or voluntary basis) is that neither staff nor students buy into them sufficiently (The International Graduate Insight Group Ltd 2011). They are frequently seen as an irritation and not part of what HE is about. The only approach is to combine a pedagogical focus within disciplines on development of 'soft' skills with specialist, compulsory modules along the lines of Macquarie.

Finally, there must be dialogue with students regarding what these skills are and how to articulate them. One of the problems is that, especially when students are paying such large sums for their HE, they want to do the course they paid for. Courses such as 'People, Planet and Participation' are not on the bill, and are perceived as a distraction.

We return inevitably to the macro-questions: the fundamental mission of HE and HEIs has to change, so that courses such as 'People, Planet and Participation' are seen as being as much a part of the student experience as any established subject.

The 'unbundling' of higher education

However, there may be a bigger set of challenges for HE to confront than just MOOCS and employability, if it is to retain its present position or to act as a driver for social mobility. Barber at al describe:

> the growing impact of technology, which threatens many components of the traditional university… [T]his new competition is not necessarily only at the level of the whole institution, it is also competition at the level of each individual component. When this happens, the unbundling of the existing institutions becomes possible, likely or even necessary. (Barber et al 2013: 32)

They describe this 'unbundling' as taking place across a range of functions of the university. In the teaching and learning space they point to how certain large corporations are already setting up their own educational pathways/institutions (The Economist 2013b). In research they describe the increasing contribution made by non-HE-based organisations. Regarding assessment they describe how the monopoly of HE in this field has now been broken. Finally, with the rise of online learning, the fragmentation of the learning experience is another aspect of this unbundling phenomenon. Barber et al **(2013) shows** how new providers are quite different from 'traditional' multi-faculty institutions. The idea of the university as a large physical site offering a range of educational and non-educational experiences becomes itself under question. Unbundling theory recognises that, as there have been in the last 30 years, there will have to be distinct changes in how HE operates in the future if it is not only to expand but also to thrive.

Some of these changes are not so new. The HE sector in England is unified in name only. In reality, it is made up of an increasing number of subsectors (hence why different 'mission group' organisations seem to be able to survive). There are also new ones as what is defined as HE moves away from full-time, three-year courses for young people to something much more diverse and packaged in a greater number of ways. What MOOCs, for example, may have demonstrated is less how technology can change the pedagogic experience and more that it is possible to deliver an 'HE experience' that is shorter and quite different.

It will be a far greater challenge, though, as has been seen so far, in using such insights to deliver economically productive education, for example to groups who at present appear a long way away from participating in HE.

Conclusions

HE appears to be entering massification, if not entirely blindly, then with blurred vision. Where once it may have been a bulwark against a problem such as the success paradox, representing a place where alternative ways of measuring value in life can be explored, it is now being pulled into it. Many HEIs appear to survive by selling a vision of success that is craven in breadth and vision.

In strategic terms, HEIs and policy makers face a choice: whether to retain the model (based around three to four years of full-time study, with the main benefit being better employment opportunities) that has served well so far in educating close to 50% of any cohort of 18-year-olds in England and a small percentage of those who are older, or to diversify what HE does and for it to act as the framework within which the increasing demand for post-compulsory education across the 21st century is met and moved beyond 50%; or, as some politicians advocate, HE could shrink in size and return to a more elitist form.

From the holistic social mobility perspective, it would be better if HE could diversify what it does and act as the framework within which post-compulsory education occurs. There remains something in the character of HE that is critical, independent, reflective and, above all, holistic. The fact that it still aspires to something more than just the transferring of skill is so important, because it enables (at least potentially) a move to a broader conception of progress via education.

The alternative approach would be to offer parallel tracks, separating more clearly the academic and the vocational. As argued in the previous chapter, so many policy makers and commentators in the UK envy such an approach, pointing to its success in Germany; however, they also usually fail to realise that these tracks end in some form of 'higher education'. Over 90% of apprenticeships in Germany are delivered at Level 3 or above (The Boston Consulting Group 2013).

It is indisputable that, if the HE system is going to be the post-secondary framework, then huge change is needed. But as a framework it is the best one available, certainly in England. There has been a continuous flow of policies attempting to build a better alternative vocational track, and none have been successful. It may be better to recognise the cultural and structural context of education in England and to build on that. As pointed out earlier, HE has assimilated thousands of students who, as recently as 20 years ago, would never have dreamed of entering HE. Crucially, though, this means extending what is understood as HE, so that it can encompass 80 or 90% of any given cohort. It will certainly not mean that all young people should 'go to university' via three-year or four-year full-time courses at 18-19, paying tuition fees of £9,000 per year; it means that we should take the goal of all young people achieving HE-level qualifications or equivalent over the lifecourse and work back from there.

Such radical change needs to be built on certain principles. Rather than massification, the main such principle could be one of 'diversification'. As a principle, it unites a number of different elements that are essential if HE is to be a vehicle for holistic social mobility. It includes both a commitment to changing those who go on to HE making the investment necessary to this via outreach activity and strategic commitment, that is, diversifying the intake. It also includes, however, diversifying what we understand as the benefits of HE increasing our knowledge regarding if and how HE participation affects well-being in the way described in Figure 5.1.

The diversification agenda for HE provides the context for the growth of the ecological university described by Barnett (2011). Unbundling is a powerful idea, but it implies that the uniqueness of what HE offers unravels. In the diversification context, this essence is retained but becomes part of a wider, richer experience. The question is whether HE itself is able to articulate a role for itself that can combine this critical and independent nature built on history with the kind of engagement with society and the economy. Can it diversify in mission and form? If the challenges that need to be overcome are too large, then it will continue to have a role to play where social mobility is concerned, enabling up to 50% of any given cohort to experience labour market progression

It may be reaching its limit, though. In the longer term, higher education participation could even be reduced. It is possible that it's role in social mobility terms could be confined to the kind of long-range economic mobility so favoured by many politicians today, delivered through a limited number of selective, research-intensive institutions with strong national and global brands.

The bulk of the other work on economic social mobility may instead be done by a rather different configuration of post-secondary institutions, or, in some occupational areas, by employers themselves (as Barber et al 2013 allude to), who may well have a much more vocational focus to their activities (IPPR 2013). If such organisations are better able to offer an educational experience that allows their learners to make economic progression (possibly because they are cheaper, or more bespoke and employer-focused), this will be good for those who participate. But they may also lack the kind of space and mission that allows learners to develop a set of skills which help outside the workplace, with negative consequences for holistic social mobility.

SIX

The shape of the labour market: hourglass, diamond or molecule?

The current changes in the labour market could have potentially seismic impacts across the whole field of social mobility. They are having an impact on both the type of jobs available and their nature in terms of the tasks associated with particular roles, including the knowledge-intensive jobs. These changes fatally undermine the idea that politicians can engineer social mobility by raising the attainment of children and hence educate their way to a more equal society.

The combination of technology and ideology driving these changes is also changing the very nature of the occupational stratification systems on which the academic study of social mobility depends. The relationship between different types of job is what underpins occupational stratification systems. There need to be clear dividing lines between jobs. When these lines become blurred and when within job categories there becomes increasing differentiation in levels of skill required, tasks performed and income levels these stratification systems become more less meaningful as indicators or social division.

In this chapter, the rise of the 'hourglass economy' is explored – as the number of mid-range jobs disappears, this leaves us not with a linear form of occupational structure, but with something more akin to an hourglass shape. This concept, however, is a rather simplistic view of the economy – useful to capture some broad changes, but less useful at describing the complexity of the changes that are currently underway. If an accurate picture of the 21st-century labour market is to be portrayed, we may need more mixed metaphors.

These changes in the labour market strengthen the case for a holistic perspective on social mobility, but they also demand an understanding of the impact they are having. It is not just the type of jobs that are changing; it is also the very meaning of work that is under question. Success and progress via work are the bedrock of the present social mobility discourse, and these fundamentals must themselves be examined. Have we gone too far in the fetishisation of work? Is it desirable – or even possible – to step back to consider how we re-position work in relation to leisure and family? And if we do, what will that mean for social mobility?

The 'hourglass economy'

There is a welter of evidence to support the argument that the seeds of the changes in the economy and the labour market now being experienced were sown in the late 1970s and early 1980s (Barnet and Cavanagh 1994, Michie and Grieve Smith 1995, Stiglitz 2003). A combination of technological change and a move in the political centre to the Right have led to increased economic and cultural globalisation, with, for example, the privatisation of utilities and services, reductions in the power of unions, increased freedoms regarding movement of capital, and a shift in attitudes regarding taxation (Hutton 1996). The recession of the early 1980s in the UK began a 'hollowing out' of mid-range jobs in the UK (Fothergill et al 1985), with many geographical areas dependent on manufacturing (including mining and shipbuilding), as well as areas dependent on such industries and the wages of those workers (for example, a large number of coastal holiday towns), propelled into a process of decline from which they have never re-emerged. This process gathered pace in the following decades to produce what researchers now describe as the 'hourglass economy', where employment is becoming polarised with increasing numbers of 'high quality' and 'low quality' jobs, but a continuing decline in routine occupations in the middle of the labour market (Sissons 2011). As Goos and Manning describe, the UK economy is becoming divided into 'lovely' and 'lousy' jobs (Goos and Manning 2007, Goos et al 2010).

Technology has displaced routine occupations such as secretarial and administrative work previously done by women, for example, and machine-based factory work, assembly line operations and so on for men (Sissons 2011). There has been some growth in knowledge-intensive work, which implies a greater need for those who understand how technology works, and in particular how to use and control it. One particular consequence has been the growth in the need for managers of seemingly a range of varieties. There are also a large number of low-skilled jobs whose existence (and even growth) may not be attributable to technology, but neither can technology readily replace them – occupations such as those in social care, construction and personal services have grown significantly in the last 30 years (Sissons 2011).

The work of Goos and Manning casts further doubt on the idea that technology will produce more knowledge-intensive jobs and lead to the withering away of low-skilled work. Goos and Manning (2007) argue that technology may be driving an increase in demand for those in more high-skilled jobs, but it is the increased supply of those willing to do low-skilled jobs who have been displaced from routine occupations that is creating the conditions for the 'hourglass economy'.

Work by Michaels et al (2014), looking at the role of technology in increasing polarisation in 11 different countries, supports this view, but only to an extent. They argue that it accounts for only up to a quarter of the growth in demand for more skilled workers, and so there must be other factors at play here. Their research suggests, for example, that the growth in some areas of low-skilled work (such as personal services) is a function of increases in demand from high earners for such services as well as increased female participation in the labour market.

The impact on wages of this occupational polarisation appears more ambiguous. Technology is mediated to a greater extent in its impact on wages by factors such as unionisation, differences between and within occupations, gender and also the availability of workers able to do what employers want (Holmes 2010). Hence, research by Holmes and Mayhew (2012) shows that the relative wages of those in these routine occupations may have held up, even though their numbers have decreased. There is also evidence to suggest that the wages of the new low-skilled workers have also held up, relative to more middle earners, despite the supply of these workers increasing (Holmes 2010), which may be due to the impact of the minimum wage legislation in the UK. This legislation has only been partially effective, though. Since the late 2000s, the stagnation in real wages in the UK economy has had a particularly serious impact on those at the low end of the wages ladder. The Resolution Foundation, a charity dedicated to looking at low pay, argues that 'since 2009 in particular, the number of workers earnings less than a living wage – the amount considered adequate to achieve a minimum standard of living – has rocketed, from 3.4 million to 4.8 million in April 2012' (Whittaker and Hurrell 2013: 4).

The evidence also shows that for a significant proportion of such workers, there is no route out of these occupations, which has significant implications for social mobility. Sissons' analysis of earnings mobility in the 2000s, using the British Household Panel Survey, showed that 60% of those in the bottom 10% of the earning distribution in 2001 had remained within the bottom three deciles by 2007. The Resolution Foundation describes the increase in those in low-pay situations in the UK as a 'structural one' (Whittaker and Hurrell 2013: 22), stemming from an increasing demand for low-paid service work resulting from changes in technology and patterns of consumption. Those receiving less than two-thirds of the average median living wage per hour, 47%

are aged 31-60. Low-paid work is not confined to the young and old, however; it is prevalent across the lifecourse, as Figure 6.1 shows.

Figure 6.1: Distribution of low pay across age groups, 1975–2011

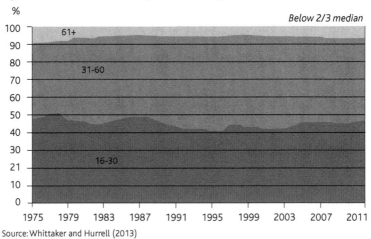

Source: Whittaker and Hurrell (2013)

Sizeable numbers of low-qualified workers are stuck in occupations that are less likely to be skilled. The disconnect in the 21st-century labour market between low-skilled and mid-range work makes the possibilities of upward mobility far lResearch by Nunn et al (2007) and Holmes (2010) reach similar conclusions regarding the solidifying of divisions between the low- and high-skilled. There may be a higher chance of workers when they enter low-skilled work remaining there throughout their careers, as the 'small rungs' in the career ladder that used to be available to them are no longer there. There may also be a continued process of what Sissons describes as 'bumping down', where routine workers, as their occupational areas shrink, come to swell the ranks of the non-routine, low-skilled workers in the labour market 'tier' below.

The shape and size of the hourglass(es)

While the aggregate analysis seems to show an increasing polarisation between high-skilled/high paid work and low-skilled/low paid work, there are significant variations in the nature, extent and shape of this divide by factors such as gender, geography and occupation.

Sissons illustrates how, while polarisation is affecting both men and women, it is doing so in very different ways, mainly because of the very strong gendering of the labour market that still exists. The fastest-growing jobs over 2001 to 2007 for men and women were ones that reflected this gendering exceptionally strongly. For men, there was a growth in over 120,000 in employment in construction, and for women, a growth in over 180,000 in childcare and related services. For all the rhetoric of a 'new' knowledge-based economy, the evidence appears to show that the old economy, structured around low-skilled, gender-differentiated work, is alive and well.

Differences within the labour market by geography are equally, if not more, striking. In 2012 Green undertook research to explore the utilisation of skills in three different parts of England and Wales as part of a four-country study into labour market structures at the local level. Green argued that:

> It was clear that there is strong variation between local labour markets in terms of the relationship between skills supply and demand. While some sub-regions exhibit characteristics of 'high skills equilibrium', with a strong supply of skills being matched by a strong demand for skills, others experience either an imbalance in skills supply and demand (leading to 'skills shortages' or 'skills surplus') or a 'low skills equilibrium' where low skills in the workforce are matched by low demand for skills amongst employers. (Green 2012: 10)

There is significant research in the UK showing the growing differences between regional economies and labour markets (Gardiner et al 2012). Neither is it clear the type of local labour market that would favour economic mobility for the low-skilled are the ones we would expect. It may be that those labour markets that retain a presence from the type of mid-range occupations threatened by technology may benefit this group more than the more 'successful' economies, as the former can provide conventional ladders out of low-skilled work. Conversely, the labour market of the UK's most knowledge-rich regional economy, London, may provide less opportunity. It is the most extreme form of hourglass – the gaps between low and high skill are more extreme, and the career ladder' is steeper and more difficult to ascend (Kaplanis 2007, Deloitte 2013).

As Green acknowledges, though, even the framework she outlines is a simplistic one. The boundaries of what a 'local labour market' constitutes are contested and contingent. Locality in labour market terms means different things to different people, often because of their differing existing skill levels and the occupational field they are in.

Most UK-born workers in the UK are still relatively geographically immobile (it is quite a different story for migrant labour; Green et al 2013). However, this differs as one moves up the skill ladder (Holmes 2010). For more highly skilled workers, their labour market is national or international. Moreover, it then differs again by occupational field. As evidence from both the UK and Europe shows for those in certain high-demand/high-skilled occupations, they operate in a global 'local labour market' (Cedefop 2011).

Nor is the picture the same for workers of different generations. Holmes and Tholen (2013) examined the labour market experiences of those who entered the labour market in the mid-1970s and the late 1980s respectively. They found that, for the younger cohort, after the recession of the late 2000s it was harder to move up through the occupational scale. Something was happening that was changing the nature of progression: 'The analysis from this paper suggests that in recent years, increased room at the top has not increased upward mobility for those already in work, implying that a growing number of these jobs are predominantly recruiting new labour market entrants rather than offering opportunities' (Holmes and Tholen 2013: 38). However, this pattern was not the same across occupations, meaning that depending on the field one worked in, the prospects looked better or worse.

While it is an appealing image in terms of its ability to make a complex thing like the labour market look simple in reality, the labour market is not really one hourglass. If anything, it is thousands of smaller hourglasses, where the relative size of the bottom, middle and top differs. And in some occupational or geographical areas, it may not resemble an hourglass at all. Occupational mobility is a complex phenomenon, experienced and lived through gender, ethnicity, region and occupation. In this context, it becomes clear that the study of it must reflect these nuances and how they interact at the individual level. This complexity also suggests that success and progress may mean very different things across individuals, groups and, in particular, localities. The fixation, among many politicians, with long-range upward occupational mobility means that the majority of occupational social mobility is being lost from political view, precisely because of these nuances. This is a contradictory outcome. Politicians understand acutely the importance of locality in shaping people's lives; their careers depend on this understanding. Yet where social mobility is concerned, they fail to make this link, preferring to fall back to the familiar celebration of long-range mobility where they find it.

The need for low-skilled work

While the shape of the hourglass may differ by region, occupation and so on, what appears certain is that there will not be a disappearance of what is presently defined as lower-skilled/lower-paid work in the foreseeable future. And this reality poses major questions for politicians. It is unrealistic to suggest that all workers will be able to benefit from any set of social mobility policies whose main aim is to facilitate upwards movement from low-skilled to higher-skilled work. Neither is it just an issue of the pressure of numbers implying that people have to remain in these jobs as there is no room for them in the other parts of the hourglass. While the desirability of upward economic mobility is taken as given at present, there will be people who do not want to move out of their social and economic locations.

As Friedman (2013) has argued, many people do not necessarily wish to move jobs; rather, they want their existing ones to improve. However, this does not mean they do not want to see progress in their working lives in the context of these jobs. Increasing pay is one obvious, essential route, to such progress of course. There are increasing numbers in poorly paid work in the UK, and a rising amount of in-work poverty. This was picked up on by the Labour Party in the early 2010s, coining the phrase 'pre-distribution' to describe the need to get employers to pay better wages to the low-skilled (Labour Party 2013).

As crucial as increasing wages is, though, it is not enough. US economist Richard Florida argued in 2010 that low-skilled work should be 'upgraded'. Florida looks back at the routine 'blue-collar' jobs, which have been lost from the middle of the occupational range. He points to how many of these jobs are now viewed with great affection for their security and status, even though they were once seen as 'bad' jobs:

> ... more than 60 million Americans toil in low-wage, low-skill service jobs in everything from food prep and retail sales to personal care. We can transform them into good, family sustaining jobs, the same way we made manufacturing jobs good jobs decades ago, by creatifying them – tapping the knowledge and creativity of workers as a source of productivity, which in turn will generate higher wages. (quoted in Business Insider 2012: 2)

This process of 'creatifying' involves tapping into the skills and knowledge that each individual has, and creating structures inside and outside the workplace that enable them to be maximised. While upgrading work might be only one way of describing it, the idea that something more could and should be done to enable those in low-paid positions to experience upward social mobility is important. Improving earnings is crucial – economic progression is at the centre of any understanding of mobility, including the one being developed in this book. Improving earnings also increases status and contributes to the perception of the job among those who do not do it (although, as will be argued later, this is problematic). But the quality and nature of the job is also vital. Increasing wages for low-skilled occupations on its own does not constitute a way of ensuring that those occupying these positions are socially mobile. The nature of the work undertaken must also be examined. The strengths of the blue-collar jobs described by Florida were founded on more than income. There were relatively high levels of job satisfaction, often rooted in the solidarity of the working experience. And recreating these conditions in the 21st century will be very difficult. As the research on job polarisation shows, the large workplaces built on routine labour are less common. Where they do exist, the fragmentation of social groupings among the workforce by gender and ethnicity makes the kind of connection between work and community on which these jobs were based far less relevant. There is also a high degree of mythologising here. The blue-collar idyll was a predominantly male, white one, and the work still routine and stultifying (Goldthorpe et al 1968, Ramdin 2007).

Moreover, it was the lack of progression afforded by this work that made so many skilled working-class families keen to ensure that their children had something better in the last quarter of the 20th century in the UK, driving up HE participation rates and helping to embed aspiration more firmly in the national value system (Goldthorpe et al 1968). If it was a lack of social mobility that was the problem for this kind of work, it may seem perverse to see it as part of the solution to social mobility problems today. Looking back, then, is only a partial remedy for the problem of social mobility and low-skilled work. Thinking about why blue-collar work was seen as good, though, highlights the importance of non-pay factors. Is it possible to experience progress in a job if you remain in the same job and your pay remains relatively unchanged (and low)?

For this to happen, both the perception and experience of lower-skilled work would have to change. There are examples of how this could be done. In 2009 nef undertook research into the social value of six different occupations. The additional social value of those working in childcare was up to £9.50 for every £1 spent, in contrast to bankers, who may collect salaries in excess of £500,000, but destroy £7 of social value for every £1 they generate. Measuring social value as opposed to pay is a different way of also capturing success where employment is concerned. If social value could be articulated as a metric of achievement, then it would greatly support attempts to broaden what social mobility means (nef 2009).

On a more practical level, Anderton and Bevan's research for the Work Foundation in 2014 examined how employers could foster greater employee engagement and involvement to enrich what they described as 'constrained jobs', where worker autonomy is limited and the kind of 'digital Taylorism' described in Chapter Two has taken hold. They list four different ways by which employers could do this:

- New performance management: shifting from traditional object and quantitative to qualitative performance measures.
- An emphasis on training, development, problem solving and career progression.
- Team work and participation in business development.
- Flexible working and supporting work–home balance (Anderton and Bevan 2014:7)

Upgrading lower-skilled work is not going to be easy. The UK has a relatively high number of jobs that are in 'low-skilled categories' (Holmes 2010).

Over 20% of workers are in jobs that require only a primary level of education. This compares to less than 10% in Sweden and Germany (Osborne 2014). And low-skilled work is overrepresented in the jobs that are rated by employees as the least satisfying (Addley 2014).

Finally, attempts that have been undertaken to upgrade occupational areas have also been controversial. The recent change in nursing in England to become a graduate occupation is an instructive example. In 2009, measures were put in place to make nursing a graduate profession by 2013 (BBC News 2009). All new nurses now need a graduate-level qualification. This was opposed by some, who felt that the academic knowledge associated with graduate study was not required for good nursing, and that it was placing new barriers in front of those who wanted to become nurses (Ford 2009). The extent to which nursing practice has been improved by this change is no doubt contested. It shows, however, that it is possible for policy makers to engineer upward economic social mobility by shifting the required skill levels of a whole group of workers.

The nature of work'

Exploring the social mobility challenges facing low-skilled workers is also important because of the wider set of questions regarding the relationship between social mobility and the nature of work it opens up. It reaffirms, for example, the importance of intra- as well as intergenerational mobility. Considering what happens when there is likely to be occupational immobility (in terms of socioeconomic classification) brings into greater focus work over the lifecourse. The concept of a career trajectory is lost when the attention remains predominantly on intergenerational mobility. The ideas of permanent income and occupational maturity described in Chapter Two may be good and accurate ways of summarising earnings or occupation over the lifecourse, but they tell us nothing about the lifecourse itself. This suggests the need for different ways of studying social mobility that may draw on qualitative as well as quantitative forms of analysis. Life history research, for example, can tell us as much about social mobility as any of the quantitative studies that have come to define the nature of study in the field (Stuart 2012).

The limitations in using the movement between jobs as a measure of social mobility are not confined to the case of the low-skilled. They are not the only group who may remain in their jobs for a considerable period of time, or within the same occupational group. While the level of job change is higher in the 21st century (Cabinet Office 2009), it still appears to be the case that the majority of workers remain in fewer than 10 jobs over their career, and job change is skewed towards the early years, when career paths are being established (Bialik 2010, National Careers Council 2013).

What happens within jobs matters as much for the high- and mid-skilled workers as for the low-skilled. Restricting a measure of mobility over the lifecourse to changes in occupation doesn't capture what happens within the experience of a particular job. This can include significant increases in pay and responsibility, even though the job title doesn't change (or decreases in pay and responsibility or demotion as well). Deciding what metrics could be used to capture progression within jobs or occupations is very difficult, though. There is significant evidence to support the view that 'job satisfaction' matters, and not just to what happens in work time but also to an individual's overall view on their well-being or progress in life (Clark 1998, 2005; Diaz-Serrano and Cabral Vieira 2005). But there is far less consensus on what 'job satisfaction' means, and whether it is so amenable to fluctuation, dependent on when it is measured (today I may feel satisfied with my job as I had a good day, but tomorrow I may lose a deal and feel unhappy that you might not be able to measure it at all (van Saane et al 2003).

More sophisticated attempts to capture job satisfaction exist, which concentrate on the more ongoing features of the working experience that may underpin people's long-term views on their work (Rose 2003). Improving these more permanent features of the working experience provides a potentially more robust approach to measuring the occupational part of social mobility than merely asking workers whether they are happy or not. However, the degree to which there are practices firmly in place that can deliver this kind of progression in the UK has to be questioned. A major part of the 'education sceptics'' argument described in the last chapter was that too many workers in the UK are underemployed. Keep and James (2010) argue that the structures are not in place to utilise and develop the skills of the workforce in the UK.

This view is supported by the UKCES (2011) and its work on high performance working (HPW). HPW touches on some of the themes described by Anderson and Bevan (2014) in their research on low-skilled occupations. It is a broad concept, summarised by Belt and Giles as:

> ... a general approach to managing organisations that aims to stimulate more effective employee involvement and commitment in order to achieve high levels of performance. The precise form HPW takes within an organisation will vary depending on context, but will include activities in the areas of: human resource management (eg pay and incentives, appraisal, workforce development), work organisation (eg team working and job design), employment relations, management and leadership (including strategic management and business development as well as line management), and organisational development. Importantly, the HPW approach is specifically designed to enhance the discretionary effort employees put into their work, and to fully utilise the skills that they possess. It needs to be underpinned by a philosophy of people management that emphasises autonomy, participation and learning. (Belt and Giles 2009: 10)

UKCES argues that there is a significant 'policy to implementation' gap where HPW is concerned. It is not well understood by employers or, for that matter, by policy makers – the incentives to drive its development are too voluntary. As Belt and Giles 2009:10) state it is a 'policy without a home' in the UK.

'The meaning of work

Even if the development of HPW could be incentivised and more clearly defined, there are still some wider questions about work that need to be addressed.

A holistic approach is required here, as examining/promoting social mobility should involve not only improving the experience of work, but also asking what it is for and what it does – or should – mean. This requires simultaneously paying more and less attention to work. Keynes predicted that as societies became richer, the time spent in work would decline, and we would move to a more leisure-based society (Keynes 1931; see also Veal 2009). Yet this has not been the case. In the UK, in particular, there has been a move in the other direction, with longer working hours, and an increasing blurring for those in higher-skilled occupations between work and non-work life. This has been described as the 'work–life' merge, where technology enables people to be constantly available for work to answer emails and so on (Hinsliff 2013). In France, however, they have recognised the impact of this work–life merge on employees and introduced legislation to curtail email communication out of work hours (de Castella 2014).

The work–life merge phenomenon is not entirely employer-driven. Work by Gershuny and Fisher in 2014 showed that (in contrast to the mid to late 20th century) in the early 21st century, the highest skilled and highest paid workers *want* to work more, as they find this both rewarding and where they get meaning in life. There has been the growth of a 'super-ordinate working class', which cuts across both genders, who are reversing historical trends by working more than those in lower-skilled/lower-earning groups (Gershuny and Fisher 2014).

The rise of the work–life merge and the super-ordinate working class has an importance that spreads wider than just this super-ordinate elite to affect how the rest of society work and see work. It is shaping how success is understood, and can filter down to influence attitudes and practices among those not paid as handsomely for answering their emails in the middle of the night. Across the workforce this kind of commitment can easily become an expectation. What some people are doing because they choose to, others then do because they have to. (This is indeed if the super-ordinate class are really engaged in the work–life merge because they want to, or because they are caught in a form of executive 'prisoner's dilemma', where everyone else is doing it, so they feel they have to too, in order to retain their position.) The rise of the super-ordinate working class may be the latest facet of what Sennett described in his 1999 book, The Corrosion of Character as the 'new economy'. Sennett argued that new opportunities for self-fulfilment in work, represented by technology and new ways of working, are actually a chimera; in reality, greater flexibility in the labour market and workplace only results in new forms of oppression.

Conclusions

This chapter set out to take a more detailed look at how contemporary changes in the labour market that have gathered pace since the 1970s have shaped, and been shaped by, how social mobility is understood. While the hourglass is a good visual metaphor for the labour market in an economy like the UK's in the early 21st century, no two hourglasses ever look the same, and neither do any two parts of the labour market. The drawback with any metaphor designed to make complex issues easier to understand is that it may mask the details that make up the real picture. In reality, the UK economy is more complex. The hourglass is a fairly one-dimensional model, where there is a clearly defined top, middle and bottom. This chapter has tried to show that the picture may be more nuanced than this, and the reality may be more three-dimensional than one-dimensional. The relationships between 'top', 'middle' and 'bottom' might actually start to be less clear-cut where work is concerned.

There are alternative metaphors for how the labour market currently looks. First, it may look more like a pyramid shape where there are those at the top whose wealth and power allow them to insulate themselves from any of the negative side effects of high-paid work. At the bottom there could be a growing group whose work is insecure, low paid and lacking satisfaction. The differentiator of the degree, for example, in deciding who is in the top half of the hourglass or the bottom, may (if the evidence in Chapter One is accepted) mean less. The title of the job, which is the basis by which researchers place people in the hourglass model, may also mean less than we think, and it might require more detailed qualitative work to really decide who is – or who is not – going up or down the occupational scale. As Lloyd and Payne argue, it is too easily assumed that we know what skill means. At present there is an 'often un-stated, question: what is "skill" and what do we mean by a "skilled job?"' (Lloyd and Payne 2008: 1).

An even better metaphor may be many molecules. Each has its own individual structure, and the atoms within are connected not by a straight line from top to bottom, but by a number of different lines: vertical, horizontal and sloping, connecting separate, distinct parts of the whole. In this more three-dimensional conception of the labour market, it is more difficult to say what sort of mobility (downward, upward or sideways) that movement between jobs represents, and how different jobs relate to each other. The appeal of this metaphor is that it at least attempts to reflect the complexities described, the more complicated nature of work as provider of income, status, meaning and social mobility, and it fits the idea of social mobility as a more complex phenomenon. It attempts to reflect the need to explore not just progression within or between jobs in terms of income or status, but also in the nature of what the work itself means to the worker. Increases in income and responsibility may be all well and good, but beyond a certain level, do they really constitute progress or success?

SEVEN

Social mobility, well-being and class

Introduction

A coherent education system that prioritises the development of a range of skills and aptitudes necessary for progress in 21st-century life (in particular, for those from lower socioeconomic groups) and a labour market that concentrates on how to enhance the capabilities of workers and the quality of their work (especially for those in low-skilled work) are the twin foundations of holistic social mobility. But both require reform in the economic and social system, if they are to be built on anything other than shifting sand.

The existing social mobility discourse stops short of connecting with a debate around the broader social and economic model. Equally, debates around the nature of the system rarely touch explicitly on social mobility. At the same time, more long-standing concerns about what 'success' means in early 21st-century capitalist economies, and whether the pursuit of purely economic goals is actually the best way of maximising societal welfare, have led to a growing literature on economic and social well-being. However, neither the literature on alternative ways of running capitalist economies nor the social mobility discourse engages with this work in a substantive way. There has been a growing literature in the last 20 years that goes beyond well-being to look at happiness and to argue that we now have sufficient evidence and methodological capability to build on the philosophical claims regarding the primacy of happiness. This chapter attempts to join the dots and connect these different sets of ideas.

A broken Britain?

There has been increasing interest since the late 2000s in the degree to which the dominant economic model in the UK, and throughout the capitalist West, is 'fit for purpose' in the wake of the most recent recession (Hutton, 1996, James 2007, Crouch 2009, Green 2009, Lawson 2009, Sainsbury 2013). There is an alternative vision for early

21st-century capitalism that rejects the 'Anglo-Saxon' consumerist/ materialist view, which has grown in prominence since the 1970s. In general, however, what this vision lacks is an appreciation of the extent to which individual behaviour needs to change. And where this is understood, the need to change what social mobility means in order for these changes to occur is not recognised by this spectrum of authors. As much as the government(s) they often set out to criticise they accept a narrow and sterile vision of social mobility.

We begin with Will Hutton. In the revised edition of his 1996 book The State We're In, Hutton argued that: 'The central proposition – that British society is fracturing, that investment is profoundly low and British democracy does suffer from structural deformations – have held up' (Hutton 1996:2).

In his 2012 essay for The Work Foundation Annual Debate, he argued that:

> Yet once companies and institutions deny any larger purpose, the vacuum is filled with incantations to efficiency, flexibility and the rationality of economic men and women – so creating alienation, disconnection and anxiety. It is a moral hollowing out in which the aggressive pursuit of material wellbeing is all that is left to provide meaning – resulting in a material arms race of being paid ever more extravagantly – from the CEO to the football star. (Hutton 2012: 11)

Both Sainsbury and Green, respectively, have picked up on Hutton's themes regarding the value system of UK capitalism. Stephen Green, ex-chair of HSBC bank as well as an ordained priest, takes a historical perspective on capitalism, arguing that it has shown itself to be the best system to improve human wealth. However, he seeks to find a way in which capitalism can be the servant of a broader morality rather than the other way round. In his 2000 book Good Value he addresses directly the issue of ambition and fulfilment in work, seeing this as inevitably limited in what it can offer. Instead, the goal should be a completeness that reflects the ambiguities of the modern world and our own imperfections within it. Green offers a more nuanced and very spiritual framework for what social mobility fits. It is not being explicitly argued here that there has to be a spiritual element to success, but it is one of the resources that can be drawn on to inform it.

Writers such as Neal Lawson and Oliver James address the faults with the values that underpin contemporary capitalism in a different way. They focus more explicitly on the negative consequences of pursuing materialistic goals at the individual and societal level. James (2007) argues that the damage to psychological well-being from a definition of success based on material grounds is huge. It has created a deep-seated emotional malaise at the societal level. Both Lawson and James suggest that the state needs to act to curb consumption and what causes it, in particular, advertising. According to James, countries like the UK are infected by the 'affluenza' virus, where what we have and own has come to define who we are. Both in terms of personal appearance and possessing goods with a high level of worth (in both financial and fashion terms), image has become far too important, with severe consequences for our psychological well-being. James argues that emotional distress is directly linked to income inequality. In a similar vein to Green, James sees a role for the spiritual in finding a way out of this malaise, acting as a form of antidote to the virus.

Lawson heads the left-of-centre think tank Compass. His 2009 book, All Consuming, is a polemic attack on the values that underpin modern consumerist capitalism. In it, he suggests a range of ways in which consumer behaviour could change, including working fewer hours, buying less but from businesses with good environmental records, and joining grassroots networks such as book-swapping schemes or Freecycle, which offers free unwanted items. However, he leaves discussions of the meaning of social mobility untouched.

While Lawson and James attack the present capitalist system from a polemic and psychological angle respectively, Colin Crouch does this from the perspective of the political scientist. Crouch has been writing about the decline in social democracy, and the threat posed by neo-liberalism, since the 1970s (Crouch 1977, 2009). In 2008, he was concerned with how the capitalist model since the 1970s had been sustainable despite undergoing several recessions, and if it could weather the latest one it was experiencing (Crouch 2008). He argued that it had been able to do this via a form of 'privatised Keynesianism', where the growth of credit and derivatives markets has enabled demand to remain high despite stagnation in real wages. This model is inherently unsustainable, as the recession of the late 2000s and early 21st century showed, but he does not see likely alternatives. The continuation of this 'mutant' model will require an ever narrowing of the economic parameters among political parties as they are forced to work even closer with multinational firms and their power in the face of these organisations diminishes. The possibility of change will depend on the ability of organisations outside of the organised political party structure to effect change.

There is little or no mention of social mobility in any of the different works described here. This is mainly because the present discourse on social mobility does not include a consideration of values. Yet the ideas outlined all require a shift in values and, in so doing, actually depend on a holistic approach to social mobility. Instigating the 'good capitalism' that Hutton, Green or Sainsbury argue for will be difficult, if success continues to be defined in terms solely of occupational progression. Hutton points to exactly this shift in values to change business practice, when he argues that business needs to take a different view of its own particular objectives, and change how it sees success. The move away from a consumer-oriented culture advocated by Lawson, or finding a mass antidote to the affluenza virus, will require a comprehensive move away from the present social mobility/success nexus at the individual level. Finally, a value shift in how we see capitalism itself is necessary to create the space for the kind of significant political change that Crouch sees as necessary but unlikely.

Welcome to well-being

For this shift in values that underpins attempts to redefine the economic model to happen, an alternative discourse for understanding individual and societal welfare is necessary. This is a delicate process in a context where marketised values are so entrenched in many capitalist countries and especially at a time of economic recession. Prime Minister David Cameron summarises the problem very well, when talking about the coalition government's attempts to understand more about well-being and how to measure it:

> … as this initiative has been coming to the fore, three objections have become very clear. First, there is the worry that this is a distraction from the major, urgent economic tasks at hand. Second, there is the criticism that we can't hope to improve people's wellbeing – that this is beyond the realm of government, so why are we trying? And third, there is a suspicion that, frankly, the whole thing is a bit woolly, a bit impractical. You can't measure wellbeing properly, so why bother doing it at all? (Cameron 2010)

The further specific risk where social mobility is concerned is that looking at well-being may somehow downplay the importance of differences in income and wealth. Keeping the spotlight on these differences is the great advantage that the present focus on social mobility brings.

An approach to well-being is required that can balance the concerns about inequality and economic welfare. It is argued here that the best chance of doing that is through utilising the ideas of Nobel Prize-winning economist Amartya Sen and his work on capability. The capability approach is an attempt to construct a system of moral philosophy grounded in what individuals do and experience, as opposed to one based on ideas either imposed by government or academics. Sen argues that the aim in terms of social justice should be to maximise the substantive freedoms that people enjoy (Sen 1989). For substantive freedom to occur, people need to have the ability to achieve things that they value. Sen's approach distinguishes between the individual and the ability to achieve, and the achievement itself. The achievements are called 'functionings', and incorporate everything from health and employment to actual states such as happiness. These functionings, however, are not the same as capabilities, which includes what we could achieve. Maximising capability implies enabling the freedom to pursue different combinations of functionings. So, for instance, in a society like the UK everyone has the 'freedom' in principle to have a million-pound-a-year job, but not everyone has that in their combination of functionings. The issue, of course, becomes the extent to which this actual 'freedom exists' in a society as structurally unequal as that in the UK. It is the capability element that is most important to Sen, in differentiating between sets of functionings that individuals have. The key challenge is, how can capability be increased to enable those in situations of poverty or oppression to achieve better such sets of functionings?

Sen does not define a priori what desirable capabilities are as such (1989). Consistent with his emphasis on how the freedom of the individual is paramount in defining justice and his unwillingness to support externally imposed systems of morality, Sen prefers to see capability defined by individuals in the context of different societies (1993). He emphasises the importance of public reasoning as the mechanism by which practical ideas around fairness and capability are reached, rather than seeking moral absolutes across different societies (Sen 2000). This malleability is a virtue of the capability approach, but also a problem for social mobility, in so far as it militates against comparative measures of progress.

Others writing in the field of capability theory have been more willing to develop scales that define capability more absolutely and objectively. Martha Nussbaum, for instance, has produced a list of 10 capabilities. These include the ability to live life to the end and not to die prematurely, enjoying good health, being able to fulfil one's education and cultural potential, the ability to enjoy play and recreation as well as control over the political and material world (Nussbaum 2000). The capability approach stands in contrast to approaches to social justice/societal progress based on the maximisation of utility or access to income or other resources. Sen would not deny the importance of access to resources within the capability approach – the central concern in his life's work is inequality and the combating of it. As he states in a 2011 interview:

> We need to ask the moral questions: Do I have a right to be rich? And do I have a right to be content living in a world with so much poverty and inequality? These questions motivate us to view the issue of inequality as central to human living. Ultimately, the whole Socratic question—'How should I live?'—has to include a very strong component of awareness and response to inequality. (quoted in The Progressive 2011)

Seeing the rationale for Sen's arguments in the case of developing economies and the fight against inequality within them is straightforward. Sen maintains that to improve quality of life and to reduce poverty in these contexts, the issue is more than one of income. He argues that the ability to enjoy political participation and uncensored speech, as well as access to education, are at least as important as increasing income (Sen 2009), and are not universally available. In richer countries, however, capability remains an equally valid idea. Both Sen and Nussbaum are aiming for an understanding of essentials in defining the nature of well-being across societies, but are doing this in different ways.

Capability theory provides a potentially strong philosophical basis for redefining social mobility. It also provides an alternative set of goals for the compulsory education system, the post-secondary system and society overall to aim for. Not only is it grounded in an understanding of well-being that embraces a broader set of material and non-materialistic variables than are usually considered, but it also does this by being anchored in a commitment to addressing inequality. The narrowness with which social mobility is defined, and the absence of any concerted efforts to maintain within its study a continued element of philosophical reflexivity based on the question of progress and success, can be addressed by locating a critique within the framework provided by capability. It is not without its challenges, though, in terms of applications to social mobility. The subjective and contested nature of capabilities, which Sen sees as central to his theories, would make the measurement of social mobility more complex and messy. If capability is defined at an individual level and also defined in terms of freedoms rather than achievements, it is surely harder to gauge whether there has – or has not – been social mobility than in the present discourse with its reliance on achievements. This has consequent effects for the political currency of social mobility as an idea. The kind of quantitatively assessed measures that lend themselves to straightforward political messages would not be as readily available.

In addition, the emphasis on freedoms and the individual, it could be argued (and some have levelled this criticism at Sen), invites a lack of appreciation of the importance of communities, groups and collectives in shaping such freedom (Dean 2009). Hence, it may encourage the kind of individualising of structural inequalities that the focus on parenting and character in relation to educational achievement risk doing. Such a move is clearly not Sen's intention. To use Sen's ideas in such a context as social mobility, it is necessary to think more widely (and holistically) on what freedoms mean. For example, the freedom to go to school is not the same as the capability and hence freedom to achieve at school. The groups who have always done poorly in the education system lacked the freedom to achieve, hence their capabilities were curtailed. The distinction between capabilities and functionings also makes Sen's approach actually close in some respects to the present political discourse on social mobility. The emphasis within it is on enhancing capabilities – by expanding the ability of those from lower socioeconomic groups to move up the occupational scale.

According to Sen, the issue around freedom and education should be subject to the most forensic public debate in an individual society, to arrive at the best way of enhancing capability. Sen favours a move away from what he describes in the capability context as a 'transcendental' approach, where the approach to rights and equalities is shaped in a uniform way across societies by a theoretical model. It is discourse and debate about how the contours of these relationships work in practice in different societies that is required. It is in this approach that Sen's work has a final contribution to make to holistic social mobility, as it has been argued in this book that social mobility should be subject to this very same approach.

Can well-being be measured?

Despite the philosophical and practical challenges that exist where measuring capabilities are concerned, there is an increasing appetite to try to do so. The OECD's 'Better Life' Initiative is the product of over a decade of work in the area of well-being. It builds explicitly on Sen's work, but gives equal weight to both functionings and capabilities. The framework developed by the OECD attempts to 'operationalise the capabilities approach and to make it measurable through indicators that can be collected and used by policymakers' (OECD 2013: 8).

It is based around 11 indicators of well-being, and attempts to give equal weight to both capabilities and functionings (see Figure 7.1).

Figure 7.1: OECD Framework for Measuring Well-being and Progress

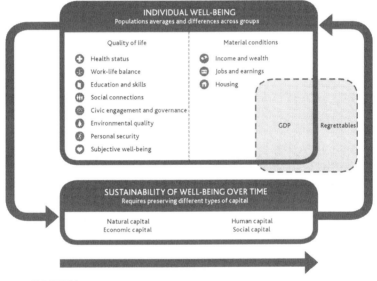

Source ONS (2014b)

The framework has been constructed in the form of a web application that individuals can visit and then create their own indices (with over 60,000 of these indices having been created by early 2015). On the basis of this sample, life satisfaction, education and health emerge as the things that have the greatest impact on well-being – above income.

The OECD argues that there are four distinctive features to the Better Life Initiative: a focus on the individual rather than the overall economy; outcomes as opposed to inputs; the distribution of well-being with differences by socioeconomic background; and inclusion of subjective as well as objective dimensions. In effect, though, the aim is to do two things: to use statistical data to produce a living tool that can be used to compare the development of countries across dimensions of well-being; and also to allow individuals to build their own well-being profiles and then mine these data to get a picture of how well-being is viewed. What it is not trying to do is to replace socioeconomic groupings as a marker of stratification. It rightly emphasises the impact of poverty and worklessness on the other dimensions of well-being. It shows that countries with higher levels of income also show, in general, higher levels of life satisfaction. But this is not a linear relationship – South American countries score higher than would be expected, given their economic circumstances.

The 'Better Life' Initiative is a comprehensive attempt to give more statistical rigour to the study of well-being and also to move the concept of progress away from pure econometrics. As a possible framework for assessing social mobility it presents some interesting questions. Including environmental quality or personal security in any concept of social mobility implies giving weight to things that are, to a large degree, outside the control of the individual – as opposed to income, which is under the individual's control (although this is open to huge debate as well, of course). It would therefore make increasing social mobility more directly the control of state actions. However, in the context of the environment and climate change, embedding action on this within the context of individual progress could be very powerful. It may be easier to sell action on the environment at the individual level, if it were framed within the narrative of individual welfare and progress.

Aside from the OECD's work, a number of other countries are involved in developing ways of understanding and measuring well-being, including Australia, Austria, Mexico and Germany (Kroll 2011). In France in 2012, former President Nicolas Sarkozy commissioned Amartya Sen and US economist Joseph Stiglitz to head a Commission on the Measurement of Economic Performance and Social Progress: 'the time is ripe for our measurement system to shift emphasis from measuring economic production to measuring people's well-being' (Stiglitz et al 2012: 12). The report went on to stress that this did not mean some form of rejection of the importance of the economic:

> Changing emphasis does not mean dismissing GDP and production measures. They emerged from concerns about market production and employment; they continue to provide answers to many important questions such as monitoring economic activity. But emphasising well-being is important because there appears to be an increasing gap between the information contained in aggregate GDP data

and what counts for common people's well-being. (Stiglitz et al 2012: 12)

In England, the ONS is leading an ongoing project to explore well-being in the UK. Its work focuses on 10 domains, as opposed to the OECD's 11. In 2013 the Measuring National Well-being programme found that well-being was most closely linked to self-reported health, employment status and relationship status (ONS 2014b). It appears on the basis of this work that it is possible to take an approach to measuring well-being that is quantitative and empirical. Figure 7.2 shows the ONS approach and how the UK was doing in 2014 across the different drivers of well-being.

Figure 7.2: ONS national well-being interactive wheel of measures, 2014

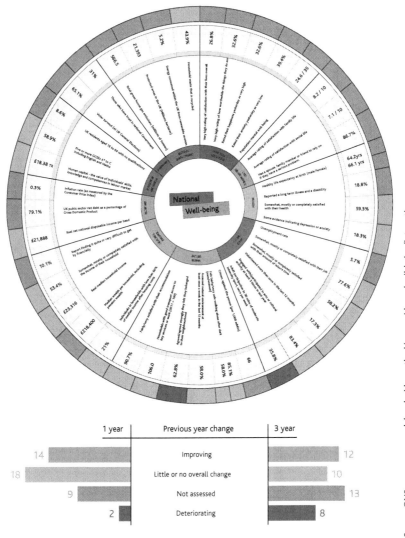

Source: ONS, www.ons.gov.uk/ons/guide-method/user-guidance/well-being/interactive-content/index.html

Is happiness everything?

One of the main objections to looking at individual well-being is that the debate becomes too subjective, although to some this is not a problem.

The economist Richard Layard has written extensively on subjective well-being and happiness (Layard 2006, 2010, 2011). His work on happiness is based on a return to the first principles of social science. In Layard's case this means Jeremy Bentham's work. Layard argues that the objective of public policy is, and always has been, to maximise happiness, but we have become overly focused on one dimension of it – the economic – to the point at which it has distorted our measures and our behaviour. Layard is scathing about the impact of materialism on happiness and the competition for status in particular. These are destructive forces, which undermine happiness by encouraging the engagement in a zero sum game that can never be won. The origins of these destructive forces are inherent in capitalism itself, but they have been exacerbated by the shift rightwards and the neo-classical economic models pursued since the 1980s. Layard argues that we need to pay far greater attention to (again) meeting spiritual needs, but in a more practical and secular way than Green alludes to, for instance (although Green does attempt to remain secular in his book (2009).

Layard co-founded the organisation Action for Happiness in 2010. It suggests a number of ways to maximise happiness, including giving, exercising, connecting with others, engaging in learning and developing greater self-awareness. Layard is also very sure that happiness can be measured. In his 2002 Lionel Robbins Memorial Lecture, he stated his definition of happiness, which is a very simple proposition on the face of it:

> So what do I mean by happiness? By happiness I mean feeling good – enjoying life and feeling it is wonderful. And by unhappiness I mean feeling bad and wishing things were different…. What we really want to understand is the average level of happiness which a person feels, when averaged over a long period of time. (Layard 2002: 4)

Layard also expressed his confidence that happiness could be measured: 'rational policy-making is possible since happiness is a real scalar variable and can be compared between people' (Layard 2002: 11).

Research into happiness across countries by Graham and Nikolova (2013) has shown that it varies by age and employment status. It dips in one's 40s and then rises again in retirement. While unemployment was a big cause of unhappiness, income declines in importance after basic needs are met (as the Easterlin paradox predicts; Easterlin 1974). As you get older, things change. Part-time, voluntary employment can bring a great deal of satisfaction for older people. Graham and Nikolova (2014) suggest that happiness research, when used in this way, can give useful pointers to policy makers in the context of ageing societies, for instance.

Layard's work, in particular, has pushed the issue of happiness to a point where it is taken much more seriously in public discourse, but there are still those who argue that it is not an appropriate goal for public policy. The most significant objections are that it is a private issue and/or that as a goal it is unattainable in policy terms.

Sen has his own concerns. He argues that it can take the focus away from understanding what essential rights or freedoms may be, which is at the heart of capability. It may also undermine the importance of distributional inequalities. People can be very adept at adjusting to poor situations; they may report that they are very happy, for instance, but this may be happiness in the face of circumstances that, as a society, we would want to see changed.

In the quest to redefine social mobility, happiness presents either another potential dimension to sit alongside the economic, or an alternative schema altogether. The present definition does not rest easily with happiness theory; it only supports the materialism that is undermining happiness. Conceiving of social mobility entirely as the progression of individuals along a continuum of happiness, subjugating occupation or income to this greater goal would no doubt satisfy Layard and the happiness theorists. However, it may also imply that we lose the fundamental insights of the present schema which, while they may be in need of reform, should not be ignored altogether.

Where does class come in?

The central argument for the holistic approach to social mobility is that measures of purely economic progression are not enough. However, those who put greatest store by the centrality of economic measures are not oblivious to the issues here. Bourdieu's work, for example, acknowledges explicitly the multidimensional nature of inequality, albeit based around the centrality of economic position (Bourdieu 1992). In 2013 Savage et al led on a major project rooted in Bourdieuian thinking to try to better understand these dimensions. The British Class Survey (BCS) was a national online survey conducted in 2011 by the

BBC, but developed and conceived by Mike Savage and Fiona Devine. It was open to anyone to complete. According to Savage and Devine:

> We devised a new way of measuring class, which doesn't define class just by the job that you do, but by the different kinds of economic, cultural and social resources or 'capitals' that people possess. We asked people about their income, the value of their home and savings, which together is known as 'economic capital', their cultural interests and activities, known as 'cultural capital' and the number and status of people they know, which are called 'social capital'. (Savage and Devine 2013)

A total of 164,000 people completed the survey and, on the basis of it, Savage and Devine developed a seven-part class schema. The schema itself is shown in Table 7.1. It compares their nationally representative sample work with just over 1,000 people (GfK) with their online

Table 7.1: The British class survey class schema

	% GfK	% GBCS	Description
Elite	6	22	Very high economic capital (especially savings), high social capital, very high highbrow cultural capital
Established middle class	25	43	High economic capital, high status of mean contacts, high highbrow and emerging cultural capital
Technical middle class	6	10	High economic capital, very high mean social contacts, but relatively few contacts reported, moderate cultural capital
New affluent workers	15	6	Moderately good economic capital, moderately poor mean score of social contacts, though high range, moderate highbrow but good emerging cultural capital
Traditional working class	14	2	Moderately poor economic capital, though with reasonable house price, few social contacts, low highbrow and emerging cultural capital
Emergent service workers	19	17	Moderately poor economic capital, though with reasonable household income, moderate social contacts, high emerging (but low highbrow) cultural capital
Precariat	15	<1	Poor economic capital, and the lowest scores on every other criterion

Source: Savage et al (2013)

survey (GBCS). It shows that the online survey seemed to attract a certain sort of respondent.

The attempts of the BCS to capture dimensions of inequality not measured by occupation alone have triggered considerable debate. For example, attempts to measure taste via questions regarding music preferences is an extremely subjective methodology. The criteria used in establishing high and low levels of cultural capital appear to ignore the spread of popular culture across social groups – listening to rap music is categorised as a lower-class activity than listening to classical music, for example.

The techniques used to produce the final schema have also come under fire from other sociologists more wedded to longer-standing forms of socioeconomic classification. Goldthorpe, for example, argues that the analysis is skewed towards a much smaller sample than the 164,000 respondents, in order to produce a workable seven-scale class schema, rather than one that may run into over 50 groups, for instance. He goes on to attack the criticisms that Savage et al (2013) make of the National Statistics Social-economic Classification (NS-SEC) system in order to justify the BCS, saying they are wholly unjustified and that the NS-SEC system can also predict things like cultural consumption (Goldthorpe 2013).

The BCS is a laudable attempt to propel the issue of socioeconomic divisions to a broader audience. The lead authors have a well-respected record in class analysis, and in exploring the social aspects of socioeconomic division. However, the key issue here is, to what extent can a framework built around class-related forms of capital capture entirely what it means for individuals and society to 'progress' and be socially mobile? And where does it sit in the holistic social mobility framework that is trying to be built here?

Cultural capital does matter. However, the impact flows through attitudes towards education development and maintenance of communication skills and networks (the survey does try to capture the latter, to be fair), rather than through taste in music or food. A problem exists when cultural capital is seen as the end itself rather than as an indicator of something more fundamental. Whether it was the fault of the researchers or not, this is how it was interpreted. It appears to reinforce cultural hierarchies, if going to the opera is seen as a superior activity to going to bingo. However, the bigger problem is that of those going to bingo, the vast majority has no desire to go to the opera. That would not constitute social mobility for them. In terms of describing 'ends', well-being actually has far more to offer than looking at taste. Virtually everyone, regardless of economic position, wishes to increase their well-being (as the OECD and ONS data show), but very few (regardless of economic position) want to go the opera.

The attempts by Savage et al (2013) to define class in a different way has led to an inevitable backlash from those who perceive a downgrading of importance for economic factors as particularly dangerous in a time of increasing economic inequality (Dorling 2013). Savage et al are adamant that this was not their intention; rather, their intention was to ensure that class (in the context of the increasing fragmentation of social stratification and the difficulties that class faces in retaining its salience as a form of identity) retains its role as the primary way in which stratification is understood. Savage et al are correct to try to do this. If new attempts are not made by academics to map out the social terrain, the risk is that marketeers, journalists and politicians will do this on the basis of their own interests.

Nevertheless, the primary importance of economic divisions must be recognised. In the holistic social mobility approach, they are likely to constitute a large part of what mobility means and to frame the role that well-being measures can have in shaping social mobility. As has been maintained throughout this book, economic inequalities define, to a significant extent, the opportunities available for progression over the lifecourse, and hence the nature of social mobility in the UK. They do not, however, tell us everything. Inequality is not necessarily a driver of social identity in the UK in the early 21st century. The experience of economic hardship is a fragmented one, consisting of individualised combinations of income, housing, education, domestic circumstances and community, as is living in relative economic comfort. Both states are lived by those with multiple identities, made up of occupational experience, educational background, ethnic and gender identity, and region.

Social division no longer lends itself to being meaningfully understood through occupation or income alone. Descriptions designed to promote solidarity, such as 'working class', or to attribute blame or pity, such as 'underclass', have little everyday collective resonance. They may describe, but do not unite in any way. The overriding importance of economic inequality today cannot be allowed to crowd out attempts to understand better the complexities in stratification and social mobility. If economic inequality does crowd out attempts in this way, as is argued throughout this book, it will undermine attempts to overcome these inequalities.

Grusky and Weeden argue for a multidimensional approach to stratification analysis, where class is set in empirical context. It continues to have huge utility as a way of (as they describe it) 'representing' multidimensional stratification space, but this utility differs across and within countries. In a similar vein to the analysis in Chapter Six, they argue that different occupational groupings represent forms of 'micro-classes', that is, smaller groups specific to place or time. It is the macro-class form that, while still useful, needs reworking.

Conclusions

There is clearly no theoretical shortfall where alternative approaches to delivering capitalism are concerned, or where alternative ways of conceiving of success are concerned. Even within the context of the orthodoxy of class, active attempts are being made to revise what success and stratification mean. Such new ways of understanding success in the 21st century are essential, if social mobility is to be redefined. None of the analysis above regarding the importance of well-being implies a wholesale rejection of class as a mechanism for either understanding capitalism or social mobility. Park et al (2013) show that, despite the economic and social changes since the 1980s, only 5% of the population is unable to place itself in a class group. Furthermore, the balance between working and middle-class self-identification has hardly changed since the 1980s – the majority of people in Britain still see themselves as working class. But the same study also shows that the link between self-ascribed social class and behaviour has weakened.

But as no less an advocate of the importance of class-based analysis than the renowned sociologist Goran Therborn recognises, the 21st century may not be the same as the 20th century where the role of class is concerned. Therborn (2012) described the 20th century as the 'age of the working class'. In the 21st century he suggests that the middle class may well predominate, although they are harder to define and their interests are more diverse, both within and between countries. Notions of struggle, but also mobility, are more complex, subjective and involve other sets of identities and concerns than class in this context. As Therborn concludes: 'Class… becomes a compass of orientation – towards the classes of the people, the exploited, oppressed and disadvantaged in all their variety – rather than a structural category to be filled with consciousness' (Therborn 2012:87).

While it may well be that some measure of socioeconomic group is the most important facet of identity that structures life chances and the possibilities of success, it may have to share the limelight with ways of understanding stratification and, in turn, social mobility.

If the stranglehold that class has over the language and understanding of social division and behaviour can be loosened, this will also strengthen the variety of attempts to redefine what capitalism means in the 21st century, described earlier. Holistic social mobility as both method and meaning has much to offer these ideas. It creates a bridge between the traditional forms of stratification within which this thinking remains, and the more expansive ideas of Sen, Stiglitz and Layard. In this vein, holistic social mobility contributes well to the kind of societal dialogue that Sen (and earlier Sandel, as described in Chapter One) view as essential, if social change is to occur.

EIGHT

A new politics of social mobility

It's [Social mobility is] very difficult to achieve, it's extremely complex, we don't know how to do it. Nobody knows how to make it popular, nobody can talk about it [in] a way that any normal person can understand. It is, in every single respect, a terrible objective for a politician. (Philip Collins, quoted in Wheeler 2013)

Philip Collins, a lead writer for *The Times*, may also be a sociologist in disguise. If social mobility were to fade from political view, then most sociologists would shed few tears. Collins echoes much of what was argued earlier in Chapter Seven: that increasing social mobility requires a reform of the whole economic and social system. But ignoring the issue is the wrong thing to do. Social mobility is a prism through which the whole system of society can viewed, and in doing so, this highlights where the flaws are. And like prisms, social mobility has many facets. The one-dimensional presentation of social mobility favoured by the majority of politicians and academics, doesn't do justice to what examining social mobility can tell us, nor what changing it could achieve. Ironically, it is those politicians with the least knowledge about it who are most able to recognise that there may be a range of ways in which individuals can be socially mobile, and that it is what 'progress' and 'success' means (as well as how 'stratification' is defined) that makes up social mobility. While ignorance should seldom be seen as a virtue where matters of policy are concerned, being unencumbered by the parameters that define previous thinking can be an advantage. And even accepting that social mobility may be about more than intergenerational occupational change (or income change) is a start.

While Collins is correct in suggesting that the present political approach to looking at social mobility has its limitations, it also has a distinctive appeal. It seems to tick a number of boxes where today's anxieties are concerned. There is no guarantee that a broader and certainly more complicated definition would do this, especially if it challenges head on the ideas and vested interests associated with the current approach. The essence of the new politics of social mobility is not just a matter of deciding what issues are now encompassed by social mobility and the policies to address them, but also whether the space to do this exists or can be created.

The space for a new politics

The first challenge faced in building a coherent political coalition based around holistic social mobility is that the parameters of political debate in the UK are broadly constrained to a centre ground, which is based on constructing a mix of policies that best deliver on short-term improvements in economic welfare targeted at specific groups of voters (Lee 2013). As argued in Chapter Three, however, political discourses are not static. The anxieties that paved the way for the rising importance of social mobility also are also creating the ground for new ideas. The possibilities of such space are heightened by the increasing loss of faith in the political process and in politicians themselves (Clark and Mason 2013). Trust in politicians has declined markedly in the last 25 years, with over a third of voters saying that they would never trust politicians on any issue (NatCen 2013), while research by ICM in 2013 showed that over 60% of voters thought politicians did not keep their promises, and nearly 50% believed them to be corrupt. The Committee on Standards in Public Life, set up to try to improve trust in politicians by acting as a watchdog on their behaviour, found, in 2013, that only 20% of the public believed that politicians told the truth (Lyons 2013).

The recent global recession has borne down particularly heavily on young people, with unemployment among those aged 18-24 in Europe running at record levels. Over 11 million young people were out of work in the early 2010s with rates rising to over 50% in Spain and Greece. In the UK, youth unemployment reached nearly 20% around the turn of the decade, the highest since 1992 (OECD 2012b). And this unemployment has not just been confined to those with few qualifications (Sparreboom and Staneva 2014).

A combination of factors means that for young people today, the future may not be rosy. The uncertain economic future described in Chapter One combines with lower wages for young people, a housing market that is increasingly hard to enter, a HE system that is more expensive than virtually anywhere in the world, and the prospect of working into old age as the pensions system has to cope with an ageing society. This is producing an 'imperfect storm' of factors, coming together to make it appear, as Danny Dorling describes in the New Statesman in 2013, that: 'If you are young in Britain today you may well be being taken for a ride' (New Statesman 2013).

This has led to a growing view that future generations will not be financially better off (Helm 2011). This is supported by research from the Social Mobility and Child Poverty Commission, which argues that these views are held by those from across social groups and the middle classes in particular (Social Mobility and Child Poverty Commission 2013a).

Young people are those most affected by higher university costs and problems in getting onto the housing ladder. Some of these changes; in particular uncertainty in the housing and employment markets, have been endemic to those in lower socioeconomic communities since at least the economic recession of the 1980s. However, they are now taking on a greater political resonance as they are starting to have an impact on middle-class groups who feel they have invested heavily in the system, particularly via education.

And there are not just disparities in wealth between those born in the 1990s compared with those born in the 1960s. Willetts, in his 2010 book The Pinch, goes further than just the economic to argue that the cultural and political hegemony of those born in the 1960s has left a poor legacy for today's young people (Willetts 2010).

The social contract

This 'imperfect storm' threatens one of the central tenets of the social contract in Western democracies: that present sacrifice and hard work are worth it, because your children will reap the benefits. To the majority of parents, if it was a choice between their own welfare and that of their children, they would always choose the latter. It is this widespread questioning of whether the present economic model can deliver for young people in particular that creates the potential space for alternative options for social mobility to be considered. It is the belief in progress at the individual, familial and societal level that holds together capitalism in the early 21st century in the West. Once that belief is questioned on a large scale, including, crucially, among those in the middle class, the whole system is up for debate.

The extent of actual 'breakdown' of this social contract is debatable though. As argued in Chapter Seven, the values that underpin a great deal of this social contract, that is, the importance of the material in defining identity and success, are still present – and worryingly so (Ramesh 2011b). The concept of the social contract itself is one that is also contested. It is a convenient and catchy way of pulling together some of the problems that capitalism faces in the early 21st century, but it is not as straightforward a set of arrangements as we may be led to think. The contract, in terms of a set of arrangements that give consent to the government to govern the people, differs across social groups. It is also an implicit relationship. It is not stated in a written or legislative form. There is also little history in the UK of actual 'breakdown' in societal norms. Urban unrest is usually taken as the real evidence. Some interpreted the riots in 2011 as an example of young people rejecting the social contract in the UK (Mason 2012), but compared to many other countries, the extent of urban unrest in the UK has always been low.

The evidence concerning the impact of the interconnected phenomena on young people's attitudes to politics is equally nuanced. There has been a long-term decline in voting among young people since the mid-1960s (Henn and Foard 2011). Research in 2013 by Demos into young people's attitudes to politics showed that six times as many viewed 'charities and social enterprises' as agents of positive change rather than politicians (60% versus 10%) (Birdwell 2014). According to the ONS, over 40% of young people have no interest in politics (ONS 2014b), although voting turnout did increase considerably in the 2010 general election to over 50% from 37% in 2006 (Dar 2013). The research by Demos also showed that:

> ... a huge majority of young people today (80%) believe their generation is more concerned with social issues than previous generations of teenagers, with two-thirds of teachers (66%) agreeing. Over four times as many teachers also feel that today's youngsters are more likely than previous generations to volunteer for good causes and community organisations (46% agree vs 11% disagree). (Birdwell 2014: 1)

So, while young people may distrust politicians, they do not necessarily reject politics.

The idea of the social contract breaking, fraying or unravelling is problematic. There is nevertheless enough evidence to suggest that there is disillusionment with politicians in the early 21st century, and certainly with those who represent 'mainstream parties'. This disillusionment may be especially acute among young people (Cramme 2011). There has been a significant growth in populist political movements in Europe on the political Right in the last 10 years. A study produced in late 2013 by the German Foundation Konrad-Adenauer-Stiftung argued that almost everywhere in Europe, right-wing populist parties have 'established themselves as relevant political forces' (Euractiv. com 2013). The growth of the United Kingdom Independence Party (UKIP) is an example of such a trend in the UK. This can at least partly be interpreted as a result of the failure of mainstream political parties, especially on the Left, to deliver economic and social policies that address the challenges of declining growth and rising inequality for those from lower socioeconomic groups.

Making equality matter

As the evidence suggests that there is space for new ways of looking at political issues, if there is the opportunity for a new politics of holistic social mobility, what should it focus on?

The most commonly offered solution to the breakdown/fraying of the social contract is greater equality. As outlined in Chapter One, the evidence regarding the increasing concentration of income and wealth among a minority are striking. The corrosive effects of inequality on a number of indicators of societal well-being have also been documented. It is hard to dispute the argument that improvements in the material standard of living would not improve social mobility, however defined, for those from lower socioeconomic groups.

The existing discourse focuses, however, on the method of producing greater equality should it be for example, by distribution of resources, opportunities, or by concentrating on raising the wage offered to the working poor through 'pre-distribution', and so on? Recent research in the US is trying to quantify the exact contribution that the direct transfer of funds to low-income families will have on educational performance (Coughlan 2013a). This is interesting research because, certainly in the UK, this direct transfer approach to reducing inequality has steadily fallen out of favour compared with extending opportunities or pre-distribution, for example, increasing wages for low-income workers.

The major challenge faced by those wishing to promote greater equality is less one of mechanism (as either direct transfer or pre-distribution would eventually improve the lot of low-income groups), and more one of morality. The evidence indicates that support for redistribution and actions to reduce inequality has declined over the last 30 years, despite increases in inequality. At present, there is simply not a strong enough level of support in the UK for the kind of redistribution necessary to arrest the progression to an increasingly polarised society. Since 1993, for example, the percentage of the population who said that unemployment benefits are too low has fallen from 55 to 22% in 2012 (Park et al 2013). Over the last 30 years there has been a quite distinct reversal regardomg attitudes towards benefits. Far more people now believe that benefits are too high rather than too low.

Where as in 1983 over 10% more people felt that benefits were too low and caused hardship than those who felt that benefits where too high and discouraged work by 2012 the situation had reversed quite markedly. In 2012 30% more respondents felt that benefits were too high and discouraged work as opposed to those who felt that they were too low and caused hardship. This is a swing of 40% over a period when benefits have reduced and the benefit system has become far more putative.

A more in-depth look at these attitudes reveals further complexities (and problems) buttressing the present social mobility discourse and highlighting the problems with it. Looking at British Social Attitudes data from the mid-2000s to early 2010s, Cavaille and Trump (2015) argue that while redistribution to those in low-income positions has declined, redistribution from the rich has remained stable in its support. Thus the majority of people are keen to see the rich give up their wealth, as long as it does not go to poorer people. Those from lower-income groups differ here, though, as their own experience makes them more likely to support redistribution. Cavaille and Trump go on to argue that the combination of more difficult economic conditions and the framing by successive governments of poor and unemployed people as responsible for their own predicaments is what has led to declining support overall for 'redistribution to'. It could be argued, though, that redistribution to the unemployed is only one element of redistribution per se; what about the overall position here? The BSA research shows that in 2012 80% of the population felt that the income gap was too large. However this is 40% more of the population than the percentage who felt that the government should redistribute income. While there have been minor fluctuations in both measures over the period this 40% gap has hardly changed. So, despite the distinct rise in inequality over the period documented in chapter 1 there has been no change in the appetite for redistribution amongst the UK population.

This evidence reveals the depth of the problem regarding redistribution. A redistribution of income and wealth, in particular from the top 1%, is (it is argued by some) the key to addressing inequality. This is important, but it will not in itself address the problems that led to such inequality in the first place, and that are at the heart of the challenges that a country like the UK faces in the 21st century. What has driven this inequality is the centrality of material consumption, the association of individual prosperity and success with economic position, and the accumulation of material wealth.

Danny Dorling argues that it is the attitudes of the richest 1%, their greed and self-interest in particular, which has led to this increase in inequality in the last 30 years (Dorling 2014). This 1% may display a level of self-interest that is exceptional, but it is only an extreme version of values that we all hold, to some extent. The research into what defines attitudes to redistribution focuses on a range of things (Alesina and Giuliano 2009), including individual economic circumstances and the risk of income decline and unemployment, the impact that welfare state institutions have on public attitudes and also the extent to which attitudes to redistribution are cumulative but shaped by the 'political-economic context in which one comes of age' (Neundorf and Niemi 2014: 16).

The genesis of these attitudes is undoubtedly the result of a number of interlinking factors. However, it does appear that the broader social and political climate in the UK since the 1980s has changed, which has influenced attitudes across most of the population, and not just the elite. This implies that any change in these attitudes requires something similarly wide-ranging.

Enlightened instrumentalism

Books such as *The Spirit Level* by Wilkinson and Pickett have provoked great academic interest, and even more so from policy makers, but they have not managed to arrest the declining support for the redistribution they advocate. The moral arguments around individual responsibility for one's welfare and the spectre of the 'undeserving' poor are winning.

It may be here, though, that a holistic approach to social mobility has a significant role to play. The Spirit Level tried to argue that inequality would have a detrimental effect on the ability of us all as individuals to progress in our lives. Rather than build an argument for greater equality as a virtue in itself, it argued for a form of 'enlightened instrumentalism'. This may not sit very comfortably with those who hold the merits of greater equality to be self-evident, and it also potentially leaves equality more vulnerable to how this instrumentalism is defined when the morality element is ducked. Sandel, for one, who offers such a cogent critique of marketisation and the limits of markets, also argues that moral questions cannot be avoided in trying to create a better society (Sandel 2012).

What is not being advocated here is absenteeism from the moral territory – it is the reframing of success – and its cousin, 'aspiration' – in such a way as to reflect the morality of the choices that it entails. An appeal to enlightened instrumentalism is what The Spirit Level tried to do, but it failed to do this as well as it could because it remained trapped by the existing 'success frame', stopping short of the 'reframing of success'. This is essentially what is being advocated in this book via the idea of holistic social mobility.

The living salary

The converse or downside of this argument, however, is that if 'money matters less', then so should its redistribution. This is the major potential drawback with attempting to move social mobility off the purely economic terrain: it loses the focus on the importance of economic position. So how can this argument be countered?

The widening of the concept of the 'living wage' could be one mechanism to do this. The most important evidence to support the diminution of the relative importance of money is the diminishing returns it provides in terms of well-being after a certain point: that is, the Easterlin paradox, as described in Chapter One. The question is, how can this idea be developed in such a way as to have wider appeal?

The living wage concept at present in the UK is used to support better living standards for the low-paid. The concept underlying it is to identify the amount of income required to live a satisfactory life free from poverty. This could be equally applied to higher levels of income. There could be debate, for example, around the 'living salary'. By the living salary what is meant is the amount required to live 'comfortably' or 'securely', or to the point beyond which the Easterlin paradox kicks in and actual happiness levels off. The societal debate around how much income is required to live an acceptable standard of life is a continual one. It is a moral judgment, which is context-specific. Different answers across societies have given rise to contrasting systems of taxation. In the UK, it has manifested itself most clearly in the 2010s in the debate around the 'squeezed middle', as those earning relatively high salaries who were previously fairly immune to economic downturns are now feeling that their incomes are not enough to maintain the kind of lives they want and expect, as increases in salaries are flat, but the cost of living is rising (Resolution Foundation 2012).

The idea of the living salary may be a powerful way of reframing this issue. Instead of restricting the debate around what income is required to maintain a standard of living to a subsistence level, it should be extended to consider the level of the 'living salary'.. The objective of developing this argument is to reframe the discussion around income. Making the level of income required to live a 'middle-class life' more specific will force more detailed debate around what that life constitutes. Most importantly, it will highlight the extent to which such a life is materially driven – or not – and hence open up the debate around social mobility and success.

Why does changing the powerful matter?

At the centre of the present politics of social mobility is the concern regarding who occupies the most powerful positions in society. The loss of faith in politics and politicians is also occurring at a time when the social background of politicians has narrowed in comparison with the late 20th century, as we have seen the ascent of the 'professional' politician:

> Over one third (35%) of MPs elected in the 2010 General Election attended independent schools, which educate just 7% of the school population, this includes just under three in ten who were educated at either Oxford or Cambridge universities. Oxford has produced 102 MPs serving in the 2010 Parliament. 38% of Conservative MPs were educated at Oxford or Cambridge compared with 20% of Labour MPs and 28% of Liberal Democrat MPs. (Sutton Trust 2010: 3)

Among leading Labour MPs there is a lesser preponderance of ex-public school pupils, but still a dominance of those educated at Oxford, Cambridge or other more selective Russell Group universities. And some question the degree to which what has been described as 'the political class' are able to relate to the rest of the population. The association between political apathy, a lack of ability to connect, and the trajectory that MPs have followed combined with their social background, has interesting implications regarding social mobility. Many prominent Labour MPs were born into middle-class or lower-middle-class backgrounds, but it is the intragenerational journey they have taken that is the issue: a 'classic' social mobility one, as they move up the occupational class structure. By passing into what is perceived to be the elite, often through the conventional pipeline to such positions in the UK i.e. through elite universities and professional jobs they are deemed to have lost their ability to relate to whom they are meant to serve, and the social mobility journey is devalued. The focus on the background of MPs has also led to attention being paid to the pathway to elected office, and a concern that the costs involved, both in terms of time and money, militate against more working-class candidates (Skelton 2013). What is less clear is why this is actually a problem. While it is taken as read that elites should be more diverse, the arguments regarding the composition of elites need a little more thinking through.

There are several reasons posited as to why elites should be more diverse. First, it is seen as efficient – given that talent or ability may be distributed across the whole population, drawing leaders from just a narrow part of it means that the whole of society may suffer. Second, it is seen as necessary for society to function – much of the way in which the idea of the social contract is deployed by politicians such as Barack Obama in the US draws significantly from functionalist sociological theory. Functionalists argue that social mobility is important because it ensures that there is at least an idea of 'fairness' at play in a society. History is littered with examples of what happens when elites self-perpetuate and the mass of the population are unable to become part of this group. The almost inevitable conflict is not functional for any society, bringing with it death, misery and so on. The phrase 'American dream' itself, for example, is a telling one. It is the possibility of entering the elite (even if it is remote) that matters, rather than it actually happening in large numbers.

As important as these reasons may be, though, is just ensuring that those in powerful positions are more diverse per se enough? If what happens, in effect, is the filling of a quota – and those who enter such positions bring the same qualities as those who occupy them at present, only they come from different backgrounds – is social mobility of this kind such an important goal?

The actual impact of greater social mobility into elite positions is not really explored much in either the present political or academic discourses. The merits of greater diversity are held to be self-evident; it is assumed, rather than proven, that a more diverse elite brings with it wider social transformation.

In the private sector, the argument that the benefits of anything are self-evident usually holds less appeal. The case for greater social mobility, therefore, has been presented in this context as offering a clear business benefit. More diversity is expected to bring with it greater insights into different markets and perspectives that will assist business (BIS 2013c).

Elites and social transformation

The principle that the socially mobile have a different impact in their new location to the incumbent as a result of their background is important. It links social mobility with social transformation, and considerably strengthens the case for the former. A practical difference in the nature of what those in elite positions do appears to be the justification for recent concerns about exclusivity at the top. The exact nature of this difference, however, is never clearly articulated and could be interpreted differently. Greater diversity among decision makers could be a platform for greater redistributive policies, which is what those on the Left would like; a way to make more money, which is what those in the private sector think will happen with more 'diverse' senior leaders, and a way of ensuring that policy and practice are more attuned to lower-class sensibilities, is what those on the political Right think.

How to weave these differing forms of societal benefit into one narrative around the overall benefit to society of long-range economic social mobility is a considerable challenge, as they are ideologically diametrically opposed. It is hard to conceive of John Major and his fellow Conservative politicians being so keen to wax lyrical about greater access to the professions being so important because the professions are lacking in members committed to redistributive politics, yet this is why many on the Left see the primary need for more diversity among those in powerful positions.

A new politics of social mobility has to involve a greater debate about exactly why making elite positions more open to those from different backgrounds is so important, relative to changing what social mobility for everybody means. It needs to aim for a greater balance in terms of the importance of such elite mobility relative to other forms of social mobility. At present, the vast majority of economic mobility is ignored in the political discourse in favour of concentrating on who makes up the elite. This is not to say that the composition of elites does not matter. The weakness in much of what is written regarding the need for an alternative form of capitalism is not in the description of what should happen, but in how it will be achieved. It is the change model that is overlooked or absent. And in any model of change that is developed, the role of decision makers is paramount. For the kind of change that Hutton or James, for example, advocate, the present decision makers have to think or act differently. However, it is precisely the difference in viewpoint and behaviour that is most important – and being really committed to greater equality is more important than who instigates the differences.

'It's the economy, stupid...'

Given the centrality of the question of economic growth to early 21st-century politics, a new social mobility politics has to relate to it. The rising importance of growth is, in many ways, just further evidence of the fragility of the present socioeconomic model in the UK (and much of the economically developed world). Continued

GDP growth is needed to allow the state to deliver on the promise of ever-increasing prosperity, and in particular the intergenerational increases in material prosperity, which, as argued earlier, are at the centre of the social contract.

Growth has come to dominate the discussion at this time in a way that it did not in previous recessions, because increasing prosperity has, if anything, become more of an expectation now than in the 1980s or 1990s. The effect of a shift to an individualistic culture and the penetration of the market into far more areas of life that began with Thatcherism in the 1980s, followed by the longest period of sustained economic growth in modern British history, may have shifted expectations. Increased prosperity and improvements in material standard of living are now expected, not hoped for.

Expectations may have been lower in previous generations – the focus on the 'squeezed middle' by Labour in opposition provides evidence of this. The problem of flat wage growth and increases in costs of living, together with a tightening of middle-class benefits, has now led to increasing numbers of those in 'middle-class' positions who have experienced a plateau in their real incomes, if not a reduction (Resolution Foundation 2012). However, this is not a problem of the magnitude of the early 1990s, when house repossessions were at record levels, and nor has unemployment reached anything like the levels and duration of the early 1980s.

In reality, for the majority it means that they have had to cut back on the kind of status expenditures which, in the early 21st-century UK, are evidence of social mobility, that is, holidays, consumer durables, home improvements, cars and so on. Much has been made of the stagnation in real wages – in early 2013, they had fallen back to 2003 levels. However, was the standard of living so low in 2003 as to merit this alarm? Broughton et al (2014) analysed the progress of families who were in the middle 20% of income distribution – the third income bracket – at the start of the economic downturn in 2007-08, and analysed what had happened to them by 2011-12. A family in this group in 2011-12 would have had a total pre-tax income of between £26,100 and £41,200. The research argued that over 40% of families had climbed into the top two income groups over the period, and only just under 20% had fallen. Most families were actually better off over this period and continue to earn relatively well.

The question as to whether this level of income is 'enough' returns us to the living salary question discussed earlier. It can also be argued that, given the debt-laden nature of UK society in the 2010s, many people, even in middle- to high-income brackets, live on a precarious line between economic success and failure, because of their dependence, through home loans in particular, on interest rates, which have been at record low levels through the 2010s. And this analysis is not oblivious to the realpolitik of the early 21st century – it is not productive to castigate the majority of the population for wanting new cars and holidays from some (usually mythical and hypocritical) higher moral ground where. Rather, there has to be some way of supporting people's aspirations for success and progress, but changing what they aspire to and what they want to succeed in.

The above evidence shows that the biggest problem in the 21st century where growth is concerned will be managing expectations, if we see the long-term decline in growth predicted by King, Gordon and Piketty in Chapter One. This means those in virtually all socioeconomic positions having to adjust to a less rapidly improving material standard of living – if indeed an improvement at all. Politicians have been understandably less keen to engage with the implications of the work of Piketty, King and others, yet if these writers are correct, they will have no choice, sooner or later, but to do so. A holistic approach to social mobility offers them some options in two different respects. Out of necessity, they will need a new way of looking at progress and success, if the old one is no longer viable. Social mobility conceived as improvements in well-being as opposed to economic position provides this. Given that such improvements may be conceivable without ever-increasing economic growth, it could enable politicians to deliver increasing social mobility in a tougher economic environment. This is an attractive option to any politician. Improving well-being will not be easy, especially when it depends to a great extent (at the moment anyway) on material resources, but it could be more feasible than relying on continued expansion in middle-class jobs and 4–5% a year growth in GDP, which the evidence suggests may be unrealistic.

Creating 'good growth'

Adjusting to lower levels of growth would require revising the growth model itself, and regardless of whether growth declines or not, there is still a case for revising this model. This means moving away from looking at bald GDP figures as indicators of success (as argued in the previous chapter), and developing models of 'good growth'.

Research with over 2,000 people by PricewaterhouseCoopers (PwC) and Demos in 2011 looked at what 'good growth' meant. They argued that:

... the public takes a wider view of the components of economic success. In the public's eyes, 'good growth' depends on creating jobs that enable their bills to be paid, but also on issues such as work-life balance, health and housing, amongst others, which are seen as critical components of good economic performance. Indeed, when forced to make trade-offs in the factors contributing to economic success, work-life balance assumes an even greater importance; working people are willing to sacrifice income to spend more time with family and friends. Overall, income and jobs only account for roughly a third of what the public thinks is important when considering what a successful economy might look like. (PwC and Demos 2011: 2)

This research reaffirms the idea that there is space for the development of new conceptions of success, but the challenge in developing such conceptions may be greater in the UK than in many other nations. The relatively impressive growth enjoyed by the UK in the 20th century was based to a large degree on consumption, as have been the gradual improvements since the recession peaked in the early 2010s (Corry et al 2011). This model is less sustainable and productive than more investment-based growth models such as those pursued by Germany, for example.

More thought-out and sustainable approaches to promoting growth require a better growth strategy than the UK has at present – the UK does not have an impressive record in terms of growth strategy (Aghion et al 2013). Any strategy in the future will have to be developed in the context of lower growth and the need for 'good growth'. It will need a way of subjecting the policies designed to deliver it to an impact audit that goes beyond the more basic metrics of GDP increase, employment increase or revenue to the exchequer.

As Aghion et al (2013: 33) state: 'changes in GDP are an inadequate measure of human wellbeing'. In a similar vein to the way in which much industrial policy is now subject to an environmental audit in deciding on its overall impact on society, a 'good growth' or even a holistic social mobility audit may be required.

Eccles and Serafeim (2013) of Harvard University in the US have been developing a model to account for the societal impact of corporate decision making. They argue that companies need a social 'licence to operate' in 21st-century capitalism, which means they have to be seen to be following certain societal norms in their practice across areas such as environmental impact, worker rights and treatment and taxation strategy. They use the example of controversies in 2013 regarding the tax avoidance strategies of major companies such as Starbucks of the impact on a company when they violate these norms and start to lose their licence. They scored a range of social issues in terms of relative importance to private sector companies' licence to operate, and equal opportunities and diversity was one of these issues. Such a framework could well be extended, however, for social mobility and well-being.

While Eccles and Serafeim provide a potential set of tools to assess the relationship between well-being and growth at the corporate level, the OECD has recently developed a set of tools that can be used by policy makers to inform the development of inclusive growth at the societal level. In its 2014 publication All Aboard: Making Inclusive Growth Happen, the OECD argues that: 'there is much to gain from going beyond income to include non-monetary dimensions of well-being. Employment prospects, job satisfaction, health outcomes and educational opportunities matter for people's well-being' (OECD 2014b: 8). It introduced the idea of 'multidimensional' living standards to account for both monetary and non-monetary dimensions of growth. In its first iteration, as in the 2014 report, these non-monetary dimensions are risk of unemployment and health status, but the OECD argues that it could be extended to include education and the environment.

The OECD's work lends further support to the idea that if we are to account for structural differences within and across societies in the 21st century, a broader approach than just looking at income/occupation is needed, particularly if we are to do this in the context of understanding and addressing inequality. As the OECD (2014b: 8) states: 'Inclusive growth … is a new approach to economic growth that aims to improve living standards and share the benefits of increased prosperity more evenly across social groups'.

Social mobility and the Left

Former leader of the Labour Party, Ed Miliband, attempted to develop ideas that could orientate a different approach to the economy at least, and to some extent the composition of the political system, by playing around with ideas such as pre-distribution and responsible capitalism (Miliband 2013). As the 2010s progress, so could these ideas, but as yet they do not have the wider intellectual or political basis of earlier attempts to underpin the renewal of social democratic thinking in the UK, such as the emergence of the Social Democratic Party (SDP) in the early 1980s or the 'third way' of the late 1990s. This is, however, part of an ongoing journey for the Left to try to fit their intellectual and moral beliefs with an era very different from when these beliefs were forged. Miliband was right to try to continue with this ongoing project of renewal, and to identify a gap where alternative approaches to delivering capitalism could be built, but what are the ideas that could fill this gap, and where does social mobility fit into them?

Social mobility, with its deep association with greater economic equality, has a more intuitively 'natural fit' with the political Left. The idea that there has been a slowdown in upward mobility is an explicit comment on a failure of the Left more than the Right. For the Right, the lack of upward mobility may be seen as an indictment of their soft underbelly as defenders and products of privilege, but they have never put as much store as the Left in reducing such disparities. Many on the Right think they are a natural part of capitalism. It is the Left who are compelled to find a place for social mobility much closer to the centre of their political narrative.

There has been a considerable amount of reflection in recent years, since the latest global recession (precipitated as it was by the inequality and agglomeration of financial power), on how this did not become a 'moment for the Left' (Policy Network 2014). Despite the widespread anger concerning the behaviour of the financial sector, and the deeper sense of unease regarding the nature of a system that allowed this to happen, the Left has been unable to really capitalise or produce a compelling enough picture of what a different system would look like (Cramme et al 2013). If anything, the tendency has been to concentrate on familiar but fairly parochial themes to achieve political differentiation. A good example here is the announcement by the Labour Party in October 2013 that it would freeze energy prices if elected in the 2015 general election. This was a laudable aim, focusing specifically on the everyday concerns of the population, centring apparently on declining standards of living (Wintour 2013a). It was well received by the electorate on its announcement, and was credited with increasing Labour's lead in the opinion polls.

But while it is an important and effective policy, it does not represent even the start of the kind of shift in the UK model of capitalism that Labour pronounce they would like to see, or that may be necessary. There is a space on the Left for new thinking, and social mobility in its present form does not occupy much of this space. Nick Pearce has written very thoughtfully on the philosophical and intellectual basis for the politics of the Left in the early 2010s. In his 2013 article 'What should social democrats believe?', he argues that in the early 2010s there has not been an intellectual revisionism on the political Left in the UK, as has followed other election defeats (Pearce 2013). But writing in 2012, he was critical of the focus that the coalition had placed on intergenerational mobility, on progression to elite positions, and the emphasis on those on low incomes. He argues that:

> This narrowing of focus, allied to recent trends that suggest the labour market has hollowed out, with more 'lousy' and 'lovely' jobs but fewer skilled middle-tier positions, means that the new social mobility strategy will have little to say to large swathes of the population who are suffering stagnant wages and declining living standards. The risk of this approach is that the promise of greater opportunities for future generations will appear too distant to command popular support. (Pearce 2012:7)

With the exception of Pearce, however, there have been relatively few attempts in the 2010s to move social mobility beyond the parameters set by the coalition government. The Compass organisation has been arguing for over 10 years for a broader understanding of the 'good life', challenging those on the Left to go beyond the purely economic in defining such a life. Lawson's book All Consuming (2009) summarises much of this thinking. But there is little emerging from Compass regarding social mobility, aside from the standard concerns about self-recruiting and self-aggrandising elites. The same could also be said from other Left-wing political organisations, such as the more centrist Progress or the statist Fabian Society. The latter's contribution amounted to a retread of these familiar themes (Bliss 2013). Holistic social mobility could be central to many of the concerns that the Left have in trying to define an alternative politics consistent with their core beliefs but appropriate to deal with the early 21st century.

One of the biggest of these concerns is how to understand stratification, especially as it relates to how consciousness is formed. In the aftermath of electoral defeat in 2010 there was much debate concerning the degree to which the Labour Party had lost touch with its core working-class constituency (Kellner 2012). This debate continues after their defeat in 2015.

Advocates of a much greater acknowledgement of the role of religion, patriotism and cultural conservatism described these ideas as 'Blue Labour' (Glasman et al 2012). They drew on the problems posed by the decline in the social and cultural infrastructure of working-class life in the last 30 years. The role of unions in articulating on an everyday basis what social class meant – via rhetoric, wage bargaining and also in underpinning much of the social and cultural infrastructure – has played a fundamental role in giving working-class identity its lived meaning. Their declining membership and political emasculation has played a huge part in the unravelling of the bonds that tied working-class life together. This emasculation has been coupled with the downsizing of some of the other organisations that fertilised working-class identity. The number of Working Men's Clubs, for example, has declined by half in the last 30 years (BBC News 2014c).

The criticism levelled at 'Blue Labour' ideas was that they were very backward-looking. As well as presenting a romanticised view of a working-class past, for example, in playing down sexism and racism, they did not speak to the need for political parties to be vehicles for progress, however defined (Goodman 2011). Blue Labour did, however, ensure that issues of identity and culture were placed under serious consideration on the Left. Pearce goes on to argue that a richer and more pluralistic form of Left politics is needed that gives greater attention to the role of institutions in civil society, and that also recognises the importance of differentials in power as well as resources. While he echoes much of the Left in seeking to retain equality as the central goal for the Left, he advocates it being 'reconceived' to recognise democratic control, human agency and social relations. In terms of the latter, he suggests: 'challenging a focus on the abstract metrics of material equality with a commitment to valuing the expressive and cultural dimensions of life' (Pearce 2013: 6).

Pearce is not the only one on the political Left in the UK in the 2010s to recognise that there is a need to reform the capitalist model, and that Left politics is about more than economism. Jon Cruddas, who took a role in the early 2010s as head of the policy review for the Labour Party, connects this concern with the history of the party. Speaking in 2013 on the identity of Labour, he says that it was: '… never simply materialistic. Labour is a political tradition that allows us to realise our potentials, to flourish as human beings – to live more rewarding lives' (Cruddas 2013).

Cruddas frames these priorities in the context of some of the bigger challenges facing the UK described in this book. He goes on to argue that the focus should be not just on what he sees as the economistic tradition of the Left 'earning', but the wider idea of being part of a society, of belonging.

The potential for a new social mobility politics

It is difficult for politicians to address the bigger questions that 21st-century capitalism faces. This requires shifting the societal goals, while at the same time not losing sight of the primacy of economic differences and economic activity. This kind of cultural change is not amenable to quick policy fixes. Exploring what social mobility means, and then by extension what success means, enables the challenges to be better mapped out and creates a platform for a more inclusive or sophisticated politics of the Left.

The cultural changes necessary may not be so daunting. The disillusionment with politics described earlier may be so profound as to appear permanent. Cultural change has, in fact, already happened; politicians are just running to catch up with it – an enhanced version of what was on offer before will not enable them to make up the ground. An approach that acknowledges and deals with the complexities of progress, success and well-being for individuals and communities in the early 21st century is not just desirable, but necessary. The perception that many politicians appear to hold at present appears to be that many young (and older) people may be turned off politics because politicians overpromise on things they cannot deliver. The solution is to make smaller, day-to-day commitments that people can relate to and that are achievable. However, a more powerful position may be that they are turned off because there is no bigger vision that resonates with them, there are no attempts to look at the big underlying things that shape their lives.

This is not to decry the depth to which individualistic economism shapes success and progress – and hence social mobility. But the pluralistic nature of both individuals and groups' lives and views in the 21st century should not be decried either. The research on well-being by the OECD and ONS described earlier shows that people do place value on things beyond the material. There is a range of other studies that shows we hold a range of non-material values alongside – and even in preference to – those focused on material gain (Barrett and Clothier 2012). Research looking particularly at the attitudes of young people shows that they hold a broader, if more demanding, set of views regarding what they aspire to. An overview of the social attitudes of young people produced in 2014 argued that there was some commonality between different age groups in what they aspired to, and this echoes the work on well-being discussed in the previous chapter: 'having good friends, health, being independent and having good partnerships are the most important things for under 25s and older groups' (Social Attitudes of Young People Community of Interest 2014: 6).

But this does not mean that there are no differences across generations. The report goes on to state: 'However, there is evidence that there has been an increase in the importance of power and achievement (social prestige and personal success), stimulation (excitement and challenge in life) and hedonism (pleasure/gratification for oneself) for younger generations' (Social Attitudes of Young People Community of Interest 2014: 18). It appears that people do expect more today from life, but not necessarily money.

Conclusions

The notion that there is something wrong in the early 21st century, due to a combination of marketisation, materialism and technology, is a familiar refrain in the early 2010s. Thomas Piketty's book *Capital in the Twenty-First Century* was the best-selling hardback book in the US in early 2014. Piketty advocates taxation rates of up to 80% on wealth, arguing that wealth plays a pivotal role in defining inequality. However, he offers no methodology of how to get support for such policies.

David Marquand, one of the foremost political writers in Britain, produced a powerful and polemical condemnation of the impact of marketisation on our values in his 2014 book, Mammon's Kingdom: An Essay on Britain Now. In it, he argues that hedonistic individualism, freedom and choice have produced both an economic and a moral crisis in capitalism. As with Piketty, while the descriptions of the problems are very good, the solutions offered are less so. Marquand advocates greater public discourse or a national conversation on these issues, and this is as argued in the conclusions (echoing Sen), but it is not evident why such a conversation would necessarily conclude that we need greater redistribution, less importance on material goods, a retreat from hedonism and so on.

There is clearly a need for some new, more concrete and achievable ways of reforming capitalism so it can better meet the grand challenges of today for the whole population and not just for some. But addressing the intergenerational disparities in economic life chances between social groups should be the start and not the end of the politics of social mobility. There is an opportunity, particularly for social democratic parties, to use social mobility as a route to articulating an approach to these challenges, although this is not the easiest route. In its present iteration, social mobility is relatively safe. The goal of raising the educational attainment of young people from lower socioeconomic groups is shared across parties, as is increasing wages for the low paid and making the elite more diverse. They are almost 'above politics', a status that is the ultimate goal for those campaigning to bring an issue to prominence.

However, consensual positions are also less attractive to political parties. They do not offer the same opportunity to construct a distinctive position. Not advancing thinking on social mobility also risks loss of support and momentum, as it becomes harder to energise politicians and others when the 'moral panic' element passes. A new politics for social mobility, centred on confronting the unsustainability of the present capitalist success model in a country like the UK, would be far less consensual. It would mean challenging deep-rooted assumptions regarding what success is and what social mobility is. The questions that form the body of new holistic social mobility politics are radical, in that they are not being confronted at present, but they are also realistic. This is not the politics of the margins, but the politics of the centre (a place that many on the Left felt Labour deserted from 2010 to 2015). They accord with challenges the majority of the population are experiencing, but politics in the early 21st century appears unable to connect with, as disillusionment with politicians and their methods reaches new heights. These questions have been encountered throughout this book, and include: how should school prepare young people for work and life? What is the point of higher education? How do I be a 'good' parent? How can work be more fulfilling (and remunerative)? What does a 'good' work–life balance mean? How can inequality be reduced? Why should elites be more diverse? How important is being healthy? What should the state provide and who for? And how can my future and that of my family and/or children be more secure, successful and happy?

Constructing realistic answers to these questions is an even bigger challenge, which the final chapter attempts to confront.

NINE

Reframing social mobility

The aim of this book has been to look at what social mobility actually means, rather than how much of it there is. It has tried to reflect on how what success means is at the heart of social mobility, arguing that the way in which social mobility is defined must be extended beyond just progression (or lack of it) in terms of occupation or income. This present definition of social mobility based soley on income/occupation risks exacerbating the corrosive impact of materialism on economic and social life in the 21st century. An alternative way of understanding social mobility is therefore essential, in order to tackle some of the biggest issues that we face in the 21st century. This means deconstructing the idea of social mobility, and understanding better what 'social' and 'mobility' means, rather than assuming that it can be reduced to economic factors, and that mobility automatically follows when economic status changes.

This new approach is best described as a holistic one. As argued in Chapter One, it is both a method and a definition. It means extending the field of social mobility to include the full range of factors that constitute progress in life. In such a holistic definition, social mobility is made up of changes in well-being which incorporate progress across a number of domains, and what constitutes these domains should be the product of more empirical work.

A starting point in understanding the kinds of relevant domains to social mobility would be the categories that the OECD used to construct its 'Better Life' Initiative (see Chapter Seven). These domains are interrelated but not autocorrelated – while one may determine another, the extent of this relationship is context-specific. Occupation and/or income in particular may be drivers of the other domains, but these domains exist independently. Nor is the relationship totally one way; much evidence exists to show that those whose well-being is low due to depression or stress, for instance, are less likely to progress in the labour market and less likely to be 'occupationally socially mobile' (Blaug et al 2007). The centrality and importance of occupation and income in defining individual welfare and progress are not being denied here, but they are not enough – and nor should they be – to capture all that it means to be 'successful' in life.

How achievable is a new approach to social mobility? I have criticised those who offer solutions to the problems associated with social mobility, such as inequality, but who do not go on to explain how solutions would actually be delivered. It is only right, then, that this conclusion at least attempts to be consistent with this critique, and tries to avoid being part of the problem by offering some workable solutions.

This final concluding chapter outlines how a holistic approach to social mobility could be advanced, and how the 'success paradox' in the early 21st-century UK could be addressed. It argues that 'success' itself needs to be reframed. The way in which a social phenomenon such as social mobility is understood and interpreted is within the constraints of a set of parameters based around language and concept. Borrowing from the work of Lakoff (1990) and Chong and Druckman (2007), among others, we can see insights into how, by changing the way in which we speak about, define and connect a concept, meanings can be reframed and a more holistic understanding reached.

I therefore describe a number of steps (as follows) which, taken together, could start this process of reframing.

Step 1: Recalibrate occupational stratification

The first step should be to change what data are collected, how it is collected, and then how it is moulded into a political discourse.

Existing approaches to examining social mobility, led by academics, are in the main historically and culturally hemmed in by a commitment to the primacy of class or income. For sociologists this makes it difficult to recognise that while class is an important marker for success, as is income, it cannot just be read off from an individual's economic position. Grusky and Weeden (2006) are quite forthright regarding the challenge that sociology faces, unless it moves away from its 'unidimensional approach to the analysis of stratification.' They go on to argue that: 'If the sociological approach to mobility is to survive, it must therefore be converted from a mere disciplinary predilection to an approach with real empirical standing' (Grusky and Weeden 2006: 104). However, the growth in the amount of objective data on individuals that is likely to become available, and the increase in the sophistication of analytical techniques, will add to the ability of those studying social mobility to produce more detailed information on how both occupation and income change. This is not in itself a bad thing – the kind of regional data on income over time that enabled Chetty et al (2014) in the US, for example, to look at differences in income mobility across different areas in quite a detailed, granular fashion would be very interesting in the UK.

However, it needs a significant injection of empirical, primary data from people themselves. Social mobility is in danger from what Davies describes as 'data fundamentalism' (Davies 2013), where big data combined from large administrative data sets start to define academic or political activity. The kind of large panel studies favoured by both sociologists and academics in social mobility analysis should start to include questions that look at what social mobility actually means to the people experiencing it (or not). When do they think they have been socially mobile? How does social mobility relate to improvements in their well-being?

This doesn't mean that there is no role for the analysis of secondary data sets on income distribution, but it needs to sit within a wider discourse based on empirical quantitative and qualitative work that contextualises this analysis. There are opportunities that already exist here. As Abdallah and Shah (2012) point out, the UK's largest annual survey, the Annual Population Survey, includes questions on well-being. Rather than imposing definitions of social mobility on society, there is the opportunity to generate them from 'society up'. This could well produce far less empirically attractive, neat categorisations for statistical analysis. What if, for instance, social mobility becomes more subjective than objective? Or definitions overlap and are inconsistent in and over time? The reality of social mobility may be far messier than it is presented at the moment, and it may also look more materialistic than we would like it to look, but at least the scale of the challenge would be clearer.

This is a political and academic challenge for a holistic approach to social mobility. The attractiveness of the research from Blanden et al described in Chapter Two that did so much to advance the position of social mobility in political discourse was the simplicity of the message. Increases or decreases in income are easy to understand. Politicians like simple messages, not messy ones. There are those contributing to the social mobility political discourse (the Social Mobility and Child Poverty Commission and, to a degree, the APPG) who are a little more attuned to the complexities around measuring and understanding social mobility, but accepting that it may have an inherently subjective nature would challenge their work.

Changing the data collected is only the basis for changing how stratification is understood. Chapter Seven looked at various alternatives to the accepted forms of occupational/income schemas. Their main weakness is that they do not, as yet, come in the form of a scale. For example, a five- or seven-part capability schema that could be applied to the UK has not yet been developed, and there has been reticence in the work of the OECD or ONS to develop such scales. However, the occupational schemas used to define social mobility at present must be questioned. The BBC BCS described in Chapter Eight may indeed be flawed, as Goldthorpe and others argue. It has been suggested, for instance, that on the basis of the methodology they used, you could end up with 77 classes (Oxford Sociology 2013). But is it more absurd to think that in the UK in the 2010s there are 77 class groups rather than 7?

Given what we know about occupational change in the last 60 years in terms of increased differentiation between jobs, the rise in the individualisation of lifestyles and the fragmentation of class infrastructures such as unions and so on, is it realistic to assume that the number of social classes is the same as it was 60 years ago? It might not be an attractive proposition for certain researchers to think that there might be 40, 50 or 60 'class'-related groupings, but it may make more sense. Attempts to construct stratification schema that are different from the government-approved NS-SEC are not new, however. Geodemographic analyses of a range of social data built for commercial use have been around in the UK for some years (Singleton and Speilman 2013). Although they have their own critiques, and such particular schemas are not being advocated as such here, the resonance of class as an identifier, if it does exist, is more refracted and nuanced now. Many of the attempts to build detailed categorisations that combine lifestyle, economic position and geography can be rightly criticised as attempts themselves to create new categories or groups that do not, in reality, exist (Goss 1995), but this does not mean that the fundamental aim of tackling the complexity of social divisions can be ignored.

Building a new understanding of social mobility will not work unless there is a mechanism to shape and legitimise such transformatory changes. Control of the message is the essence of 'framing' an issue. And the framework to forge this new, more empirical understanding of what social mobility means already exists in England. The existence of the Social Mobility and Child Poverty Commission is in itself ground-breaking internationally. There is also a strong programme of research developed by the ONS looking at well-being, with cross-sector support.

There is a strong argument for some reconfiguration and alignment here, forming a new Commission for Social Mobility and Well-Being to champion the holistic social mobility approach. Child poverty would become the business of a separate office or commission, with the power to audit a range of organisations with a responsibility for child poverty. As argued earlier, while child poverty and social mobility are intimately related, the latter is a much broader issue than the former. Moreover, the importance of child poverty is such that it actually demands its own mechanism of change.

Step 2: Change the mission of education as well as the method

Trying to shift, even subtly, what success means in a country like the UK in the early 21st century means tackling the 'mission' of education. Even if relatively rapid increases in the attainment of children from lower socioeconomic backgrounds could be achieved, it is naive in the extreme to suggest that their peers from higher socioeconomic groups will stand still. By creating a culture where a narrow version of educational achievement is the marker of progress in society, it inevitably makes it more difficult for those with fewer resources to compete in that race. I am not arguing here that the pursuit of increased attainment for all pupils is wrong, or that the dominance of elite universities and professions by those educated at private school is acceptable, but the 'end game' has not been thought through. If the present education strategy was successful, the result would be a lot of disappointed (young) people – there are simply not enough 'good' jobs (as such jobs are defined at present) to absorb such a qualified workforce.

If, as a society, we wish to pursue educational excellence for all, the purpose of education must be better worked out. This means conceiving of a broader range of productive outcomes for educational achievement. The idea that education can lead to better health, greater happiness, and contribute to a better civil society is extremely important, but we need to know more about how exactly these effects are produced. The arguments presented by James Heckman in Chapter Two have had a very powerful impact on how early years education and parenting is perceived, and they may be equally important for holistic social mobility.

Heckman argues that if all the population could achieve a form of minimum education threshold, many negative outcomes such as poverty, crime and ill health could be minimised. If this threshold could be achieved, would this mean that the importance of differences in attainment could be reduced? There may still be big differences by social background, but if the 'floor' level of attainment could be achieved to enable those who achieve this floor to be relatively well educated, these individuals would presumably avoid the poor parenting and subsequent poverty that Heckman describes. Think, for instance, of a society where everyone, with the exception of those with really challenging circumstances, has a degree. Would they all then be able to experience the broad range of benefits described in the Figure 5.1 in Chapter Five? Would we then need to worry as much whether there were differences in overall attainment? This kind of society is not a hypothetical one, of course. It is the UK in the future – if present trends continue, at some point, probably over the next 100 years, almost everyone will have the equivalent of a HE qualification. The problem in labour market terms is that by the time everyone has a degree, it probably won't be worth much in the labour market – the economic 'floor' will have become somewhat higher. But would it still deliver the range of other crucial, non-economic benefits in the 'quadrant diagram' that are so important? Would it mean that society was inculcated with a set of attitudes and characteristics that make the behaviours that underpin some of the negative outcomes Heckman describes rare? If this is the case, is there a way of conceiving of the benefits of education in different terms, that is, as a mechanism of enabling everyone to develop the capabilities necessary to engage meaningfully in society, rather than as a positional good burdened with overcoming what are essentially societal inequalities inherent in capitalism?, are the benefits that we see as accruing to education independent of any inequalities in attainment and intrinsic to the level of education achieved, or would they dissipate if these inequalities continued despite the level of education being achieved?

The work on the framing of political ideas by Lakoff (1990) illustrates that it is difficult to shift understanding by playing the game within rules set by the opposition. You need to set your own. Education requires holistic social mobility in equal if not greater measure than holistic social mobility requires a different educational system. This idea of a broader range of outcomes should be the main focus of any policy and research agenda here. This doesn't mean detracting from the value of achievement in academic subjects or the investment and efforts to raise achievement. These efforts must be matched with an equal amount of investment in what the outcomes of these efforts should be.

Step 3: Connect success with society

The study of social mobility was not designed to be an end in itself. When Sorokin (1959) and Glass (1954) began the study of social mobility, it was for its value in helping us understand how society was, or was not, changing. However, as the field developed to where it is today, the debate has been constructed primarily around the progress (or not) of the individual. As argued in Chapter Seven, even where increased social mobility is seen to benefit society, in the case of the more diverse elites, the arguments justifying such changes are weakly developed. As a consequence, the connection between success and society is weak – which is one of the central features of the paradox: success at the individual level causes problems at the societal level. The best way to tackle this is to look to connect success with its impact on society as much as on the individual, emphasising the connections between society and the individual.

This requires much greater multidisciplinarity in the study of social mobility. The legitimacy in terms of what social mobility scholarly work pertains to must be overhauled. The measurement of social mobility should remain key to the study of it, but needs to act as a foundation from which much more diverse and wide-ranging work occurs, drawing in ideas and researchers from economics, sociology, psychology, political studies, labour market studies and education. At the centre of the holistic method is the idea that social mobility is shaped in a reflexive way by the actions it informs. This reflexive relationship has been discussed in this book over a range of contexts, including the labour market, education, societal attitudes towards redistribution and the impact (or not) of long-range social mobility to elite positions on the use of political power. This reflexivity needs to be combined with a greater willingness to illustrate how success and social mobility connect to the big issues of our age.

There has been surprisingly little consideration, for instance, of the ramifications for society stemming from the increasing numbers going to higher education. England has changed from a society where less than 17% of its population were graduates in 1992 to one where over 38% were in 2013 (ONS 2013). Globally there will be a quarter of a billion students by 2030, which is an increase of two-thirds in only 20 years. What impact is this having on the big societal challenges, such as climate change? The single most important factor in defining the level of knowledge and awareness of climate change is years spent in education. A Gallup survey of over 200,000 people in 2009 found that adults with 9-15 years' education were twice as likely to be aware of climate change as those with eight years' education or less (Pugliese and Ray 2009). To what extent, at present, are research and policy looking at social mobility connecting education and climate change?

Alongside climate change, the movement of people and the growth of multi-ethnic and multi-faith societies is another such challenge. The tensions this creates between host and immigrant groups are being played out across the world and in particular in Europe with dramatic results as witnessed in Madrid, London and Paris over the last decade. As argued in Chapter Five, crafting a notion of social mobility that can benefit groups with both lower levels of income and occupying the 'lower-skilled jobs' that society needs doing (as many immigrants do) is essential, if tensions and conflict related to movement of people is to be avoided.

It is not only an issue of income, though. As Western societies, and in particular certain urban regions within Western societies, become what has been described as 'super diverse' (Spoonley 2014) – London, for example, now has more non-white than white residents – what does social mobility mean? There are now communities intertwining with each other with quite different belief systems, grounded in contrasting cultural mores and religious belief systems whose views on success contrast greatly. The need for a holistic approach to social mobility is a pressing one in this context.

I believe that there is a clear road to reframing the concept of social mobility, if the desire is there to do so.

Step 4: Take middle-class social mobility seriously

It is an inevitable, if slightly disconcerting, reality that the most important ingredient in any reframing of success will be how it handles 'middle-class' aspirations. Defining this group may be fraught with difficulties, as argued earlier, but there is a significant percentage of the population who are not the super-rich but who are far from the poverty line. They tend to be those who shape opinion and control – if not the commanding heights – of what gets done in the economy. Achieving any form of social change without this group is difficult, if not impossible.

While the Social Mobility and Child Poverty Commission, for instance, is now doing valuable work to extend the social mobility discourse to include those in work, and to recognise progression to a broader range of educational institutions, the concern (which is not confined to the political Right) with self-recruiting elites continues to skew the social mobility focus. The academic study of social mobility is certainly not guilty of this bias, but the linear, ordinal, hierarchical structures within which it operates also means that there are limits to the upward mobility of those in higher occupational or income groups. The drawback of a definition of social mobility that confines the upward element of it effectively to those in lower socioeconomic groups is that it implies that those in higher groups are either happy to remain where they are, or that they are not striving to progress in their lives. However, the reality is that the majority of those in higher-skilled and higher-earning occupations make upward economic progression in their working lives, earning more money and achieving work promotions (UKCES 2011, ONS 2013).

In the US, President Obama has successfully tapped into the collective anxiety of middle-class groups over their life progression with his attempts to turn the social mobility lens on the pressures they face (The White House 2013). The problem with the approach that he takes, however, is that it locks in the idea that individual and collective welfare is a product of improvements in income. This therefore re-emphasises the belief that success can only be defined in terms of increased income.

How do we deal with this? Chapter Five looked at the 'work–life merge' and the trickledown effect of this to those across occupational categories. Banning people from receiving emails after 6pm is not necessarily the answer. Many of those most committed to work behave in this way because of their belief in a cause as much as a desire to earn more money. Exploring how breaking away from the 'merge' could be better incentivised for those who wish to is very important, but is not the only answer.

Reframing needs to take the form of a more coherent approach to the success question, covering lexicon, policy and discourse. The kind of national conversation that Sen (2009) advocates is crucial.

It is a losing battle to impose value change, be that for the middle class or any other group. Any change needs ownership, especially in the less deferential times of the early 21st century. What we also know is that any approach has to be aspirational and individualised – more affluent groups are characterised by these twin qualities. But the conversation itself is not enough – there needs to be action to give it any kind of momentum. This means weaving some of the ideas in this book together into a manifesto for holistic social mobility and success.

Step 5: Creating a manifesto for holistic social mobility and success

Creating such a manifesto means linking social mobility with issues right across the policy spectrum. A number of ideas have already been outlined in this book, such as a living salary; the upgrading and 'creatification' of low-skilled work; placing pupils at the centre of schooling and moving beyond attainment as the only goal of schooling; the 'diversification' of HE and prioritising inclusive growth which includes non-monetary and monetary dimensions.

But there is no magic bullet here. Although new policies themselves are important, not everything can be changed. What is as, if not more, important, is the way in which ongoing issues and the policies in place to address them are approached. A manifesto for holistic social mobility means looking at all policy decisions pertaining to the question of success (which is most policy decisions in this context) through this particular lens. It means looking systematically to recast the relationship between the different aspects of well-being described in Chapter Eight and income and wealth, but doing so in gradual ways so as not to denigrate the importance of economic factors. In practice this means looking for ways in which improving health, engagement with civic issues or education are not associated solely with money. To an extent, this sounds like a defence of the encroaching forces of the market that Sandel is so keen to advocate (Sandel 2012), which can also be identified within much social democratic thinking. Holistic social mobility provides another way of framing economic factors in the context of individual empowerment and aspiration as well as utilising them as a vehicle toward value change.

Finally, creating such a manifesto means confronting the issues of spiritual fulfilment and ethical behaviour touched on in Chapter Six through the work of Stephen Green and Oliver James, for example (Green 2009, James 2007) . The starting point here may be with the institutions of society. From education and the legal system to business and politics, should there be greater and more explicit debate and concern with their goals, purposes and behaviour? There have been repeated instances in recent years of 'unethical' institutional behaviour in the business world (as highlighted by Eccles and Serafeim (2013). In 2015 the Governor of the Bank of England, Mark Carney, in his annual Mansions House speech, pointed to the need for markets to have what he called a 'social licence': 'Markets are not ends in themselves, but powerful means for prosperity and security for all. As such they need to retain the consent of society – a social licence – to be allowed to operate, innovate and grow' (Carney 2015).

However, while there is some agreement over what institutions should not do, that is, avoid tax in the case of business, or falsify expense claims in the case of politicians, there is less about what they should aspire to do. An imaginative policy approach to institutional behaviour would start by looking at how they can provide a vision that supports the improvement in well-being of their stakeholders. The recent discussions in the UK on inclusive capitalism have been a useful starting point, but they need to be underpinned by more ambitious set of questions that go beyond asking what business should *do* to what business is *for*. They must also embrace the other institutions that are equally essential for a capitalist society to flourish within state and civil society, to avoid accusations of scapegoating a business or being anti-business, but also because they are equally important to any value change project (Boleat 2014, Byrne and Cruddas 2014, OECD 2014b, Mian 2015).

The creation of a holistic social mobility manifesto is the final step in the reframing exercise suggested here. It requires further research and analysis, but as this book has argued, the case for this is compelling.

The case for holistic social mobility

This book began by asking whether the recent attention paid to social mobility was little more than a moral panic. It has been argued that while the way in which many politicians and political commentators have picked up on the issue is consistent with the phenomenon of moral panic, the focus on it also highlights the more fundamental challenges facing the UK in the early 21st century.

The way in which social mobility is addressed by policy makers and academics, however, is set within narrow orthodoxies, which means that social mobility is not connected to these challenges as well as it could be. It is benefiting from too much attention, if anything, in how it is conceived at present. As Pearce argues, talking about the need for a broader 'statecraft' in such a scenario: 'Social mobility aspirations would be set alongside wider economic and social ambitions, and they would be one chapter in a longer book, not the beginning and end of social policy' (Pearce 2012: 2).

In contrast, however, a holistic approach to social mobility offers a route into the exact set of bigger questions regarding what sort of society we want and need, which Pearce thinks the present 'moral panic' social mobility discourse is diverting attention away from. It enables a more tangible approach to these anxieties to be developed. The major issues facing not just one country but all countries are not currently being met with great political (or academic) vision. Many of political leaders in the West appear cowed by the threat of economic recession and voter disillusionment. They seem more keen to focus on the achievement of minor goals that they think they can deliver on ('kitchen table politics', as it is described), rather than striving for anything more ambitious.

It is essential that politicians focus on the daily challenges of the population, but they must connect these with the same broader issues that are both part of and frame these daily discussions.

Examining these major issues through a holistic social mobility approach, however, still enables a focus on everyday issues to be retained. In this vein, it makes it a potentially appealing proposition, as it appears in the spirit of the times. However, as important as it is to have the ability to deconstruct these challenges and to find practical ways forward, the need for a broader vision is inescapable. Creating more space in how success is defined for a broader range of factors requires a coherent narrative that articulates why this should be done and how it would work. It requires those from politics, and from academia as well, to have the courage to develop, own and personify this vision, and to give it credibility. And there should be no illusions about the scale of this task. There are significant vested interests where social mobility is concerned, with some who may be as resistant to change as the forces that constrain much (upward) social mobility. But the task itself is too important to avoid. Unless the balance in people's motivations for themselves and their family can be shifted towards a different idea of progress, then the adjustment required by any move to a new industrial age will be far more painful, and the consequences for the planet and future generations who inhabit it far more severe.

Facing our future challenges is going to take more than extending educational opportunities or creating more high-skilled jobs, but it requires a change in values'. We can no longer afford social mobility to be just one chapter of a longer book. It has to be the whole story.

Bibliography

Abdallah, S and Shah, S, 2012, *Well-Being Patterns Uncovered: An Analysis of UK Data*, London: New Economics Foundation

Addley, E, 2014, Vicars report greatest job satisfaction while publicans are least happy, *The Guardian*, 21 March, www.theguardian.com/money/2014/mar/21/vicars-greatest-job-satisfaction-publicans-least-happy

Agarwal, A, 2013, Unbundled: Reimagining higher education, *Huffington Post*, 12 September, www.huffingtonpost.com/anant-agarwal/unbundled-reimagining-higher-education_b_4414048.html

Aghion, P, Besley, T, Browne, J, Caselli, F, Lambert, R, Lomax, R, Pissarides, C, Stern, N and van Reenen, J, 2013, Investing for Prosperity, Report of the LSE Growth Commission Skills, *Infrastructure and Innovation*, London: London School of Economics

Aldrich, R (ed) 2001, *A Century of Education*, London: Routledge

Alesina, A F, and Giuliano, P, 2009, Preferences for Redistribution, Working Paper 14825, Cambridge, MA: The National Bureau of Economic Research

Altbach, P G, Reisberg, L and Rumbley, E, 2009, *Trends in Global Higher Education: Tracking an Academic Revolution*, Report prepared for the UNESCO 2009 World Conference on Higher Education, Paris: UNECSO

All-Party Parliamentary Group on Social Mobility (APPG), 2012, *Seven Key Truths about Social Mobility*, London: APPG

All-Party Parliamentary Group on Social Mobility (APPG), 2013, *Social Mobility Goldspots: Capital Mobility*, London: APPG

Anderson, P, 2009, *Intermediate occupations and the conceptual and empirical limitations of the hourglass economy thesis, Work, Employment & Society*, 23, 1, 169-80

Anderson, R, 2014, *Making Education Work: A Report from an Independent Advisory Group chaired by Professor Sir Roy Anderson*, London: Pearson

Anderton, E and Bevan, S, 2014, *Constrained Work? Job Enrichment and Employee Engagement in Low Wage, Low Skill Jobs*, London: The Work Foundation

Archer, W and Davison J, 2008, *Graduate Employability: the Views of the Employers*. London, the Council for Industry and Higher Education (CIHE).

Archer, L, Hollingworth, S and Halsall, A, 2007, University's not for me – I'm a Nike person': Urban, working-class young people's negotiations of 'style', identity and educational engagement, *Sociology*, 41, 2, 219-37

Atherton, G, 2010, Allocating Resources to Widen Participation in Higher Education for Young People in England, in Jones, P, Storan, J, Hudson, T and Braham, J (eds) *Towards a New Agenda for Lifelong Learning: Access, Diversity and Participation*, London: University of East London

Atherton, G, 2012, AccessHE: can collaborative outreach work continue in London after Aimhigher?, *Widening Participation and Lifelong Learning*, 13, 1, 93-9

Atherton, G and Jenkins, P M, 2015, *Children as Change Agents*, Liverpool: University of Liverpool,

Atherton, G, Roberts, K, Remedios, R and Page, L, 2009, *How Young People Formulate Views of the Future: Exploratory Research with Year 7 Pupils*, London: Department for Children, Schools and Families

Atik, N, 2012, We aren't freaks: Women who don't want children should not be made outcasts, *The Mirror*, 22 June, www.mirror.co.uk/lifestyle/women-are-not-freaks-just-because-905131#ixzz31XZuWSJ2

Autor, D H and Katz, L, 2010, *Grand challenges in the study of employment and technological change: A white paper prepared for the National Science Foundation*, www.aeaweb.org/econwhitepapers/white_papers/David_Autor.pdf

Ball, S J, 2002, *Class Strategies and the Education Market: The Middle Classes and Social Advantage*, London: Routledge

Ball, S J, 2010, *New voices, new knowledges and the new politics of education research: The gathering of a perfect storm?*, European Educational Research Journal, 9, 2

Ball, S J, 2011, Back to the 19th century with Michael Gove's education bill, *The Guardian*, 31 January, www.theguardian.com/commentisfree/2011/jan/31/michael-gove-education-bill

Barber, M, Donnelly, K and Rizvi, S, 2013, *An Avalanche is Coming: Higher Education and the Revolution Ahead*, London: Institute for Public Policy Research

Barnet, R J and Cavanagh J, 1994, *Global Dreams: Imperial Corporations and the New World Order*, New York: Touchstone

Barnett, R, 2011, The Idea of the University in the Twenty-First Century: Where's the Imagination? *International Higher Education Congress: New Trends and Issues*, 27-29 May, Istanbul, Turkey

Barnett, R, 2012, *Imagining the University (New Studies in Critical Realism and Education)*, London: Routledge

Barnett, R, 2013, Wanted: New visions of the university, *University World News*, 16 March

Barrett, R and Clothier, P, 2012, *The United Kingdom Values Survey: Increasing Happiness by Understanding What People Value*, London: Barrett Values Centre, www.valuescentre.com/uploads/2013-01-23/UK%20National%20Values%20Values%20Assessment%20Report%20-%20Jan%2024th%202013.pdf

BBC News, 2009, Nursing to become graduate entry, 12 November, http://news.bbc.co.uk/1/hi/health/8355388.stm

BBC News, 2014a, Character can and should be taught in school, says Hunt, 12 February, www.bbc.co.uk/news/uk-england-london-26140607

BBC News, 2014b, Graduate starting salaries 'drop 11% over five years', 14 April, www.bbc.co.uk/news/education-26992728

BBC News, 2014c, Working Men's Clubs fight for survival, 5 February, www.bbc.co.uk/news/magazine-26015247

Beechler, S and Woodward, I C, 2009, The global 'war for talent', *Journal of International Management*, 15, 273-85

Bell, D, 1973, *The Coming of Post-Industrial Society: A Venture in Social Forecasting*, New York: Basic Books

Belt, V and Giles, L, 2009, *High Performance Working: A Synthesis of Key Literature*, London: United Kingdom Commission for Employment and Skills

Bennet, R and Kottasz, R, 2012, Public attitudes towards the UK banking industry following the global financial crisis, *International Journal of Bank Marketing*, 30, 2, 128-47

Bialik, C, 2010, Seven careers in a lifetime? Think twice, researchers say, *Wall Street Journal*, 4 September, http://online.wsj.com/news/articles/SB10001424052748704206804575468162805877990

Binkley, M, Erstad, O, Herman, J, Raizen, S, Ripley, M, Miller-Ricci, M and Runble, M, 2012, Defining twenty-first century skills, in Griffin, P, McGraw, B and Care, E (eds) *Assessment and Teaching of 21st Century Skills*, Netherlands: Springer, 17-66

Birdwell, J, Grist, M & Margo, J, 2011, *the forgotten half a demos and private equity foundation report* London:Demos

Birdwell, J, 2014, *Introducing Generation Citizen*, London: Demos

Blair, A, 2001, Full text of Tony Blair's speech on education, *The Guardian*, 23 May, www.theguardian.com/politics/2001/may/23/labour.tonyblair

Blair, A, 2007, Our nation's future: The role of work, www.number10.gov.uk/output/Page11405.asp

Blanden, J, 2009, *How Much Can We Learn From International Comparisons of Intergenerational Mobility?*, London: Centre for the Economics of Education

Blanden, J and Machin, S, 2004, Inequality in the expansion of higher education, *Scottish Journal of Political Economy*, Special Issue on Education, 51, 230-49

Blanden, J, Goodman, A, Gregg, P and Machin, S, 2001, *Changes in Intergenerational Mobility in Britain*, London: Centre for Economic Performance

Blanden, J, Gregg, P and Machin, S, 2005, *Intergenerational Mobility in Europe and North America: A Report Supported by the Sutton Trust*, London: Centre for Economic Performance

Blanden, J, Gregg, P and Macmillan, L, 2007, Accounting for intergenerational income persistence: Non-cognitive skills, ability and education, *Economic Journal*, 117, 43-60

Blanden, J, Gregg, P and Macmillan, L, 2011, Intergenerational Persistence in Income and Social Class: The Impact of Within-Group Inequality, IZA Discussion Paper 6202, Bonn: IZA

Blau, P M, 1956, Social mobility and interpersonal relations, *American Sociological Review*, 21, 3, 290-5

Blau, P M and Duncan, O, D, 1967, *The American Occupational Structure Paperback*, New York: Wiley Press

Blaug, R, Kenyon, A and Lekhi, R, 2007, *Stress at Work*, London: The Work Foundation

Bliss, O, 2013, Grammar schools are broken, and I should know, *Fabian Society*, 20 November, www.fabians.org.uk/grammar-schools-are-broken-and-i-should-know/

Boleat, M, 2014, Inclusive capitalism: searching for a purpose beyond profit, *The Guardian*, 27 May

Boliver, V, 2010, Maximally Maintained Inequality and Effectively Maintained Inequality in Education: Operationalizing the Expansion Inequality Relationship, *Sociology Working Papers Paper Number* 2010-05, Oxford: University of Oxford

Bolton, P, 2012, *Education: Historical Statistics*, London: House of Commons Library

Boudon, R, 1974, *Education, Opportunity, and Social Inequality: Changing Prospects in Western Society*, New York: Wiley

Bourdieu, P, 1992, *Language and Symbolic Power*, Cambridge: Polity Press

Bourdieu, P, 1996, *The State Nobility: Elite Schools in the Field of Power*, Cambridge, Polity Press

Brant, P, 2014, Who's frightened of being middle class?, *Social Mobility and Child Poverty Commission*, 26 February, https://smcpcommission.blog.gov.uk/2014/02/26/whos-frightened-of-being-middle-class/

Breen, R and Goldthorpe, J, 1999, Class inequality and meritocracy: a critique of Saunders and an alternative analysis, *British Journal of Sociology*, 5, 1, 1-27

Breen, R and Luijx, R, 2004, Social mobility in Europe between 1970 and 2000, in Breen, R, (ed) *Social Mobility in Europe*, Oxford: Oxford University Press, 37-75

Binkley, M, Erstad, O, Herman, J, Raizen, S, Ripley, M and Rumble, M, 2010, *Defining 21st Century Skills. Assessment and Teaching of 21st Century Skills: Draft White Paper.* The University of Melbourne.

Broughton, N, Ezeyi, O and Hupkau, C, 2014, *Riders on the Storm: Britain's Middle Income Households since 2007*, London: Social Market Foundation

Brown, P and Hesketh, A, 2004, *The Mismanagement of Talent: Employability and Jobs in the Global Economy*, Oxford: Oxford University Press

Brown, P, Ashton, D and Lauder, H, 2012, *The Global Auction: The Broken Promises of Education, Jobs, and Incomes*, Oxford: Oxford University Press

Brown, P, Ashton, D, Lauder, H and Theron, G, 2008, *Towards a High-Skilled, Low-Waged Workforce? A Review of Global Trends in Education, Employment and the Labour Market*, ESRC Funded Centre on Skills, Knowledge and Economic Performance (SKOPE), Cardiff and Oxford Universities

Brown, R and Carasso, H, 2013, *Everything for Sale? The Marketisation of UK Higher Education*, London: Routledge

Brynjolfsson, E and McAfee, A, 2014, *The Second Machine Age: Work, Progress, and Prosperity in a Time of Brilliant Technologies*, New York: W W Norton & Co

Bukodi, E and Goldthorpe, J H, 2009, *Class Origins, Education and Occupational Attainment: Cross-cohort Changes among Men in Britain*, London: Centre for Longitudinal Studies Institute of Education, University of London

Business Insider, 2012, *Richard Florida: It's up to the cities to bring America back*, 3 February, www.businessinsider.com/richard-florida-its-up-to-the-cities-to-bring-america-back-2012-2#ixzz31LbROlUa

Byrne, L and Cruddas, J, 2014, Liam Byrne and Jon Cruddas: Labour's plan for a capitalism that works for all, *London Evening Standard*, 5 June, www.standard.co.uk/comment/comment/liam-byrne-and-jon-cruddas-labours-plan-for-a-capitalism-that-works-for-all-9491828.html

Cabinet Office, 2009, *Panel on Fair Access to the Professions, Unleashing Aspiration: The Final Report of the Panel on Fair Access to the Professions*, London: HM Government

Cabinet Office, 2011, *Opening Doors, Breaking Barriers: A Strategy for Social Mobility*, London: HM Government

Cabinet Office, 2012, *Fair Access to Professional Careers: A progress report by the Independent Reviewer on Social Mobility and Child Poverty*, London: HM Government

Cameron, D, 2006, We are the party of class mobility, *The Guardian*, 3 December, www.theguardian.com/commentisfree/2006/dec/03/comment.politics2

Cameron, D, 2010, Prime Minister's speech on wellbeing: A transcript of a speech given by the Prime Minister on wellbeing on 25 November, www.gov.uk/government/speeches/pm-speech-on-wellbeing

Carney, M, 2015, Building real markets for the good of the people, Speech given at the Lord Mayor's Banquet for Bankers and Merchants of the City of London at the Mansion House, London, 10 June, Bank of England, www.bankofengland.co.uk/publications/Pages/speeches/2015/821.aspx

Causa, O and Johansson, A, 2010, *Intergenerational Social Mobility in OECD Countries*, Paris: OECD

Cavaille, C, and Trump, K-S, 2015, The Two Facets of Social Policy Preferences, http://papers.ssrn.com/sol3/papers.cfm?abstract_id=2110010, forthcoming in *The Journal of Politics*

CBI, 2009, *Future fit: Preparing graduates for the world of work*, London:CBI

Cedefop, 2011, *Labour Market Polarisation and Elementary Occupations in Europe: Blip or Long-Term Trend?*, Luxembourg: Publications Office of the European Union

Cedefop, 2013, Roads to Recovery: Three Skill and Labour Market Scenarios for 2025, *Greece: European Centre for Vocational Training*, Luxembourg: Publications Office of the European Union

Chetty, R, Hendren, N, Kline, P and Saez, E, 2014, *Where is the Land of Opportunity? The Geography of Intergenerational Mobility in the United States*, January, http://obs.rc.fas.harvard.edu/chetty/mobility_geo.pdf

Chong, D and Druckman, J N, 2007, Framing theory, *Annual Review of Political Science*, 10, 103-26

Christensen, C M, 1997, *The Innovator's Dilemma: When New Technologies Cause Great Firms to Fail*, Boston, MA: Harvard Business School Press

Cisco, 2010, *Education and Economic Growth: From the 19th to the 21st Century*, Cisco Systems Inc, www.cisco.com/web/strategy/docs/education/Education-and-Economic-Growth.pdf

Clark, A E, 1998, Measures of Job Satisfaction – What Makes a Good Job? Evidence from OECD Countries, Labour Market and Social Policy, Occasional Paper No 34, Paris: OECD

Clark, A E, 2005, Your money or your life: Changing job quality in OECD countries, *British Journal of Industrial Relations*, 43, 3, 377–400

Clark, T and Mason, R, 2013, Fury with MPs is main reason for not voting – poll, *The Guardian*, 26 December, www.theguardian.com/politics/2013/dec/26/fury-mps-not-voting-poll

Clegg, N, 2010, Nick Clegg delivers speech on social mobility, 18 August, www.libdems.org.uk/nick_clegg_delivers_speech_on_social_mobility

Clegg, N, 2013, Nick Clegg's speech to the Liberal Democrat conference: full text, *New Statesman*, 18 September, www.newstatesman.com/politics/2013/09/nick-cleggs-speech-liberal-democrat-conference-full-text

Clifton J, Thompson S, and Thorley, C, 2014, *Winning the Global Race*, London: Institute for Public Policy Research

Cohen, S, 2011, *Folk Devils and Moral Panics*, London: Routledge

Cohen, T and Bloom, B, 2014, Too many Old Etonians in No 10, declares Michael Gove: Domination of one school in public life is 'ridiculous', *Daily Mail*, 15 March, www.dailymail.co.uk/news/article-2581299/Eton-mess-Michael-Gove-attacks-ridiculous-number-wealthy-ministers-Cabinet-claims-exclusive-developed-world.html

Collier, P, 2000, Economic causes of civil conflict and their implications for policy, in Chester, A, Hampson, C and Aall, P (eds) *Managing Global Chaos*, Washington DC: US Institute of Peace and World Bank

Collini, S, 2012, *What Are Universities For?*, London: Penguin

Collins, N, 2012, Nature vs nurture: outcome depends on where you live, *Telegraph online*, 12 June, www.telegraph.co.uk/science/science-news/9326819/Nature-vs-nurture-outcome-depends-on-where-you-live.html

Collins, N, 2013, Poorer pupils held back by 'soft bigotry of low expectations': Michael Gove says Britain has failed to create a 'colour-blind' society, *Telegraph*, 22 November, www.telegraph.co.uk/education/educationnews/10468677/Poorer-pupils-held-back-by-soft-bigotry-of-low-expectations.html

Commission on Social Justice, 1994, *Social Justice: Strategies for National Renewal (The Report of the Commission on Social Justice)*, London: Vintage

Corak, M, 2006, Do poor children become poor adults? Lessons from a cross country comparison of generational earnings mobility, IZA Discussion Papers, No 1993, Berlin: IZA

Corak, M, 2012, Inequality from generation to generation: The United States in comparison, in Rycroft, R (ed) *The Economics of Inequality, Poverty, and Discrimination in the 21st Century*, New York: Praeger

Corry, D, Valero, A and van Reenen, J, 2011, *UK Economic Performance since 1997: Growth, Productivity and Jobs*, London: Centre for Economic Performance, London School of Economics and Political Science

Cowen, T, 2013, *Average is Over: Powering America Beyond the Age of the Great Stagnation*, New York: EP Dutton & Co

Coughlan, S, 2013a, Harvard plans to boldly go with 'Spocs', 24 September, www.bbc.co.uk/news/business-24166247

Coughlan, S, 2013b, Would $4,000 make poor children cleverer?, 13 November, www.bbc.co.uk/news/business-24821383

Cramme, O, 2011, *The Changing Space for EU Politics: Democracy and Ideology in Times of Crisis*, London: Policy Network

Cramme, O, Diamond, P and McTernan, M, 2013, *Progressive Politics After the Crash: Governing from the Left*, London: Policy Network

Crawford, C and Wenchao, J, 2014, *Payback Time? Student Debt and Loan Repayments: What Will the 2012 Reforms Mean for Graduates?*, London: Institute for Fiscal Studies

Crossick, G, 2012, *The Future is More than just Tomorrow: Higher Education, the Economy and the Longer Term*, London: Universities UK

Crouch, C, 1977, *Class Conflict and the Industrial Relations Crisis*, London: Ashgate

Crouch, C, 2008, What will follow the demise of privatised Keynesianism?, *Political Quarterly*, 79, 4, 476-87

Crouch, C, 2009, *Post-Democracy*, London: Polity Press

Cruddas, J, 2013, Jon Cruddas's speech to the Resolution Foundation: full text, *New Statesman*, 6 February, www.newstatesman.com/politics/2013/02/jon-cruddass-speech-resolution-foundation-full-text

Cummings, C, Laing, K, Law, J, McLaughlin, J, Papps, I, Todd, L and Woolner, P, 2012, *Can Changing Aspirations and Attitudes Impact on Educational Attainment? A Review of Interventions*, York: Joseph Rowntree Foundation

Danczuk, S, 2013, Business rates are becoming an attack on social mobility, *Telegraph*, 3 December 2013, www.telegraph.co.uk/news/politics/10491602/Business-rates-are-becoming-an-attack-on-social-mobility.html

Dar, A, 2013, Elections: Turnout, *House of Commons Library*, 3 July

Davies, W, 2013, Policymakers are mistaken if they think legitimacy is merely a question of being led by evidence-based data, www.thersa.org/fellowship/journal/archive/issue-4-2013/features/emperical-limit

Dean, H, 2009, Critiquing capabilities: the distractions of a beguiling concept, *Critical Social Policy*, 29, 2, 261-73

DeBoer, J, Stump, G S, Breslow, L and Seaton, D T, 2013, Diversity in MOOC Students' Backgrounds and Behaviors in Relationship to Performance in 6.002x, *Proceeding of Sixth International Conference of MIT's Learning International Networks Consortium (LINC)*

de Castella, T, 2014, Could work emails be banned after 6pm?, *BBC News*, 10 April, www.bbc.co.uk/news/magazine-26958079

Deem, R, Hillyard, S and Reed, M, 2007, *Knowledge, Higher Education, and the New Managerialism: The Changing Management of UK Universities*, Oxford: Oxford University Press

Deloitte, 2013, London is the world's biggest employer of high skill people, 11 November, www.deloitte.com/view/en_GB/uk/about/931b4764c0742410VgnVCM2000003356f70aRCRD.htm

Department for Business, Innovation and Skills (BIS), 2013a, *Participation Rates in Higher Education: Academic Years 2006/07-2011/12*, London: BIS

Department for Business, Innovation and Skills (BIS), 2013b, *The Benefits of Higher Education Participation for Individuals and Society: Key Findings and Reports, 'The Quadrants'*, BIS Research Paper, London: BIS

Department for Business, Innovation and Skills (BIS), 2013c, *The Business Case for Equality and Diversity: A Survey of the Academic Literature*, London: BIS

Department for Business, Innovation and Skills (BIS), 2014, *National Strategy for Access and Student Success in Higher Education*, London: BIS

Department for Education (DfE), 2010, *The Importance of Teaching: The Schools White Paper*, London: DfE

Department for Education (DfE), 2014, Michael Gove speaks about the future of education reform, London: DfE, www.gov.uk/government/speeches/michael-gove-speaks-about-the-future-of-education-reform

Department for Education and Skills (DfES), 2003, *The Future of Higher Education*, London: DfES

Department for Innovation, Universities and Skills (DIUS), 2007, *World Class Skills: Implementing the Leitch Review of Skills in England*, London: DIUS

Diaz-Serrano, L and Cabral Vieira, J A, 2005, Low pay, higher pay and job satisfaction within the European Union: Empirical evidence from fourteen countries, IZA Discussion Papers No 1558, Berlin: Institute for the Study of Labour (IZA), http://ideas.repec.org/p/iza/izadps/dp1558.html

Dorling, D, 2011, *Fair Play: A Daniel Dorling Reader on Social Justice*, Bristol: Policy Press

Dorling, D, 2013, Debates about the cultural aspects of class risk distracting us from the brute material reality of how much class actually matters, LSE Politics and Policy Blog, 30 April, http://blogs.lse.ac.uk/politicsandpolicy/archives/32797

Dorling, D, 2014, Is the British education system designed to polarise people?, *The Guardian*, 4 February, www.theguardian.com/education/2014/feb/04/education-system-polarises-people-economic-inequality

Drucker, P, 1959, *Landmarks of Tomorrow*, New York: Harper

Easterlin, R, 1974, Does economic growth improve the human lot? Some empirical evidence, in David, P A and Reder, M W (eds) *Nations and Households in Economic Growth: Essays in Honor of Moses Abramovitz*, New York: Academic Press, Inc

Easterlin, R and Angelescu, N, 2009, Happiness and growth the world over: Time series evidence on the happiness-income paradox, Discussion Paper No 4060, http://ftp.iza.org/dp4060.pdf

Easterlin, R A, McVey, L A, Switek, M, Sawangfa, O and Zweig, J S, 2010, The happiness-income paradox revisited, *Proceedings of the National Academy of Sciences*, 107, 52

Eccles, R G and Serafeim, G, 2013, The performance frontier: Innovating for a sustainable strategy, *Harvard Business Review*, May

Elias, P and Purcell, K, 2012, Higher education and social background, in McFall, S L (ed) *Understanding Society: Findings 2012*, Colchester: Institute for Social and Economic Research, University of Essex

Erikson, R and Goldthorpe, J H, 2010, Has social mobility in Britain decreased? Reconciling divergent findings on income and class mobility, *British Journal of Sociology*, 61, 2, 211-30

Euractiv.com, 2013, EU threatened by 'rampant right-wing populism', warns German think tank, 5 December 2013, www.euractiv.com/eu-elections-2014/rampant-right-wing-populism-thre-news-532119

Federation of Small Businesses, 2013, Reform of GCSEs – what small businesses want, www.fsb.org.uk/policy/assets/fsb-gcse-paper.pdf

Feinstein, L and Duckworth, K, 2006, *Development in the Early Years: Its Importance for School Performance and Adult Outcomes*, London: Centre for Research on the Wider Benefits of Learning, Institute of Education, University of London

Felstead, A, Gallie, D, Green, F and Hande, I, 2012, *Skills at Work in Britain: First Findings from the Skills and Employment Survey 2012*, London: Centre for Employment Research

Florida, R, 2005, *The Flight of the Creative Class: The New Global Competition for Talent*, Boston, MA: HarperBusiness

Ford, S, 2009, Nursing to become degree only profession, *Health Service Journal*, 12 November

Fothergill, S, Kitson, M and Monk, S, 1985, *Urban Industrial Change: The Causes of the Urban-Rural Contrast in Manufacturing Employment Trends*, London: HMSO

Frey, C and Osborne, M, 2013, The future of employment: how susceptible are jobs to computerisation?, www.oxfordmartin.ox.ac.uk/downloads/academic/The_Future_of_Employment.pdf

Friedman, S, 2013, The price of the ticket: Rethinking the experience of social mobility, *Sociology*, 18 July

Fuller, A and Unwin, L, 2012, Banging on the door of the university: The complexities of progression from apprenticeship and other vocational programmes in England, *Monograph No 14*, Southampton: LLAKES Centre, Institute of Education, University of Southampton

Gander, K, 2014, Maths teachers in England must learn from China to end '15 year stagnation' says government minister, *Independent*, 26 February, www.independent.co.uk/news/uk/home-news/maths-teachers-in-england-must-learn-from-china-to-end-15-year-stagnation-says-government-minister-9154976.html

Gardiner, B, Martin, R and Tyler P, 2012, *Spatially Unbalanced Growth in the British Economy*, Cambridge: Centre for Geographical Economic Research

Garner, R, 2013, Michael Gove creating 'neo Victorian' curriculum for primary schools, says professor who led massive review into sector, *Independent*, 24 September, www.independent.co.uk/news/education/education-news/michael-gove-creating-neo-victorian-curriculum-for-primary-schools-says-professor-who-led-massive-review-into-sector-8837223.html

Gershuny, J and Fisher, K, 2014, Post-industrious society: Why work time will not disappear for our grandchildren, Sociology Working Papers Number 2014-03, Oxford: University of Oxford

Glasman, M, Rutherford, J, Stears, M and White, S, 2012, *The Labour Tradition and the Politics of Paradox*, London: Lawrence Wishart

Glass, D V, 1954, *Social Mobility in Britain*, London: Routledge

Goldthorpe, J H, 1996, Class analysis and the reorientation of class theory: The case of persisting differentials in educational attainment, *British Journal of Sociology*, 47, 481-505

Goldthorpe, J H, 2007, Cultural capital: Some critical observations, *Sociologica*, 2

Goldthorpe, J H, 2012, Understanding – and misunderstanding – social mobility in Britain: The entry of the economists, the confusion of politicians and the limits of educational policy, Oxford: Oxford University Press, www.spi.ox.ac.uk/fileadmin/documents/PDF/Goldthorpe_Social_Mob_paper_01.pdf

Goldthorpe, J H, 2013, Five minutes with John Goldthorpe: More equal mobility chances are unlikely to be achieved without having a generally more equal society, London School of Economics and Political Science Blog, 13 August, http://blogs.lse.ac.uk/politicsandpolicy/archives/35681

Goldthorpe, J H and Erikson, R, 1992, *The Constant Flux: A Study of Social Mobility in Industrial Societies*, Oxford: Clarendon

Goldthorpe, J H and Jackson, M, 2007, Intergenerational class mobility in contemporary Britain: Political concerns and empirical findings, *The British Journal of Sociology*, 58, 525-46

Goldthorpe, J H and Mills, C, 2008, Trends in intergenerational class mobility in modern Britain: Evidence from national surveys, 1972-2005, *National Institute Economic Review*, 205, 83-100

Goldthorpe, J H, Llewellyn, C and Payne, C, 1980, *Social Mobility and Class Structure in Modern Britain*, Oxford: Oxford University Press

Goldthorpe, J H, Lockwood, D, Bechofer, F and Platt, J, 1968, *The Affluent Worker: Political Attitudes and Behaviour*, London: Cambridge University Press

Goode, E and Ben-Yahuda, N, 2009, *Moral Panics*, London: Wiley Blackwell

Goodman, A and Gregg, O (eds), 2010, *Poorer Children's Educational Attainment: How Important Are Attitudes and Behaviours?*, York: Joseph Rowntree Foundation

Goodman, H, 2011, *Tradition and Change: Four People: A Response to the Politics of Paradox by Helen Goodman MP*, http://liberalconspiracy.org/images/misc/Helen%20Goodman%20MP%20-%20Tradition%20and%20Change.pdf

Goos, M and Manning, A, 2007, Lousy jobs and lovely jobs: the rising polarization of work in Britain, *The Review of Economics and Statistics*, 89, 1, 118-33

Goos, M, Manning, A and Salomons, A, 2010, Explaining job polarization in Europe: The roles of technology, globalization and institutions, CEP Discussion Paper No 1026

Gorard, S, 2008, A re-consideration of rates of 'social mobility' in Britain: or why research impact is not always a good thing, *British Journal of Sociology of Education*, 29, 3, 317-24

Gorard, S, Adnett, N, May, H, Slack, K, Smith, E and Thomas, L, 2006, *Review of Widening Participation Research: Addressing the Barriers to Participation in Higher Education*, Bristol: HEFCE

Gordon, D, Mack, J, Lansley, S, Main, G, Nandy, S, Patsios, D, Pomati, M and the Poverty and Social Exclusion team, 2013, The impoverishment of the UK: PSE UK First results: Living standards, www.poverty.ac.uk/system/files/attachments/The_Impoverishment_of_the_UK_PSE_UK_first_results_summary_report_March_28.pdf

Gordon, R J, 2012, Is US economic growth over? Faltering innovation confronts the six headwinds, NBER Working Paper No 18315, August, Cambridge, MA: The National Bureau of Economic Research, www.nber.org/papers/w18315

Goss, J, 1995, Marketing the new marketing: The strategic discourse of geodemographic information systems, in Pickles, J (ed) *Ground Truth*, New York: Guilford, 130-70

Gove, M, 2013, *Oral statement by Michael Gove on education reform*, 11 June, London: Department for Education

Graham, C and Nikolova, M, 2013, Happy peasants and frustrated achievers? Agency, capabilities, and subjective well-being, Human Capital and Economic Opportunity Global Working Group, Working Paper No. 2013-013, Chicago, IL: Economics Research Center, University of Chicago

Graham, C and Nikolova, M, 2014, Why aging and working makes us happy in 4 charts, 28 March, Brookings Upfront, www.brookings.edu/blogs/up-front/posts/2014/03/27-happiness-economics-employment-graham

Greater London Authority (GLA), 2013, *The London Annual Education Report 2013*, London: GLA

Green, A, 2012, Skills for competitiveness: Country report for United Kingdom, OECD Local Economic and Employment Development (LEED) Working Papers, 2012/05, Paris: OECD, http://dx.doi.org/10.1787/5k9bb1vc6skf-en

Green, A, 2013, *Education and State Formation: Europe, East Asia and the USA*, London: Palgrave

Green, A, Atfield, G, Adam, D and Staniewicz, T, 2013, *Determinants of the Composition of the Workforce in Low Skilled Sectors of the UK Economy Lot 2 Qualitative Research – Final Report*, University of Warwick: Warwick Institute for Employment Research

Green, S, 2009, *Good Value: Reflections on Money, Morality and an Uncertain World*, London: Atlantic Monthly Press

Grice, A, 2013, Alan Milburn and Gillian Shephard: 'The Government must be judged by its actions, not words. Our job is to judge the actions', *Independent*, 21 April, www.independent.co.uk/news/uk/politics/alan-milburn-and-gillian-shephard-the-government-must-be-judged-by-its-actions-not-words-our-job-is-to-judge-the-actions-8582000.html

Group of Eight, 2013, The Changing PhD, Melbourne: Group of Eight

Grove, J, 2014, Sodexo-Times Higher Education University Lifestyle Survey results, *Times Higher Education*, 13 March

Grusky, D B and Weeden, K A, 2006, Does the sociological approach to studying social mobility have a future?, in Morgan, S, Fields, G and Grusky, D B (eds) *Mobility and Inequality: Frontiers of Research from Sociology and Economics*, Stanford, CA: Stanford University Press, 85-108

Hackett, L, Shutt, L and Maclachlan, N, 2012, The way we'll work: Labour market trends and preparing for the hourglass, London: University Alliance, The-way-we-ll-work-Labour-market-trends-and-preparing-for-the-hourglass

Hall, M, 2012, *Inequality and Higher Education: Marketplace or Social Justice?*, London: Leadership Foundation on Higher Education

Hannon, C and Tims, C, 2010, *An Anatomy of Youth*, London: Demos

Harris, M, 2010, *What More Can Be Done to Widen Access to Highly Selective Universities?*, Bristol: Office for Fair Access

Heath, A F, 1981, *Social Mobility*, London: Fontana

Heckman, J J, 1995, Lessons from the bell curve, *Journal of Political Economy*, 103, 5, 1091-120

Heckman, J J, 2008, Schools, skills, and synapses, economic inquiry, *Western Economic Association International*, 46, 3, 289-324

Heckman, J J, 2012, *Giving Kids a Fair Chance*, Cambridge, MA: The MIT Press

Heckman, J J and Mosso, S, 2013, *The Economics of Human Development and Social Mobility*, 8 October, Lecture, www.sv.uio.no/econ/english/research/news-and-events/events/guest-lectures-seminars/Thursday-seminar/2013/papers/heckman-the-economics-of-human-development.pdf

Heckman, J J, Stixrud, J and Urzua, S, 2006, The effects of cognitive and noncognitive abilities on labor market outcomes and social behavior, NBER Working Paper No 12006, January, Cambridge, MA: The National Bureau for Economic Research

Heckman, J J, Seong Hyeok Moon, S H, Pinto, R, Savelyev, P and Yavitz, A, 2009, The rate of return to the high/scope perry preschool program, NBER Working Paper No 15471, November, Cambridge, MA: The National Bureau of Economic Research

Helliker, A, 2010, Old school ties in David Cameron's camp, *Daily Express*, 4 July, www.express.co.uk/comment/columnists/adam-helliker/184878/Old-school-ties-in-David-Cameron-s-camp

Helm, T, 2011, Most Britons believe children will have worse lives than their parents – poll, *The Guardian*, 3 December, www.theguardian.com/society/2011/dec/03/britons-children-lives-parents-poll

Henn, M and Foard, N, 2011, Young people, political participation and trust in Britain, EPOP Annual Conference, University of Exeter, 9-11 September, Nottingham Trent University

Hennessy, P, 2008, Gordon Brown: Britain is ready for a new wave of social mobility, *Telegraph*, 20 September, www.telegraph.co.uk/news/politics/labour/3023545/Gordon-Brown-Britain-is-ready-for-a-new-wave-of-social-mobility.html

Higher Education Funding Council for England (HEFCE), 2013, *Higher Education and Beyond: Outcomes from Full-Time First Degree Study*, Bristol: HEFCE

Higher Education Funding Council for England, 2015, *Delivering Opportunities for Students and Maximising their Success: Evidence for Policy and Practice 2015-2020*, Bristol: HEFCE

Higher Education Statistical Agency (HESA), 2014, *Statistical First Release 197 – Student Enrolments and Qualifications*, Cheltenham: HESA

Hinsliff, G, 2013, The merge: how our work–life balance is changing, *The Guardian*, 1 January, www.theguardian.com/money/2013/jan/01/merge-work-life-balance

HM Government, 2011, *Opening Doors, Breaking Barriers: A Strategy for Social Mobility*, London: HM Government

HM Treasury, 2006, *Leitch Review of Skills – Prosperity for All in the Global Economy – World Class Skills*, London: HM Treasury

Holmes, C, 2010, Job polarisation in the UK: An assessment using longitudinal data, SKOPE Research Paper No 90, Oxford: SKOPE, University of Oxford

Holmes, P and Mayhew, K, 2012, *The Changing Shape of the UK Job Market and its Implications for the Bottom Half of Earners*, London: Resolution Foundation

Holmes, C and Tholen, G, 2013, Occupational mobility and career paths in the 'hourglass' labour market, SKOPE Research Paper No 113, Oxford: SKOPE, University of Oxford

Huberman, A M, 1973, *Understanding Change in Education: An Introduction*, Paris: UNESCO

Hutton, W, 1996, *The State We're In: Why Britain Is in Crisis and How to Overcome It*, revised edition, London: Vintage

Hutton, W, 2003, *The World We're In*, London: Abacus

Hutton, W, 2012, *The Work Foundation 2012 Annual Debate: Does the Economy Need a New Kind of Business?*, Lancaster: The Work Foundation

Institute for Public Policy Research (IPPR) Commission on the Future of Higher Education, 2013, *A Critical Path: The Future of Higher Education in England*, London: IPPR

James, O, 2007, *Affluenza*, London: Vermilion

Johnson, P and Floud, R, 2014, *The Cambridge Economic History of Modern Britain*: Volume 3, Cambridge: Cambridge University Press

Kaplanis, I, 2007, *The Geography of Employment Polarisation in Britain*, London: Institute for Public Policy Research

Keep, E, 2013, Education, Skill and Empowering the Individual in the Labour Market, Public lecture at the University of Cardiff, 17 January, www.skope.ox.ac.uk/events/2013/01/17/public-lecture-prof-ewart-keep-titled-education-skill-and-empowering-individual-la

Keep, E and James, S, 2010, What incentives to learn at the bottom end of the labour market?, SKOPE Research Paper No 94 July, Cardiff University and SKOPE: University of Oxford, www.skope.ox.ac.uk/sites/default/files/RP94.pdf

Kellner, P, 2012, Labour's lost votes, *Prospect Magazine*, 17 October, www.prospectmagazine.co.uk/features/labour-voters-election-europe-immigration

Kelly, U and McNicol, P, 2011, *Through a Glass, Darkly: Measuring the Social Value of Universities*, National Centre for Public Engagement

Kerr, C J, Dunlop, J T, Harbison, F H and Myers, C A, 1973, *Industrialism and Industrial Man*, Harmondsworth: Penguin (first published 1960)

Keynes, J M, 1931/72, *Economic Possibilities for Our Grandchildren, in Essays in Persuasion*, New York: Harcourt, Brace & Company, 358-74

Kinchelloe, J L, Gresson, A and Steinberg, S, 1997, Measured lies: The liberal theories of industrialism, *Bell Curve Examined*, New York: Palgrave Macmillan

King, S, 2014, When the money runs out: The end of Western affluence, *New Haven*, CT: Yale University Press

King, R, Marginson, S and Naidoo, R, 2013, *The Globalization of Higher Education*, London: Edward Elgar Publishing

Kirkup, J, 2015, Well done, David Cameron: Social mobility and equal opportunities are Conservative ideas again, *The Telegraph*, 7th October 2015 www.telegraph.co.uk/news/politics/david-cameron/11916975/Well-done-David-Cameron-Social-mobility-and-equal-opportunities-are-Conservative-ideas-again.html

Korenman, S and Winship, C, 1995, A re-analysis of the bell curve, NBER Working Paper Series, w5230, Cambridge, MA: The National Bureau of Economic Research

Kroll, C, 2011, *Measuring Progress and Well-Being Achievements and Challenges of a New Global Movement*, Berlin: Friedrich-Ebert-Stiftung

Labour Party, 2011, Ed Miliband warns British promise being broken, www.labour.org.uk/ed-miliband-warns-british-promise-being-broken

Labour Party, 2013, Ed Miliband's speech to Policy Network – Labour's new agenda, www.labour.org.uk/labours-new-agenda

Lakoff, G, 1990, *Don't Think of an Elephant: Know Your Values and Frame the Debate*, New York: Chelsea Green Publishing Company

Lambert, P, Prandy, K and Bottero W, 2007, By slow degrees: Two centuries of social reproduction and mobility in Britain, *Sociological Research Online*, 12, 1, www.socresonline.org.uk/12/1/prandy.html

Langley, E, Hooley, T and Bertuchi, D, 2014, *A Career Postcode Lottery? Local Authority Provision of Youth and Career Support Following the 2011 Education Act*, Derby: University of Derby, Institute of Guidance Studies

Lawson, N, 2009, *All Consuming*, London: Penguin

Layard, R, 2002, Happiness: Has Social Science a Clue?, Lionel Robbins Memorial Lectures 2002/3, Delivered on 3, 4, 5 March 2003 at the London School of Economics

Layard, R, 2006, Happiness and public policy: A challenge to the profession, *Economic Journal*, 116, 24-C33

Layard, R, 2010, Measuring subjective well-being, *Science*, 327, 534-5, www.sciencemag.org/cgi/content/full/327/5965/534?ijkey=1TYZ drZNS.0Qs&keytype=ref&siteid=sci

Layard, R, 2011, *Happiness: Lessons from a New Science*, second edn, London: Penguin

Lee, M, 2013, Are British political parties converging at the 'centre ground'?, *Journal of Politics & International Studies*, 9, Summer

Lee Hotz, R, 2011, As brain changes, so can IQ, *The Wall Street Journal*, 11 October, http://online.wsj.com/news/articles/SB10001424052 9702037526045766411333332697322

Levitas, R, 1998, *The Inclusive Society? Social Exclusion and New Labour,* Basingstoke: Palgrave

Li, Y and Devine, F, 2011, Is social mobility really declining? Intergenerational class mobility in Britain in the 1990s and the 2000s, *Sociological Research Online*, 16, 3

Lipset, S M and Bendix, R, 1959, *Social Mobility in Industrial Society*, Berkeley, CA: University of California

Lloyd, C and Payne, J, 2008, What Is a Skilled Job? Exploring Worker Perceptions of Skill in Two UK Call Centres, SKOPE Research Paper, 81, July, Cardiff: SKOPE, Cardiff University

London School of Economics, 2013, Five minutes with John Goldthorpe: More equal mobility chances are unlikely to be achieved without having a generally more equal society, http://blogs.lse.ac.uk/politicsandpolicy/archives/35681

Lyons, J, 2013, Public's faith in politicians hits record low despite David Cameron pledge to restore trust, *Mirror*, 23 September, www.mirror.co.uk/news/uk-news/public-faith-politicians-hits-record-2296348#ixzz31RbRKrUG

Lupton, R and Obolenskaya, P, 2013, *Labour's Record on Education: Policy, Spending and Outcomes 1997-2010*, London: London School of Economics

Macmillan, L, Tyler, C and Vignoles, A, 2013, *Who Gets the Top Jobs? The Role of Family Background and Networks in Recent Graduate's Access to High Status Professions*, London: Institute of Education

Malanchuk, M, Messersmith, EE and Eccles, JS, 2010, The ontogeny of career identities in adolescence, *New Directions for Child and Adolescent Development*, 130, 97-110 (special issue)

Marginson, S and van der Wende, M, 2007, Globalisation and Higher Education, Education Working Paper Number 8, London: OECD, www.cshe.unimelb.edu.au/people/marginson_docs/OECD-Globalisation&HigherEd.pdf

Marquand, D, 2014, *Mammon's Kingdom: An Essay on Britain Now*, London: Penguin

Mason, P, 2012, *Why It's Kicking Off Everywhere: The New Global Revolutions*, London: Verso

Mason, R, 2015, Arts world must address lack of diversity, says Labour's Chris Bryant, *The Guardian*, 16 January, www.theguardian.com/politics/2015/jan/16/arts-diversity-chris-bryant-eddie-redmayne

McKibbin, R, 2007, The potential of British social democracy, *Renewal*, 15, 2/3

McKinsey Global Institute, 2012, *The World at Work: Jobs, Pay and Skills for 3.5 Billion People*, McKinsey Company

McMahon, W, 2008, *Higher Learning, Greater Good: The Private and Social Benefits of Higher Education*, New York: Johns Hopkins University Press

Mian, R, 2015, *Employment, Skills and Growth*, London: Social Market Foundation

Michaels, E, Handfield-Jones, H and Axelrod, B, 2001, *The War for Talent*, Boston, MA: Harvard Business School

Michaels, G, Natraj, A and van Reenen, J, 2014, Has ICT polarized skill demand? Evidence from eleven countries over twenty-five years, *The Review of Economic Statistics*, 96, 1, 60-77

Michie, J and Grieve Smith, J (eds), 1995, *Managing the Global Economy*, Oxford: Oxford University Press

Miliband, E, 2013, What responsible capitalism is all about, *The Guardian*, 22 May, www.theguardian.com/commentisfree/2013/may/22/google-corporate-responsibility-ed-miliband-speech

Morozov, E, 2011, Two decades of the web: a utopia no longer, *Prospect Magazine*, 22 June, www.prospectmagazine.co.uk/science-and-technology/morozov-web-no-utopia-twenty-years-short-history-internet

Mourshed, M, Farrell, D and Barton, D, 2012, *Education to Employment: Designing a System that Works*, McKinsey Centre of Government

Müller, EN, 1985, Income inequality, regime repressiveness, and political violence, *American Sociological Review*, 50, 1, 47-61

Müller, EN, 1988, Inequality, repression, and violence: issues of theory and research design, *American Sociological Review*, 53, 5, 799-806

National Careers Council, 2013, *An Aspirational Nation: Creating a Culture Change in Careers Provision*, London: Department for Business, Innovation and Skills

National Centre for Social Research (NatCen), 2013, *British Social Attitudes 30*, London: NatCen

National HE STEM Programme (date unknown) Embedded Employability: A guide to enhancing the university curriculum, National HE STEM Programme, www.wimcs.ac.uk/document_repository/Employability%20Skills%20Guide.pdf

Neundorf, A and Niemi, R, 2014, Beyond political socialization: New approaches in age, period, cohort analysis, *Electoral Studies*, 33, 1-6

New Economics Foundation (nef), 2009, *A Bit Rich: Calculating the Real Value to Society of Different Professions*, London: nef

New Economics Foundation (nef), 2011, *Degrees of Value: How Universities Benefit Society*, London: nef

New Statesman, 2013, Danny Dorling: If you are young in Britain today, you are being taken for a ride, 7 November, www.newstatesman.com/2013/10/defrauding-young-britain

Newsome, D, 1961, *Godliness and Good Learning*, London: John Murray

Noyes, A, 2005, Pupil voice: purpose, power and the possibilities for democratic schooling, *British Educational Research Journal*, 31, 4, 533-40

Nunn, A, Johnson, S, Monro, S, Bickerstaffe, T and Kelsey, S, 2007, *Factors Influencing Social Mobility*, Research Report No 450, London: Department for Work and Pensions

Nussbaum, M C, 2000, *Women and Human Development: The Capabilities Approach*, Cambridge: Cambridge University Press

OECD, 2001, *The Well-being of Nations: The Role of Human and Social Capital*, Paris: OECD

OECD, 2009, *Higher Education to 2030, Volume 2: Globalisation*, Paris: OECD

OECD, 2010, *Education at a Glance*, Paris: OECD

OECD, 2011, *Education at a Glance*, Paris: OECD

OECD, 2012a, *Equity and Quality in Education: Supporting Disadvantaged Students and Schools*, Paris: OECD

OECD, 2012b, G20 Labour Ministers must focus on young jobseekers, Newsroom, 15 May, Paris: OECD

OECD, 2013, How's Life? 2013: Measuring Well-being, *The OECD Better Life Initiative: Concepts and Indicators*, Paris: OECD

OECD 2014a, Focus on inequality and growth, December 2014, www.oecd.org/social/FocusInequalityandGrowth2014.pdf

OECD, 2014b, All Aboard, *Making Inclusive Growth Happen*, Paris: OECD

Office for National Statistics (ONS), 2012a, *Graduates in the Labour Market*, London: ONS

ONS, 2012b, Chapter 4: Mortality, *2010-Based NPP Reference Volume*, London: ONS

ONS, 2013, *Graduates in the Labour Market*, London: ONS

ONS, 2014a, *Young People in the Labour Market*, London: ONS

ONS, 2014b, *Measuring National Well-being: Life in the UK 2014*, London: ONS

O'Malley, J P, 2013, Michael Sandel interview: the marketization of everything is undermining democracy, 22 May, http://blogs.spectator.co.uk/books/2013/05/michael-sandel-interview-the-marketization-of-everything-is-undermining-democracy/

Osborne, H, 2014, Employment: a fifth of UK jobs 'need only primary education', *The Guardian*, 26 February, www.theguardian.com/education/2014/feb/26/employement-fifth-uk-jobs-need-only-basic-education

Ostry, J D, Berg, A and Tsangarides, C G, 2014, *Redistribution, Inequality, and Growth*, Washington, DC: International Monetary Fund

Owen, R, 1813, *Essays on the Formation of Character*, London: W. Strange

Oxford Sociology, 2013, *The Great British Class Fiasco*, 11 April, http://oxfordsociology.blogspot.co.uk/2013/04/the-great-british-class-fiasco.html

Park, A, Bryson, C, Clery, E, Curtice, J and Phillips, M, 2013, *British Social Attitudes 30*, London: National Centre for Social Research

Parr, C, 2014, The Best University Workplace Survey: the results, *Times Higher Education*, 30 January

Paterson, C, Tyler, C and Lexmond, J, 2014, *Character and Resilience Manifesto*, London: All Party Parliamentary Group on Social Mobility

Paterson, L and Iannelli, C, 2007, Patterns of absolute and relative social mobility: A comparative study of England, Wales and Scotland, *Sociological Research Online*, 12, 6

Paton, G, 2012, Michael Gove: 'progressive' teaching undermines social mobility, *Telegraph online*, 24 May, www.telegraph.co.uk/education/educationnews/9288095/Michael-Gove-progressive-teaching-undermines-social-mobility.html

Paton, G, 2014, School leavers 'lack skills needed to get entry level jobs', *Telegraph*, 24 February, www.telegraph.co.uk/education/educationnews/10658100/School-leavers-lack-skills-needed-to-get-entry-level-jobs.html

Payne, G, 1990, Social mobility in Britain: A contrary view, in Clark, J, Modgil, C and Modgil, S (eds) *John Goldthorpe: Consensus and Controversy*, Abingdon: Routledge

Payne, G, 2012, Labouring under a misapprehension: Politicians' perceptions and the realities of structural mobility in Britain 1995-2010, in Lambert, P, Connelly, R, Blackburn, R M and Gayle, V (eds) *Social Stratification: Trends and Process*, Aldershot: Ashgate Publishing

Payne, G, 2013, How much 'more social mobility' do we really want?, *New Statesman*, 10 June

Payne, G and Roberts, J, 2002, Opening and closing the gates: Recent developments in male social mobility in Britain, *Sociological Research Online*, 6, 4

Payne, J, 1999, All things to all people: Changing perceptions of 'skill' among Britain's policy makers since the 1950s and their implications, SKOPE Research Paper No 1, August

Pearce, N, 2012, Beyond social mobility, *Ethos*, March, www.ethosjournal.com/topics/politics/item/308-beyond-social-mobility

Pearce, N, 2013, What should social democrats believe?, *Juncture*, 20, 2, Autumn

Phillips, D and Ochs, K (eds), 2004, *Educational Policy Borrowing: Historical Perspectives*, Oxford: Oxford University Press

Piketty, T, 2014, *Capital in the Twenty-First Century*, Boston, MA: Harvard University Press

Pinker, S, 2011, *The Better Angels of Our Nature: A History of Violence and Humanity*, London: Penguin

Policy Network, 2014, How social democracy can triumph in the 5–75–20 society, in Policy Network (eds) *Making Progressive Politics Work*, London: Policy Network

Porter, A, 2007, Diplomas could become 'qualification of choice', *Telegraph*, 23 October, www.telegraph.co.uk/news/uknews/1567013/Diplomas-could-become-qualification-of-choice.html

PricewaterhouseCoopers (PwC) and Demos, 2011, Good growth, London: PwC and Demos, www.pwc.co.uk/en_UK/uk/assets/pdf/pwc_good_growth.pdf

Protoa, E and Rustichini, A, 2012, A reassessment of the relationship between GDP and life satisfaction, www2.warwick.ac.uk/fac/soc/economics/staff/academic/proto/workingpapers/manuscript-23july.pdf

Pugliese, J and Ray, J, 2009, Gallup presents … A heated debate global attitudes toward climate change, *Harvard International Review*, Fall, 31, 4, 64-8

Ramdin, R, 2007, *Making of the Black Working Class in Britain*, London: Ashgate

Ramesh, R, 2011a, Income inequality growing faster in UK than any other rich country, says OECD, *The Guardian*, 5 December, www.theguardian.com/society/2011/dec/05/income-inequality-growing-faster-uk

Ramesh, R, 2011b, UK children stuck in 'materialistic trap', *The Guardian*, 14 September, www.theguardian.com/society/2011/sep/14/uk-children-stuck-materialistic-trap

Ramesh, R, 2012, Nick Clegg's social mobility speech condemned by inequality experts, *The Guardian*, 24 May, www.theguardian.com/society/2012/may/24/nick-clegg-social-mobility-speech

Raymond, L, 2001, Student involvement in school improvement: From data source to significant voice, *Forum*, 43, 2, 58-61

Reed, J, Robinson, P and Delorenzi, S, 2005, *Maintaining the Momentum: Promoting Social Mobility and Life Chances from Early Adulthood*, London: Institute for Public Policy Research

Reich, R, 1991, *The Work of Nations: Preparing Ourselves for 21st Century Capitalism*, New York: Vintage

Resolution Foundation, 2012, *Essential Guide to Squeezed Britain*, London: Resolution Foundation

Richardson, W and Wiborg, S, 2010, *English Technical and Vocational Education in Historical and Comparative Perspective*, London: Baker Dearing Educational Trust

Ridley, M, 2011, *The Rational Optimist*, London: Fourth Estate

Ridley, M, 2012, Cheer up! 17 reasons it's a great time to be alive, *Reader's Digest*, April

Romano, F, 2005, *Clinton and Blair: The Political Economy of the Third Way*, London: Routledge

Rose, M, 2003, Good deal, bad deal? Job satisfaction in occupations, *Work Employment & Society*, September, 17, 3, 503-30

Rowlingson, K, 2011, *Does Income Inequality Cause Health and Social Problems?* York: Joseph Rowntree Foundation

Rudduck, J and Flutter, J, 2004, *How to Improve Your School: Giving Pupils a Voice*, London: Continuum

Russell Group, 2011, Government should focus on main barriers to fairer access, 21 July, www.russell-group-latest-news/137-2011/4923-government-should-fous-on-main-barriers-to-fairer-access/

Sainsbury, D, 2013, *Progressive Capitalism: How to Achieve Economic Growth, Liberty and Social Justice*, London: Biteback

Sandel, M, 2011, *Justice*, New York: Farrar, Straus and Giroux

Sandel, M, 2012, *What Money Can't buy: The Moral Limits of Markets*, New York: Farrar, Straus and Giroux

Sassi, F, Devaux, M, Church, J, Cecchini, M and Borgonovi, F, 2009, Education and obesity in four OECD countries, OCED Education Working Papers No 39, Paris: OECD

Saunders, P, 1997, Social mobility in Britain: An empirical evaluation of two competing explanations, *Sociology*, May, 31, 2, 261-88

Saunders, P, 2010a, *Beware False Prophets: Equality, the Good Society and the Spirit Level*, London: Policy Exchange

Saunders, P, 2010b, *Social Mobility Myths*, London: Civitas

Saunders, P, 2012, *Social Mobility Delusions*, London: Civitas

Savage, L, 2011, *Snakes and Ladders: Who Climbs the Rungs of the Earnings Ladder?*, London: The Resolution Foundation

Savage, M, 2000, *Class Analysis and Social Transformation*, Milton Keynes: Open University Press

Savage, M and Devine, F, 2013, The British Class Survey – Results, 3 April, www.bbc.co.uk/science/0/21970879 BBC Science

Savage, M, Devine, F, Cunningham, N, Taylor, M, Li, Y, Hiellbrekke, J, Le Roux, B, Friedman, S and Miles, A, 2013, Survey experiment: A new model of social class? Findings from the BBC's Great British Class Survey, *Sociology*, 47, 219

Schofer, E and Meyer, J W, 2005, The worldwide expansion of higher education in the twentieth century, *American Sociological Review*, 70, 6, 898-920

Scott, P, 2013, MOOCS: if we're not careful so-called 'open' courses will close minds, *Times Higher*, 5 August

SecEd, 2014, Post-16 performance measures to focus on progression from 2016, 3 April, www.sec-ed.co.uk/news/post-16-performance-measures-to-focus-on-progression-from-2016

Sen, A, 1988, The concept of development, in J Behram and TN Strinivasan (eds) *Handbook of Development Economics*, North Holland: Elsevier, 2-23

Sen, A, 1989, Development as capability expansion, *Journal of Development Planning*, 19, 41-58

Sen, A, 1993, Capability and well-being, in M Nussbaum and A Sen (eds) *The Quality of Life*, New York: Oxford Clarendon, 30-53

Sen, A, 2000, *Development as Freedom*, New York: Anchor

Sen, A, 2009, *The Idea of Justice*, Cambridge, MA: The Belknap Press of Harvard University Press

Sennett, R, 1999, *The Corrosion of Character: Personal Consequences of Work in the New Capitalism*, New York: W W Norton & Company

Sharma, Y, 2013, Asia's parents suffering 'education fever', BBC News online, www.bbc.co.uk/news/business-24537487

Shavit, Y and Blossfeld, H P, 1993, *Persistent Barriers: Inequality of Educational Opportunity in 13 Countries*, Boulder, CO: Westview Press

Silva, E, 2009, Measuring skills for 21st-century learning, *Phi Delta Kappa*, 90, 9, 630-4

Simon, B, 1998, *The Search for Enlightenment: Working Class and Adult Education in the Twentieth Century*, Leicester: NIACE

Singleton, A D and Spielman, S E, 2013, The past, present and future of geodemographic research in the United States and United Kingdom, *The Professional Geographer*, 66, 4, 558-67

Siraj-Blatchford, I, Mayo, A, Melhuish E, Taggart, B, Sammons, P and Sylva, K, 2011, *Performing Against the Odds: Developmental Trajectories of Children in the EPPSE 3-16 Study*, London: Department for Education

Sissons, P, 2011, *The Hourglass and the Escalator: Labour Market Change and Mobility*, London: The Work Foundation

Skelton, D, 2013, Nick Clegg has stolen the social mobility agenda, *Telegraph*, 6 June, www.telegraph.co.uk/news/politics/nick-clegg/10102847/Nick-Clegg-has-stolen-the-social-mobility-agenda.html

Snowdon, C, 2010, *The Spirit Level Delusion*, Ripon: Little Dice

Social Attitudes of Young People Community of Interest, 2014, *HM Government Horizon Scanning Programme Social Attitudes of Young People, A Horizon Scanning Research Paper*, London: HM Government

Social Mobility and Child Poverty Commission, 2013a, *State of the Nation 2013: Social Mobility and Child Poverty in Britain*, London: HMSO

Social Mobility and Child Poverty Commission, 2013b, *Social Mobility: The Next Steps*, London: The Stationery Office

Sorokin, P A, 1959, *Social and Cultural Mobility*, Glencoe, IL: Free Press

Sparreboom, T and Staneva, A, 2014, *Is Education the Solution to Decent Work for Youth in Developing Economies?*, Geneva: International Labour Organization

Sparrow, A, 2008, PM backs apprenticeships to boost UK in 'global skills race', *The Guardian*, 28 January, www.theguardian.com/politics/2008/jan/28/labour.uk

Spoonley, P, 2014, Superdiversity, social cohesion, and economic benefits, *IZA World of Labor*, 46

Stevenson, B and Wolfers, J, 2008, Economic growth and subjective well-being: Reassessing the Easterlin paradox, Discussion Paper No 3654, August, http://ftp.iza.org/dp3654.pdf

Stiglitz, J, E, 2003, *Globalization and its Discontents*, New York: Penguin

Stiglitz, J E, 2012, *The Price of Inequality: How Today's Divided Society Endangers Our Future*, New York: W.W. Norton & Company

Stiglitz, J, E, Sen, A and Fitoussi, J P, 2012, Report by the Commission on the Measurement of Economic Performance and Social Progress, www.stiglitz-sen-fitoussi.fr/documents/rapport_anglais.pdf

Street, H and Temperley, J (eds) 2005, *Improving Schools Through Collaborative Enquiry*, London: Continuum

Stuart, M, 2012, *Social Mobility and Higher Education: The Life Experiences of First Generation Entrants in Higher Education*, Stoke: Trentham Books

Suto, I, 2013, 21st Century skills: Ancient, ubiquitous, enigmatic?, Cambridge: Cambridge Assessment, www.cambridgeassessment. org.uk/Images/130437-21st-century-skills-ancient-ubiquitous-enigmatic-.pdf

Sutton Trust, 2010, *The Educational Backgrounds of Members of Parliament in 2010*, London: The Sutton Trust

Sutton Trust, 2015, *Parliamentary Privilege – the MPs*, London: The Sutton Trust

Swift, A, 2004, Would perfect mobility be perfect?, *European Sociological Review*, 20, 1, 1-11

The Boston Consulting Group, 2013, *Real Apprenticeships: Creating a Revolution in English Skills*, London: Sutton Trust

The Economist, 2013a, Fries with that, 27 April, www.economist.com/news/international/21576656-degree-burgerologyand-job-too-fries

The Economist, 2013b, The American Dream, RIP?, 21 September, www.economist.com/news/united-states/21586581-economist-asks-provocative-questions-about-future-social-mobility-american

The Economist, 2014, Is college worth it?, 5 April, www.economist.com/news/united-states/21600131-too-many-degrees-are-waste-money-return-higher-education-would-be-much-better

The Equality Trust, 2014, *The Cost of Inequality*, London: The Equality Trust

The Independent, 2013, Controversial Help to Buy scheme aids social mobility, claims David Cameron, 11 November, www.independent. co.uk/news/uk/politics/controversial-help-to-buy-scheme-aids-social-mobility-claims-david-cameron-8932794.html

The International Graduate Insight Group Ltd, 2011, *Supporting Graduate Employability: HEI Practice in Other Countries*, London: BIS

The Progressive, 2011, Amartya Sen, http://progressive.org/amartya_sen_interview.html

The White House, 2013, Remarks by the President on economic mobility, www.whitehouse.gov/the-press-office/2013/12/04/remarks-president-economic-mobility

Therborn, G, 2012, Class in the 21st century, *New Left Review*, 78, Nov/Dec

Tobin, L, 2014, 245%: That's the postcode premium for living in catchment area of top London school, *London Evening Standard*, www.standard.co.uk/lifestyle/london-life/245-thats-the-postcode-premium-for-living-in-catchment-area-of-top-london-school-8953893.html

Tough, P, 2013, *How Children Succeed*, New York: Random House

Trow, M and Burrage, M, 2010, *Twentieth Century Higher Education: Elite to Mass to Universal*, Baltimore, MD: The Johns Hopkins University Press

Tzankiis, M, 2011, Bourdieu's social reproduction thesis and the role of cultural capital in educational attainment: A critical review of key empirical studies, *Educate*, 11, 1, 76-90

United Kingdom Commission for Employment and Skills (UKCES), 2010, *Skills for Jobs: Today and Tomorrow*, London: UKCES

United Kingdom Commission for Employment and Skills (UKCES), 2011, *The Role of Skills from Worklessness to Sustainable Employment with Progression Evidence Report 38 September 2011*, London: UKCES

United Kingdom Commission for Employment and Skills (UKCES), 2015, *Growth Through People: Evidence and Analysis* London:UKCES

Universities UK (UUK), 2013, Massive open online courses, London: UUK, www.universitiesuk.ac.uk/highereducation/Documents/2013/MassiveOpenOnlineCourses.pdf

University of Sheffield, 2012, Inequality in UK at highest since pre-WW2, www.sheffield.ac.uk/news/nr/inequality-world-war-two-danny-dorling-1.190103

University of Oxford, 2015, *International Trends in Higher Education 2015*, Oxford: Oxford University Press

Usher, A, 2009, Ten years back and ten years forward: Developments and trends in higher education in Europe Region, Paper at the UNESCO Forum on Higher Education in the Europe Region: Access, Values, Quality and Competitiveness, 21-24 May, Bucharest, Romania, www.educationalpolicy.org/publications/pubpdf/0905_UNESCO.pdf

van Saane, N, Sluiter, J K, Verbeek, A M and Frings-Dresen, H W, 2003, Reliability and validity of instruments measuring job satisfaction – a systematic review, *Occupational Medicine*, 53-191

Veal, A J, 2009, The Elusive Leisure Society, 4th Edition, School of Leisure, Sport and Tourism Working Paper 9, Sydney: University of Technology, www.leisure source.net

Vincent, C, 2012, *Parenting: Responsibilities, Risks and Respect*, London: Institute of Education

Walker, I and Zhu, Y, 2013, *The Impact of University Degrees on the Lifecycle of Earnings: Some Further Analysis*, London: Department for Business, Innovation and Skills

Walker, T, 2007, Why economists dislike a lump of labor, *Review of Social Economy*, 65, 3, 279-91

Watson, D, 2006, *How to Think about Widening Participation: A Discussion Paper for HEFCE*, Bristol: Higher Education Funding Council for England

Wheeler, B, 2013, Nick Clegg told to ditch goal of 'social mobility', BBC News Online, 18 September, www.bbc.co.uk/news/uk-politics-24132678

Whittaker, M and Hurrell, A, 2013, *Low Pay Britain 2013*, London: Resolution Foundation

White House, 2012, *Economic Report of the President Transmitted to Congress 2012*, Washington; White House

Wilkinson, R and Pickett, K, 2010, *The Spirit Level: Why Equality is Better for Everyone*, London: Penguin

Willetts, D, 2010, *The Pinch: How the Baby Boomers Took Their Children's Future – And How They Can Give it Back*, London: Atlantic Books

Willetts, D, 2011, Universities and social mobility, Ron Dearing Lecture, 17 February, University of Nottingham, www.gov.uk/government/speeches/ron-dearing-lecture-universities-and-social-mobility

Winship, S, 2012, Scott Winship offers a response to Miles Corak on the economics of the Great Gatsby Curve, Guest post for *National Review*'s 'The Agenda' blog, 18 January, www.nationalreview.com

Wintour, P, 2004, Blair to bank on social mobility, *The Guardian*, 12 October, www.theguardian.com/politics/2004/oct/12/socialexclusion.labour

Wintour, P, 2013a, John Major 'shocked' at privately educated elite's hold on power, *The Guardian*, 11 December, www.theguardian.com/politics/2013/nov/11/john-major-shocked-elite-social-mobility

Wintour, P, 2013b, Labour would freeze energy prices until 2017, says Ed Miliband, *The Guardian*, 24 September, www.theguardian.com/politics/2013/sep/24/ed-miliband-labour-freeze-prices-2017

Wolf, A, 2002, *Does Education Matter? Myths About Education and Economic Growth*, London: Penguin

Wolf, A, 2011, *Review of Vocational Education – The Wolf Report*, London: Department for Education

Working Group on 14-19 Reform, 2004, *14-19 Curriculum and Qualifications Reform: Final Report of the Working Group on 14-19 Reform Summary*, October

World Economic Forum, 2015, *Outlook on the Global Agenda 2015*, Geneva: World Economic Forum

Yaish, M and Andersen, R, 2012, Social mobility in 20 modern societies: The role of economic and political context, *Social Science Research*, 41, 527-38

Young, M, 1958, *The Rise of the Meritocracy 1870-2033: An Essay on Education and Equality*, London: Penguin

Young, M, 2001, Down with meritocracy, *The Guardian*, 29 June

Index